Bootstrap 4 Site Blueprints

Explore the robust features of Bootstrap 4 to create exciting websites through this collection of excellent hands-on projects

Bass Jobsen
David Cochran
Ian Whitley

BIRMINGHAM - MUMBAI

Bootstrap 4 Site Blueprints

Copyright © 2016 Packt Publishing

First published: February 2014

Second edition: October 2016

Production reference: 1241016

Published by Packt Publishing Ltd.
Livery Place
35 Livery Street
Birmingham
B3 2PB, UK.
ISBN 978-1-78588-965-3

www.packtpub.com

Credits

Authors

Bass Jobsen

David Cochran

Ian Whitley

Reviewer

Silvio Moreto

Commissioning Editor

Ashwin Nair

Acquisition Editor

Smeet Thakkar

Content Development Editor

Sachin Karnani

Technical Editor

Rupali R. Shrawane

Copy Editor

Safis Editing

Project Coordinator

Ritika Manoj

Proofreader

Safis Editing

Indexer

Rekha Nair

Graphics

Abhinash Sahu

Production Coordinator

Melwyn Dsa

About the Authors

Bass Jobsen lives in Orthen in the Netherlands. Bass tries to combine his interests in web technology with his compassion for a sustainable lifestyle. He therefore not only owns a web development company, but is also board member at the Energie Cooperatie 073. In his spare time, he plays tennis and spends a lot of time with his kids Kiki, Dries, Wolf, and Helena.

Bass has been programming the web since 1995, ranging from C to PHP. He is always looking for the most accessible interfaces. He has a special interest in the processes between designer and programmer. Web interfaces should work independently of devices or browsers in his opinion. He also works on the accessibility of Bootstrap and his JBST WordPress starters theme.

Delivering readable and maintainable code is important for his daily job so that's why he loves CSS preprocessors and other tools that stimulate DRY (Don't Repeat Yourself) coding in web development. Also, Bootstrap helps him to work faster and make his clients and users more content.

With over 5 years of experience with Bootstrap, Bass has been actively contributing to the community with his blogs (http://bassjobsen.weblogs.fm/) and Git repos (https://github.com/bassjobsen). He has created sites such as http://www.streetart.com/ with Bootstrap. The newest version of JBST for Bootstrap 4 is already available at https://github.com/bassjobsen/jbst-4-sass. He released a CLI for Bootstrap 4 in March 2016 (https://github.com/bassjobsen/bootstrap-cli).

In the summer of 2016, Bass started teaching programming Scratch for primary school kids using the Massive Open Online Courses (MOOCs) on the edX-platform offered by Delft University of Technology.

He is also the author of, among others, Sass and Compass Designer's Cookbook with Packt Publishing and some other books on Less (Leaner CSS).

I would also like to thank Smeet and Sachin from Packt for their support and feedback. Last but not least, the critical and useful reviews of Silvio helped me to right a better book. Without the support of those wonderful people I could not wrote this book!

David Cochran serves as an Associate Professor of Communication at Oklahoma Wesleyan University. He has been teaching Interactive Design since 2005. A passion for best practices induced him to avoid shortcuts and hew towards web standards. When Twitter Bootstrap was first released in August 2011, he recognized it as a tool that would speed up development while supporting best practices. Thus, he began folding Bootstrap into his university courses, much to the benefit of his students. In 2012, David produced a Bootstrap 2.0 tutorial series for webdesign.tutsplus.com. He also published a first short book about Bootstrap, Twitter Bootstrap Web Development How-To, Packt Publishing.

Ian Whitley developed a passion for writing and literature at a young age. In 2010, he developed a deep interest in web development and decided to get involved in it. When the opportunity to help write a book on web development came up, it seemed like too good of an offer to pass up. He was one of the early adopters of Twitter Bootstrap when it was first released in 2011. With the help of David Cochran, he quickly conquered the system and has used it for many different web projects. Currently, he uses Bootstrap in relation to WordPress, using both in conjunction to create custom and creative solutions for his client.

Living in the Bartlesville, OK, Ian is the lead developer for BitBrilliant, the company that David Cochran founded. He is always looking to further his skills—both for the web and in the many hobbies he pursues, which include leather working and writing.

About the Reviewer

Silvio Moreto is a developer with more than 8 years of experience with frontend technologies and has created many websites and web applications using the Bootstrap framework. From simple pages to complex ones, he has always used the Bootstrap framework. Silvio is also the creator of the bootstrap-select plugin (`http://silviomoreto.github.io/bootstrap-select/`), which is a very popular plugin among the community. It is for replacing a selected element by a Bootstrap button drop-down element. Silvio foresaw that a plugin such as this one was missing in the original framework, and it could be useful for the community. Silvio is the writer of the book Bootstrap by Example, published by Packt Publishing as well. Besides this, he is very active in the open source community, participating in some open source repository and issue communities, such as Stack Overflow. Also, he finished third in the worldwide Django Dash 2013 challenge.

www.PacktPub.com

For support files and downloads related to your book, please visit www.PacktPub.com.

Did you know that Packt offers eBook versions of every book published, with PDF and ePub files available? You can upgrade to the eBook version at www.PacktPub.com and as a print book customer, you are entitled to a discount on the eBook copy. Get in touch with us at service@packtpub.com for more details.

At www.PacktPub.com, you can also read a collection of free technical articles, sign up for a range of free newsletters and receive exclusive discounts and offers on Packt books and eBooks.

https://www.packtpub.com/mapt

Get the most in-demand software skills with Mapt. Mapt gives you full access to all Packt books and video courses, as well as industry-leading tools to help you plan your personal development and advance your career.

Why subscribe?

- Fully searchable across every book published by Packt
- Copy and paste, print, and bookmark content
- On demand and accessible via a web browser

Table of Contents

Preface   1

Chapter 1: Getting Started with Bootstrap   7

  Quantity and quality   8

    Improving with age   8

    The power of Sass   9

    Downloading the compiled code   10

    The Flexbox enabled version   10

    The grid only versions   10

    Running Bootstrap from CDN   10

      Subresource Integrity (SRI)   11

  Downloading Bootstrap's source files   11

    The files you'll have   12

    Other ways to download and integrate Bootstrap 14

  Tooling setup   14

    The HTML starter template   15

      Responsive meta tag   15

      The X-UA-Compatible meta tag   16

      Bootstrap's CSS code   16

      The JavaScript files   16

  Using Bootstrap CLI   17

  Preparing a new Bootstrap project   17

  Setting up major structural elements   18

    Providing a navbar markup   19

      The CSS classes of the navbar   21

      Placement of the navbars   22

      Adding collapsible content to the navbar 22

      Responsive features and breakpoints 23

      Responsive utility classes   25

      Completing the responsive navbar   25

      The new Reboot module and Normalize.css. 28

      Box-sizing   29

      Predefined CSS classes   29

      Sass variables and mixins   30

  Browser support   32

    Vendor prefixes   32

    Flexible boxes   33

  The Yeoman workflow   34

Troubleshooting   34
Summary   35
Chapter 2: Creating Your Own Build Process with Gulp   37
What are we going to build?   38
    Requirements   39
        What is Gulp and why should you use it?   39
Bootstrap's build process   39
Installing Gulp in your project   40
    Creating the Gulpfile.js which holds your tasks   41
    The clean task   41
Setting up environments for development and production   42
Installing Bootstrap via Bower   43
Creating a local Sass structure   43
    Compiling Bootstrap's Sass code into CSS code   44
    CSS sourcemaps for debugging   46
    Running the postCSS autoprefixer   47
    Getting your CSS code ready for production   48
    Linting your SCSS code   49
Preparing the JavaScript plugins   51
    Getting your JavaScript code ready for production   51
Modularization of your HTML   53
    Installing the Gulp task to compile the Panini HTML templates   54
    Validating the compiled HTML code   54
Creating a static web server   55
    Start watching your file changes   56
    Copying and minifying your images   56
Putting it all together and creating the default task   57
Using the build process to finish your project   59
    The layout template   59
    The page header   60
        Custom CSS code for the page header   62
        Fine tuning of your CSS and HTML code   63
        Styling the navbar and hero unit   64
Styling the features   68
Styling the footer of your page   70
Running your template with Bootstrap CLI   72
JavaScript task runners are not required   72
Publishing your work on GitHub   72
Summary   73

Chapter 3: Customizing Your Blog with Bootstrap and Sass   75

   Expected results and the process   75
   Setting up your project and requirements   77
   The power of Sass in your project   78
      Nested rules   78
      Variables   80
      Mixins   81
      Operations   82
   Importing files   83
      The modular file organization   83
   Using the SCSS-linter for cleaner and more readable code   84
   Strategies for customization with Sass   84
      Using variables for customization   84
      Extending Bootstrap's predefined CSS classes   86
      (Re)Using Bootstrap's mixins   87
      Sass functions   88
      Reusing others' code   88
         Compass   88
   Writing your own custom SCSS code   89
      The color scheme   89
      Preparing the HTML templates   90
      Styling the page header   92
      Styling the navbar   94
         A navbar without Bootstrap's predefined CSS classes   99
   The main part of your blog page   100
   Styling the blog posts   102
   Styling the side bar   106
   The page footer   107
      The left footer column   109
      The right footer column   110
   Reusing the SCSS code of the social buttons   111
   Source code of this chapter   113
      Using the CLI and running the code from GithHub   113
   Summary   113

Chapter 4: Bootstrappin' a WordPress Theme   115

   Installing WordPress and other requirements   116
      Installing WordPress   116
      Node.js, Gulp, and Bower   116
   Installing the JBST 4 theme   117

Installing the theme	118
Reusing the Sass code	120
Conflicts between WordPress and Bootstrap – predefined classes	123
Turn the navigation into a Bootstrap navbar	125
About the grid	127
Configuring the navbar	128
Updating the HTML code	130
Adding your photo to the middle of the navbar	130
Giving your blog a page header	132
Don't forget the page footer	133
Styling your blog posts	135
The side bar of your blog	136
The off-canvas side bar	141
Applying style to the buttons	147
Other tweaks in your Sass	148
The pagination	148
Search form button	149
Styling the user comments on your pages	149
Adding a carousel to your page	153
Using Font Awesome in your theme	156
Building the social links with Font Awesome	156
Using the masonry template	158
Child theming	160
Download at GitHub	160
Summary	160
Chapter 5: Bootstrappin' Your Portfolio	**161**
What we'll build	161
Surveying the exercise files	164
Marking up the carousel	169
How does the carousel work?	173
Changing the carousel by adding new animations	173
JavaScript events of the Carousel plugin	177
Creating responsive columns	178
Turning links into buttons	181
Understanding the power of Sass	182
Customizing Bootstrap's Sass according to our needs	182
Customizing variables	184
Customizing the navbar	185
Adding the logo image	187
Adding icons	190

Styling the carousel 192
Adding top and bottom padding 192
Repositioning the carousel indicators 193
Styling the indicators 194
Tweaking the columns and their content 196
Styling the footer 200
Recommended next steps 204
Summary 205

Chapter 6: Bootstrappin' Business 207

Sizing up our beginning files 210
Setting up the basics of your design 211
Adding drop-down menus to our navbar 212
Setting the bottom border for the page header 214
Adding images with holder.js 214
Creating a complex banner area 215
Placing a logo above the navbar 216
Reviewing and checking navbar drop-down items 218
Adding utility navigation 222
Making responsive adjustments 225
Implementing the color scheme 227
Styling the collapsed navbar 229
Customizing the drop-down menus 230
Styling the horizontal navbar 231
Enabling Flexbox support 232
Designing a complex responsive layout 233
Adjusting the large and extra-large layout 236
Adjusting the medium layout for tablet-width viewports 237
Adjusting headings, font sizes, and buttons 242
Enhancing the primary column 246
Adjusting the tertiary column 249
Fine touches for multiple viewports 252
Laying out a complex footer 252
Setting up the markup 252
Adjusting for tablet-width viewports 256
Adding a targeted responsive clearfix 257
Refining the details 258
Summary 263

Chapter 7: Bootstrappin' E-Commerce 265

Surveying the markup for our products page   267
Styling the breadcrumbs, page title, and pagination   269
Adjusting the products grid   273
   Don't forget the Card module   278
     Cards with the CSS3 Flexbox layout module 281
Styling the options sidebar   285
   Setting up basic styles   286
   Styling the Clearance Sale link   287
   Styling the options list   290
   Adding Font Awesome checkboxes to our option links   292
   Using Sass mixins to arrange option links in columns 296
   Adjusting the options list layout for tablets and phones 298
   Collapsing the options panel for phone users   301
Adding a search form to your designing   304
   Using the Typeahead plugin   305
Summary   308

Chapter 8: Bootstrappin' a One-Page Marketing Website   309
Overview   309
Surveying the starter files   312
Viewing the page content   314
Adding Font Awesome to our project   315
Adjusting the navbar   315
Customizing the jumbotron   318
   Refining the jumbotron message design   322
Beautifying the features list   325
Tackling customer reviews   329
   Positioning and styling captions   332
   Refining the caption position   333
     Adjusting for tiny screens   335
Creating attention-grabbing pricing tables   336
   Setting up the variables, files, and markup   336
   Beautifying the table head   339
   Styling the table body and foot   341
   Differentiating the packages   342
   Adjusting for small viewports   345
   Providing a visual hierarchy to our tables   346
Adding the final touches   348
Adding ScrollSpy to the navbar   351
   Animating the scroll   353

Summary	355
Chapter 9: Building an Angular 2 App with Bootstrap	357
Overview	357
Setting up your first Angular app	358
Adding routing to our app	359
Setting up navigation	361
Adding Bootstrap's HTML markup code to your app	362
Integrating Bootstrap's CSS code into the application	364
Setting up the Sass compiler	364
Adding the post-processors	366
Using the ng-bootstrap directives	367
Using other directives	369
Using the ng2-bootstrap directives as an alternative	370
Downloading the complete code	371
What about Angular CLI?	372
Using React.js with Bootstrap	372
Using React Bootstrap 4 components	373
Other tools for deploying Bootstrap 4	375
Yeoman	376
Summary	377
Index	379

Preface

Since its debut in August 2011, Twitter Bootstrap, now simply Bootstrap, has become by far the most popular framework for empowering and enhancing frontend web design.

With over 5 years of experience with Bootstrap, I'm happy to write this book for you and share my experience with you. Since Bootstrap helps me to implement best practices for both CSS and HTML. Bootstrap enables me to work faster and deliver stable results. Bootstrap definitely made me a better web developer.

With version 4, Bootstrap reaches an exciting new milestone, a lean code base optimized for modern browsers. Bootstrap enables you to build applications and websites that look good and work well on all types of devices and screen sizes from a single code base.

Bootstrap is open source and released under the MIT license. It's hosted, developed, and maintained on GitHub.

This book is a hands-on guide to the inner workings of Bootstrap. In an easy-to-follow, step-by-step format, you'll experience the power of customizing and recompiling Bootstrap's Sass files and adapting Bootstrap's JavaScript plugins to design professional user interfaces.

At the end of the day, this book is about something bigger than Bootstrap. Bootstrap is but a tool—a means to an end. By the end of this book, you will become a more adept and efficient web designer.

What this book covers

Chapter 1, *Getting Started with Bootstrap*, teaches us how to download Bootstrap, set up a site template based on the HTML5 boilerplate, and practice compiling Bootstrap's Sass files to CSS.

Chapter 2, *Creating Your Own Build Process with Gulp*, teaches us how to create a build process for your Bootstrap projects with Gulp. You can reuse the build process for your newer projects. The build process compiles your Sass code into CSS code, prepares your JavaScript code, and runs a static web server to test the results.

Chapter 3, *Customizing Your Blog with Bootstrap and Sass*, enables us to get a grip on Sass. You now know how to use Sass to customize Bootstrap's components. You will build a web page for your web log and apply different strategies to style it with Sass.

Chapter 4, *Bootstrappin' a WordPress Theme*, enables us to take the portfolio design and turn it into a WordPress theme. We'll start with the excellent JBST 4 Starter Theme and customize template files, Sass, CSS, and JavaScript to suit our needs.

Chapter 5, *Bootstrappin' Your Portfolio*, helps us to build a basic portfolio site with a full-width carousel, three columns of text, and social icons provided by Font Awesome—customizing Bootstrap's Sass files and adding your own in the process.

Chapter 6, *Bootstrappin' Business*, shows us how to create a complex banner area, add drop-down menus and utility navigation, build a complex three-column page layout, and add a four-column footer, and ensures that all these things remain fully responsive.

Chapter 7, *Bootstrappin' E-Commerce*, guides us through the design of a products page capable of managing multiple rows of products in a complex responsive grid. While at it, we will provide a fully responsive design for options to filter products by category, brand, and so on.

Chapter 8, *Bootstrappin' a One-Page Marketing Website*, gives a detailed outline of how to design a beautiful one-page scrolling website with a large welcome message, a grid of product features with large icons, customer testimony in a masonry layout, and a set of three thoughtfully designed pricing tables.

Chapter 9, *Building an Angular 2 App with Bootstrap*, enables you to learn how to set up an Angular 2 app with Bootstrap 4. At the end, you will be introduced to some other tools to deploy your projects.

What you need for this book

To complete the exercises in this book, you will need the following software:

- A modern web browser
- A text or code editor
- The NodeJS installed on your system

Who this book is for

This book is assumed to be good for readers who are comfortable with handcoding HTML and CSS and are familiar with the fundamentals of valid HTML5 markup and well-structured style sheets. Basic familiarity with JavaScript is a bonus, as we will be making use of Bootstrap's jQuery plugins. We will work a great deal with LESS to customize, compose, and compile style sheets. Those who are familiar with LESS will gain significant experience working with the details of Bootstrap's LESS files. Those who are new to LESS will find this book a reasonably thorough primer.

Conventions

In this book, you will find a number of text styles that distinguish between different kinds of information. Here are some examples of these styles and an explanation of their meaning.

Code words in text, database table names, folder names, filenames, file extensions, pathnames, dummy URLs, user input, and Twitter handles are shown as follows: "Mount the downloaded `WebStorm-10*.dmg` disk image file as another disk in your system."

A block of code is set as follows:

```
.btn-tomato {
  color: white;
  background-color: tomato;
  border-color: white;
}
```

Any command-line input or output is written as follows:

```
npm install --global gulp-cli
```

New terms and **important words** are shown in bold. Words that you see on the screen, for example, in menus or dialog boxes, appear in the text like this: "The shortcuts in this book are based on the `Mac OS X 10.5+` scheme."

 Warnings or important notes appear in a box like this.

Tips and tricks appear like this.

Reader feedback

Feedback from our readers is always welcome. Let us know what you think about this book-what you liked or disliked. Reader feedback is important for us as it helps us develop titles that you will really get the most out of. To send us general feedback, simply e-mail feedback@packtpub.com, and mention the book's title in the subject of your message. If there is a topic that you have expertise in and you are interested in either writing or contributing to a book, see our author guide at www.packtpub.com/authors.

Customer support

Now that you are the proud owner of a Packt book, we have a number of things to help you to get the most from your purchase.

Downloading the example code

You can download the example code files for this book from your account at http://www.packtpub.com. If you purchased this book elsewhere, you can visit http://www.packtpub.com/support and register to have the files e-mailed directly to you.

You can download the code files by following these steps:

1. Log in or register to our website using your e-mail address and password.
2. Hover the mouse pointer on the **SUPPORT** tab at the top.
3. Click on **Code Downloads & Errata**.
4. Enter the name of the book in the **Search** box.
5. Select the book for which you're looking to download the code files.
6. Choose from the drop-down menu where you purchased this book from.
7. Click on **Code Download**.

Once the file is downloaded, please make sure that you unzip or extract the folder using the latest version of:

- WinRAR / 7-Zip for Windows
- Zipeg / iZip / UnRarX for Mac
- 7-Zip / PeaZip for Linux

The code bundle for the book is also hosted on GitHub at `https://github.com/PacktPubl ishing/Bootstrap-4-Site-Blueprints`. We also have other code bundles from our rich catalog of books and videos available at `https://github.com/PacktPublishing/`. Check them out!

Downloading the color images of this book

We also provide you with a PDF file that has color images of the screenshots/diagrams used in this book. The color images will help you better understand the changes in the output. You can download this file from `http://www.packtpub.com/sites/default/files/downloads/Bootstrap4SiteBlueprints_ ColorImages.pdf`.

Errata

Although we have taken every care to ensure the accuracy of our content, mistakes do happen. If you find a mistake in one of our books-maybe a mistake in the text or the code-we would be grateful if you could report this to us. By doing so, you can save other readers from frustration and help us improve subsequent versions of this book. If you find any errata, please report them by visiting `http://www.packtpub.com/submit-errata`, selecting your book, clicking on the **Errata Submission Form** link, and entering the details of your errata. Once your errata are verified, your submission will be accepted and the errata will be uploaded to our website or added to any list of existing errata under the Errata section of that title.

To view the previously submitted errata, go to `https://www.packtpub.com/books/conten t/support` and enter the name of the book in the search field. The required information will appear under the **Errata** section.

Piracy

Piracy of copyrighted material on the Internet is an ongoing problem across all media. At Packt, we take the protection of our copyright and licenses very seriously. If you come across any illegal copies of our works in any form on the Internet, please provide us with the location address or website name immediately so that we can pursue a remedy.

Please contact us at copyright@packtpub.com with a link to the suspected pirated material.

We appreciate your help in protecting our authors and our ability to bring you valuable content.

Questions

If you have a problem with any aspect of this book, you can contact us at questions@packtpub.com, and we will do our best to address the problem.

1
Getting Started with Bootstrap

Bootstrap's popularity as a front-end web development framework is easy to understand. It provides a palette of user-friendly, cross-browser, tested solutions for most standard UI conventions. Its ready-made, community-tested, combination of HTML markup, CSS styles, and JavaScript plugins greatly accelerates the task of developing a frontend web interface, and it yields a pleasing result out of the gate. With the fundamental elements quickly in place, we can customize the design on top of a solid foundation.

Bootstrap uses **Grunt** for its CSS and JavaScript build system, and Jekyll for the written documentation. Grunt is a JavaScript task runner for **Node.js**. Other tools and technologies can also be used to build Bootstrap. In this book you will get introduced to some alternative solutions to build Bootstrap.

But not all that is popular, efficient, and effective is good. Too often, a handy tool can generate and reinforce bad habits; not so with Bootstrap, at least not necessarily so. Those who have watched it from the beginning know that its first release and early updates have occasionally favored pragmatic efficiency over best practices. The fact is that some best practices, right from semantic markup, to mobile-first design, to performance-optimized assets, require extra time and effort to implement. In this chapter you will get introduced to Bootstrap and will learn:

Creating a solid HTML5 markup structure with many current best practices baked-in

- Setting up a new Bootstrap project with Bootstrap CLI
- Building collapsing content into your project pages
- Creating a navbar for page navigation
- Turning your navbar into a responsive component

Quantity and quality

If handled well, I will suggest that Bootstrap is a boon for the web development community in terms of quality as well as efficiency. Since developers are attracted to the web development framework, they become part of a coding community that draws them increasingly into current best practices. From the start, Bootstrap has encouraged implementation of tried, tested, and future-friendly CSS solutions, from Nicholas Galagher's CSS normalize to CSS3's displacement of image-heavy design elements. It has also supported (if not always modeled) HTML5 semantic markup.

Improving with age

With the release of v2.0, Bootstrap helped take responsive design into the mainstream, ensuring that its interface elements could travel well across devices, from desktops, to tablets, to handhelds.

With the v3.0 release, Bootstrap stepped up its game again by providing the following features:

- The responsive grid was now mobile-first friendly.
- Icons now utilize web fonts and thus were mobile and retina-friendly.
- With the drop of support for IE7, markup and CSS conventions were now leaner and more efficient.
- Since version 3.2, the **autoprefixer** was required to build Bootstrap.
- This book is about the v4.0 release. This release contains many improvements and also some new components while other components and plugins are dropped. In the overview below, you will find the most important improvements and changes in Bootstrap 4:
    - **Less** (Leaner CSS) has been replaced with **Sass**
    - Refactoring of CSS code to avoid tag and child selectors
    - Improved grid system with a new grid tier to better target mobile devices
    - Replaced the navbar
    - Opt-in **flexbox** support
- A new HTML reset module called **Reboot**. Reboot extends **Nicholas Galagher's CSS normalize** and handles the `box-sizing: border-box` declarations.
- jQuery plugins are written in **ES6** now and come with **UMD** support.
- Improved auto-placement of tooltips and popovers, thanks to the help of a library called **Tether**.

- Dropped support for Internet Explorer 8 which enables us to swap pixels with rem and em units.
- Added the Card component, which replaces the Wells, Thumbnails, and Panels in earlier versions.
- Dropped the icons in font format from the **Glyphicon Halflings** set.
- Dropped the **Affix plugin**, which can be replaced with the `position: sticky` polyfill (`https://github.com/filamentgroup/fixed-sticky`).

The power of Sass

When working with Bootstrap, there is the power of Sass to consider. Sass is a preprocessor for CSS. It extends the CSS syntax with variables, mixins, and functions, and helps you in **DRY (Don't Repeat Yourself)** coding your CSS code. Sass was originally written in Ruby. Nowadays, a fast port of Sass written in C++, called **libSass** is available. Bootstrap uses the modern **SCSS** syntax for Sass instead of the older Sass's indented syntax.

> Those who work with CSS in their daily job and have some experience with functional programming language, won't find learning Sass very difficult. However, those who want to get more out of Sass should read my *Sass and Compass Designer's Cookbook* (`https://www.packtpub.com/web-development/sass-and-compass-designers-cookbook`) too.

In Bootstrap 4, Sass replaced Less. Less is another preprocessor for CSS. The Bootstrap team preferred Sass over Less, because of the increasingly large community of Sass developers. If you are used to Less and have to switch to Sass now, you should realize that Sass is more like a functional programming language in contrast to the more declarative nature of Less. In Sass you cannot use variables before declaring them first, so you have to modify your variables at the beginning of your code. Bootstrap's variables have default values which can be overwritten by declaring and assigning a new variable with the same name before the default declaration.

In contrast to Less, Sass does support `if-else-then` constructs and `for` and `foreach` loops.

When we move beyond merely applying classes to markup and take the next step to dig in and customize Bootstrap's SCSS files, we gain tremendous power and efficiency. Starting with a solid basis using Bootstrap's default styles, we can move on to innovate and customize to our heart's content. In other words, Bootstrap is a powerful resource. I intend to help you leverage it in exciting and serious ways, working with efficiency, adhering to best practices, and producing beautiful, user-friendly interfaces.

Downloading the compiled code

On `http://getbootstrap.com/`, you will find some button links which enable you to download the compiled code of Bootstrap. These downloads contain the compiled CSS and JavaScript code ready to use in your projects. The compiled code contains the CSS and JavaScript code for all of Bootstrap's components and features. Later on, you will learn to create a custom version of Bootstrap, which includes only those components and features that you really use.

Instead of the default code, you can also choose to download the Flexbox-enabled or grid-only versions.

The Flexbox enabled version

On `http://getbootstrap.com/`, you can also download a compiled version of Bootstrap with the optional Flexbox support already enabled. Since switching to the Flexbox version does not require any HTML changes, you will only have to change the CSS source.

The grid only versions

Bootstrap ships with a 12 column, responsive, and mobile first grid. People who only want to use the grid for their projects can download the grid only version. The grid only version provides the predefined grid classes and does not require any JavaScript. Those who only use the grid should add their own HTML reset which includes the `box-sizing: borderbox` setting as described in the *Box-sizing* section of this chapter.

Beside the predefined grid classes, you can also have the option of using Sass variables and mixins to create custom, semantic, and responsive page layouts.

Running Bootstrap from CDN

Instead of downloading your own copy of Bootstrap, you can also load it from **CDN** (Content Delivery Network) inside your projects. CDNs help to distribute bandwidth across multiple servers and allow users to download static content from a closer source.

 Bootstrap can be loaded from `https://www.bootstrapcdn.com/`. BootstrapCDN is powered by MaxCDN which can be found at `https://www.maxcdn.com/`.

Subresource Integrity (SRI)

CDN can be quite a risk, because others can get control over the CDN code and may inject arbitrary malicious content into files. You can prevent this risk by adding the integrity attribute to the `<script>` and `<link>` elements which loads the file from CDN. The integrity attribute should be set to a string with `base64-encoded sha384` hash. You should also add the `crossorigin` attribute. The script element to load jQuery into your project from MaxCDN may look like the following:

```
<script   src="http://code.jquery.com/jquery-2.2.3.min.js"
integrity="sha256-a23g1Nt4dtEYOj7bR+vTu7+T8VP13humZFBJNIYoEJo="
crossorigin="anonymous"></script>
```

 You can read more about Subresource Integrity checking at `https://www.w3.org/TR/SRI/`.

Downloading Bootstrap's source files

There are many other ways to download Bootstrap, but not all ways of downloading Bootstrap are equal. For what follows, we must be sure to get the Sass files, as these files give us the power to customize and innovate upon Bootstrap's underlying style rules. For this exercise, we'll go straight to the source, that is, `http://getbootstrap.com/`. You will encounter the following screenshot:

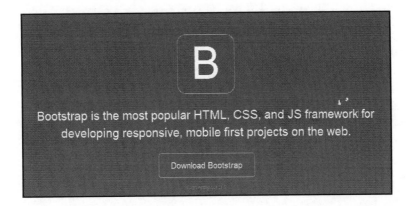

Once there, the large **Download source** button is your friend. At least as of Version 4.0, this is the second largest button on the homepage of Bootstrap:

Download source

In case something should change, you can always follow the GitHub project link at `https:/` `/github.com/twbs/bootstrap`, and once at the GitHub repository, click on the **Download ZIP** button. Or run the following command in your console to clone the repo:

```
git clone https://github.com/twbs/bootstrap.git
```

The files you'll have

Once you've downloaded the Bootstrap source files, you should see a file structure that is similar to the following screenshot:

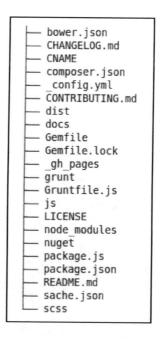

```
├── bower.json
├── CHANGELOG.md
├── CNAME
├── composer.json
├── _config.yml
├── CONTRIBUTING.md
├── dist
├── docs
├── Gemfile
├── Gemfile.lock
├── _gh_pages
├── grunt
├── Gruntfile.js
├── js
├── LICENSE
├── node_modules
├── nuget
├── package.js
├── package.json
├── README.md
├── sache.json
└── scss
```

The preceding files contain not only Bootstrap's source files, including the SCSS code and EM6 code for the jQuery plugins, but also the files to set up Bootstrap's build process. Bootstrap is built with Grunt by default. Admittedly, that's a lot of files, and we don't need them all. On the plus side, we have everything we want from Bootstrap. Notice that the source does not contain font files since the Glyphicon Halflings set has been dropped as described earlier. Bootstrap's default fonts are set by CSS only and do not require a font file.

While the exact contents of the repository will change over time, the main contents will remain relatively consistent. Most notably, in the `scss` folder, you will find all the important Sass files, which are key to every project in this book. Another benefit is that the `js` folder contains Bootstrap's individual JavaScript plugins so that these may be selectively included as needed.

On the other hand, if you want Bootstrap's default, precompiled CSS or JavaScript files (such as `bootstrap.css` or `bootstrap.min.js`), they are still available within the `dist` folder. The structure of the precompiled files will look like the following:

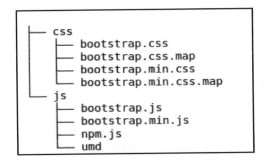

The `umd` folder in the preceding screenshot contains the plugin files ready to `require()` this file in a **CommonJS** environment. These files are **UMD** ready (**Universal Module Definition**). Both CommonJS and **AMD** are script loaders which ensure that different JavaScript components load in the right order and play nice together. The universal pattern of UMD supports both CommonJS and AMD.

As a bonus, you'll find the example HTML templates in the `docs/examples` folder. In fact, we'll use one of these examples to set up our first project template folder.

Other ways to download and integrate Bootstrap

Instead of directly downloading Bootstrap, you can also use other tool and package managers to get the files. In the overview below, you will find a list of commands and tools:

- Install with **npm**: `npm install bootstrap`
- Install with **Meteor**: `meteor add twbs:bootstrap`
- Install with **Composer**: `composer require twbs/bootstrap`
- Install with **Bower**: `bower install bootstrap`
- Install with **NuGet**:
  - **CSS**: `Install-Package bootstrap -Pre`
  - **Sass**: `Install-Package bootstrap.sass -Pre`

Tooling setup

To use the Grunt file and run Bootstrap's documentation locally, you'll need a copy of Bootstrap's source files, Node, and Grunt. Use the following steps to start working with Bootstrap's build process:

- Install the Grunt command line tools, `grunt-cli`, with `npm install -g grunt-cli`
- Navigate to the `root /bootstrap` directory and run `npm install` to install our local dependencies listed in `package.json`
- Install Ruby and install Bundler with `gem install bundler`, and finally run `bundle install`. This will install all Ruby dependencies, such as Jekyll and plugins

Now you can run the documentation locally by running the following command from the `root /bootstrap` directory in your console:

```
bundle exec jekyll serve
```

After the preceding step, the documentation and examples are available at `http://localhost:/9010`.

The HTML starter template

After downloading the Bootstrap source files, you can link the compiled CSS and JavaScript files from the `dist` folder to your HTML. You can do this by creating a new HTML template. Your HTML template should look like the following:

```
<!DOCTYPE html>
<html lang="en">
  <head>
    <!-- Required meta tags always come first -->
    <meta charset="utf-8">
    <meta name="viewport" content="width=device-width, initial-scale=1,
shrink-to-fit=no">
    <meta http-equiv="x-ua-compatible" content="ie=edge">
    <!-- Bootstrap CSS -->
    <link rel="stylesheet"
href="https://maxcdn.bootstrapcdn.com/bootstrap/4.0.0-alpha.2/css/bootstrap
.min.css">
  </head>
  <body>
    <h1>Hello, world!</h1>
    <!-- jQuery first, then Bootstrap JS. -->
    <script
src="https://ajax.googleapis.com/ajax/libs/jquery/2.1.4/jquery.min.js"></sc
ript>
    <script
src="https://cdnjs.cloudflare.com/ajax/libs/tether/1.1.2/js/tether.min.js">
</script>
    <script
src="https://maxcdn.bootstrapcdn.com/bootstrap/4.0.0-alpha.2/js/bootstrap.m
in.js"></script>
  </body>
</html>
```

As seen above, your HTML code should start with the HTML5 doctype: `<!DOCTYPE html>`

Responsive meta tag

Because of the responsive and mobile first nature of Bootstrap, your HTML code should also contain a responsive meta tag in the head section which looks like the following:

```
<meta name="viewport" content="width=device-width, initial-scale=1, shrink-
to-fit=no">
```

The mobile first strategy of Bootstrap means that the code is optimized for mobile devices first. CSS media queries are used to add more features for larger screen sizes.

The X-UA-Compatible meta tag

The `X-UA-Compatible` is another important meta tag which should be added to the head section of your HTML template. It should look like the following:

```
<meta http-equiv="x-ua-compatible" content="ie=edge">
```

The preceding meta tag is forcing Internet Explorer to use its latest rendering mode.

Bootstrap's CSS code

Of course you should also link Bootstrap's CSS code to your HTML document, the example template above loads the CSS code from CDN. You can replace the CDN URI with your local copy found in the `dist` folder as follows:

```
<link rel="stylesheet" href="dist/css/bootstrap.min.css">
```

The JavaScript files

And finally, you should link the JavaScript files at the end of your HTML code for faster loading. Bootstrap's JavaScript plugin requires jQuery, so you have to load jQuery before the plugins. The popover and plugins also require the Tether library which requires jQuery too. Link Tether after jQuery and before the plugins. Your HTML should look like the following:

```
<script
src="https://ajax.googleapis.com/ajax/libs/jquery/2.1.4/jquery.min.js"></script>
<script
src="https://cdnjs.cloudflare.com/ajax/libs/tether/1.1.2/js/tether.min.js">
</script>
<script
src="https://maxcdn.bootstrapcdn.com/bootstrap/4.0.0-alpha.2/js/bootstrap.min.js"></script>
```

Of course you can link local copies of the files instead of the CDN URIs too.

Using Bootstrap CLI

In this book you will be introduced to Bootstrap CLI. Instead of using Bootstrap's bundled build process, you can also start a new project by running the Bootstrap CLI.

Bootstrap CLI is the command-line interface for Bootstrap 4. It includes some built-in example projects, but you can also use it to employ and deliver your own projects.

You'll need the following software installed to get started with **Bootstrap CLI**:

- Node.js 0.12+: Use the installer provided on the Node.js website, which can be found at the follow URL: `https://nodejs.org/en/`
- With Node installed, run `[sudo] npm install -g grunt bower`
- Git: Use the installer for your OS
- Windows users can also try Git for Windows

Gulp is another task runner for the Node.js system. Notice that when you prefer Gulp over Grunt, you should install gulp instead of grunt with the following command:

```
[sudo] npm install -g gulp bower
```

You can read more about Gulp in Chapter 2, *Creating Your Own Build Process with Gulp*.

The Bootstrap CLI is installed through npm by running the following command in your console:

```
npm install -g bootstrap-cli
```

This will add the `bootstrap` command to your system.

Preparing a new Bootstrap project

After installing Bootstrap CLI, you can create a new Bootstrap project by running the following command in your console:

```
bootstrap new --template empty-bootstrap-project-gulp
```

Enter the name of your project for the question: "What's the project called? (no spaces)". A new folder with the project name will be created. After the setup process, the directory and file structure of your new project folder should look like that shown in the following screenshot:

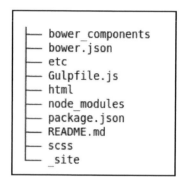

```
─── bower_components
─── bower.json
─── etc
─── Gulpfile.js
─── html
─── node_modules
─── package.json
─── README.md
─── scss
└── _site
```

The project folder also contains a `Gulpfile.js` file. In `Chapter 2`, *Creating Your Own Build Process with Gulp*, you can read how to set up a Bootstrap project with a Gulp build process yourself.

Now you can run the bootstrap watch command in your console and start editing the `html/pages/index.html` file. The HTML templates are compiled with Panini. Panini is a flat file compiler which helps you to create HTML pages with consistent layouts and reusable partials with ease.

You can read more about Panini at `http://foundation.zurb.com/sites/docs/panini.html`.

Panini compiles the HTML templates into a single `index.html` file like the base template described in the preceding sections.

Setting up major structural elements

We're almost ready for page content. Specifically, we'll create the following:

- A banner space with our logo and navigation
- A main content space for page content
- A footer area for copyright information and social links

We'll set this up using current HTML5 best practices with the support of major **Accessible Rich Internet Applications (ARIA)** role attributes (with roles such as `banner`, `navigation`, `main`, and `contentinfo`).

Run the `bootstrap watch` command, and your browser should open automatically on `http://localhost:8080/`. Then start editing the `html/pages/index.html` file; you can use your favorite text editor, and write down the following HTML code into it:

```
---
layout: default
title: Home
---
<header role="banner">
  <nav role="navigation">
  </nav>
</header>

<main role="main">
  <h1>Main Heading</h1>
  <p>Content specific to this page goes here.</p>
</main>

<footer role="contentinfo">
  <p><small>Copyright &copy; Company Name</small></p>
</footer>
```

This gives us some basic page structure and content. Let's keep rolling. Notice that the content you have added to the `html/pages/index.html` file is compiled into the `html/layout/default.html` layout template. The layout template contains the main HTML structure and links the compiled CSS and JavaScript code.

The JavaScript code has been linked at the end of the HTML code for faster performance. Notice that Gulp bundles **jQuery**, **Tether**, and the Bootstrap jQuery plugins into a single `_site/js/app.jss` file. Loading jQuery on Tether from CDN is an alternative solution.

Providing a navbar markup

The compiled CSS code is already linked to the compiled HTML code and can be found in the `_site/css` folder. We'll learn how to customize the CSS with Sass shortly. But first, let's put at least one Bootstrap-specific element in place, that is, the navbar.

Initially, we want only Bootstrap's basic navbar (we'll add other details later). I've used the markup taken from Bootstrap's documentation. This leads to the following result, nested within our `header` element:

```
<header role="banner">
<nav class="navbar navbar-light bg-faded" role="navigation">
  <a class="navbar-brand" href="index.html">Navbar</a>
  <ul class="nav navbar-nav">
    <li class="nav-item">
      <a class="nav-link active" href="#">Home <span class="sr-
only">(current)</span></a>
    </li>
    <li class="nav-item">
      <a class="nav-link" href="#">Features</a>
    </li>
    <li class="nav-item">
      <a class="nav-link" href="#">Pricing</a>
    </li>
    <li class="nav-item">
      <a class="nav-link" href="#">About</a>
    </li>
  </ul>
  <form class="form-inline pull-xs-right">
    <input class="form-control" type="text" placeholder="Search">
    <button class="btn btn-success-outline" type="submit">Search</button>
  </form>
</nav>
</header>
```

Save your results, and the browser will automatically refresh. You should now see Bootstrap's default navigation styles, and you'll also see some typographic enhancements as shown in the following screenshot. This is Bootstrap CSS at work. Congratulations!

We now have the default Bootstrap styles in place.

The CSS classes of the navbar

As you can see in the preceding navbar example, you can construct the navbar with standard HTML elements, such as the `<nav>`, `<a>` and `<ul>`, and Bootstrap's CSS classes.

First inspect the classes added to the `<nav>` element in the following snippet:

```
<nav class="navbar navbar-light bg-faded" role="navigation"></nav>

The .nav class sets the basic styles for the navbar.
```

The `.navbar-light` and `.navbar-dark` classes set the color of the texts and links in the navbar. You should use the `.navbar-light` classes when the background color of the navbar has a light color and the .navbar-dark class for dark colored navbars.

Finally, the `.bg-*` classes set the background color of the navbar; you can use one of the following classes to do this: `.bg-inverse`, `.bg-faded`, `.bg-primary`, `.bg-success`, `.bg-info`, `.bg-warning` and `.bg-danger`. These classes are part of Bootstrap's contextual backgrounds and can also be used for other elements and components.

The title or heading of the navbar can be an `<a>` or `<span>` element with the `.navbar-brand` class.

The navbar items are built with an unnumbered list (`<url>`), wherein each list item (`<li>`) gets the `.nav-item` tag and contains an anchor (`<a>`) tag with the `.navbar-link` class. Active items not only have the `.navbar-link` class but also the `.active` class.

Finally, notice the `.sr-only` class in the following snippet of the navbar HTML code:

```
<span class="sr-only">(current)</span>
```

HTML elements with the `.sr-only` class are only available for screen readers.

More information about this can be found at
`http://a11yproject.com/posts/how-to-hide-content/`.

Placement of the navbars

By default, navbars have rounded corners and are statically placed on the page. Special CSS classes can be used to fix the navbar at the top (`.navbar-fixed-top`) or bottom (`.navbar-fixed-bottom`) of the page or remove the rounded corners and set the z-index of the navbar (`.nav bar-full`). Now, let's complete our navbar by making it responsive. As a bonus, this will test to ensure that Bootstrap's JavaScript plugins are working as they should.

Adding collapsible content to the navbar

Bootstrap's collapsible plugin allows you to create collapsible content by simply using a `<a>` and `<button>` tag to toggle hidden content. You can add the toggle button to your navbar too.

First create your collapsible content and wrap it in a `<div class="collapse">` with a unique id as follows:

```
<div class="collapse" id="collapsiblecontent">
Collapsible content
</div>
```

Then create the button with `.navbar-toggler` class and `data-toggle` and `data-target` attributes like that shown in the HTML code shown as follows:

```
<button class="navbar-toggler" type="button" data-toggle="collapse" data-target="#collapsiblecontent">
≡;
; </button>
```

In the above code snippet, the `data-toggle` attribute should be set to `collapse` to trigger the collapse plugin, and the `data-target` attribute should refer to the unique ID set for your collapsible content. Notice that the `&#9776`HTML code defines the so-called *hamburger sign* which looks like this:

Now you can bring the preceding codes together and place the button in the navbar. Write down the following HTML in the `html/pages/index.html` file and inspect the results in your browser:

```
<header>
  <div class="collapse" id="collapsiblecontent">
    Collapsible content
  </div>
  <nav class="navbar navbar-light bg-faded" role="navigation">
  <button class="navbar-toggler" type="button" data-toggle="collapse" data-
target="#collapsiblecontent">
      ≡
  </button>
  </nav>
</header>
```

If you are still running the bootstrap watch command, your browser should automatically reload. The result should look like that shown in the following screenshot:

Click the *hamburger* and you should find that the collapsible content becomes visible. Now you can be sure that the collapse plugin works as expected. The collapse plugin is also used for a responsive navbar as discussed in the next section.

Content wrapped in the .collapse is hidden by default. By clicking the toggle button, the plugin adds the .in class which sets the display to visible. The plugin starts with adding a temporary .collapsing class which sets a CSS animation that ensures the transition goes ahead smoothly.

Responsive features and breakpoints

Bootstrap has got four breakpoints at 544, 768, 992 and 1200 pixels by default. At these breakpoints your design may adapt to and target specific devices and viewport sizes. Bootstrap's mobile-first and responsive grid(s) also use these breakpoints. You can read more about the grids later on.

You can use these breakpoints to specify and name the viewport ranges as follows; the extra small (xs) range for portrait phones with a viewport smaller than 544 pixels, the small (sm) range for landscape phones with viewports smaller than 768 pixels, the medium (md) range for tablets with viewports smaller than 992 pixels, the large (lg) range for desktop with viewports wider than 992 pixels, and finally the extra large (xl) range for desktops with a viewport wider than 1200 pixels. The break points are in pixel values as the viewport pixel size does not depend on the font size and modern browsers have already fixed some zooming bugs.

Some people claim em values should be preferred.

To learn more about this, have a look at the following link: `http://zellwk .com/blog/media-query-units/`.

Those who still prefer em values over pixel values can simply change the `$grid-breakpoints` variable declaration in the `scss/includes/_variables.scss` file. To use em values for media queries, the SCSS code should look like the following:

```scss
$grid-breakpoints: (
  // Extra small screen / phone
  xs: 0,
  // Small screen / phone
  sm: 34em, // 544px
  // Medium screen / tablet
  md: 48em, // 768px
  // Large screen / desktop
  lg: 62em, // 992px
  // Extra large screen / wide desktop
  xl: 75em //1200px
);
```

Notice that you also have to change the `$container-max-widths` variable declaration. You should change or modify Bootstrap's variables in the local `scss/includes/_variables.scss` file, as explained at `http://bassjobsen.weblogs.fm /preserve_settings_and_customizations_when_updating_bootstrap/`. This will ensure that your changes are not overwritten when updating Bootstrap.

Responsive utility classes

Bootstrap contains some predefined utility classes for faster mobile-friendly development. You can use these classes to show or hide content by device and viewport via media query.

The .hidden-*-up classes, where the asterisks can be replaced with one of the breakpoint shorthand names, hide everything for viewports wider than the given breakpoint. So for instance, the .hidden-md-up class hides an element on medium, large, and extra-large viewports. On the other hand, the .hidden-md-down classes go in the other direction and hide an element when the viewport is smaller than the breakpoint.

Bootstrap's media query ranges, or breakpoints are also available via Sass mixins. The media-breakpoint-up() mixin with one of the breakpoint shorthands as an input parameter sets the min-width value of the media query to hide content for viewports wider than the breakpoint. The max-width of the media query to hide everything for viewports smaller than the breakpoint can be set with the media-breakpoint-down() mixin.

Consider the following SCSS, which can be written down at the end of the scss/app.scss file:

```
p {
font-size: 1.2em;
    @include media-breakpoint-up(md) {
      font-size: 1em;
    }
}
```

```
The preceding SCSS code compiles into static CSS code as follows:
p {
    font-size: 1.2em;
}

@media (min-width: 768px) {
  p {
    font-size: 1em;
  }
}
```

Completing the responsive navbar

To completely make our navbar take advantage of Bootstrap's responsive navbar solution, we need to add two new elements, with appropriate classes and data attributes.

We'll begin by adding the toggle button to the navbar code we have used before. The HTML code of your button should look like the following:

```
<button class="navbar-toggler hidden-md-up pull-xs-right" type="button"
data-toggle="collapse" data-target="#collapsiblecontent">
    ≡
</button>
```

As you can see in the preceding HTML code, the button has the same data attributes as before, from the collapsible content example, since the responsive navbar uses the collapse plugin too. The button has a `.hidden-md-up` utility class, as described before, to hide the button for viewports wider than 768px. The `.pull-xs-right` class ensures that the button floats on the right side of the navbar.

Secondly, you have to add the classes of the element which should collapse. We collapse the `<ul>` that holds the navigation links. Add the `.navbar-toggleable-sm` that ensures that the elements do not collapse on viewports larger than the breakpoint, while the `.collapse` class hides the element by default. Finally, set the unique ID specified on the `data-target` attribute of the button before. Your HTML code should look like the following now:

```
<ul class="nav navbar-nav navbar-toggleable-sm collapse"
id="collapsiblecontent"></ul>
```

The complete HTML code of your responsive navbar should look as follows. You can add it to the `html/pages/index.html` file to test it in your browser:

```
<header role="banner">
  <nav class="navbar navbar-light bg-faded" role="navigation">
  <a class="navbar-brand" href="index.html">Navbar</a>
   <button class="navbar-toggler hidden-md-up pull-xs-right" type="button"
data-toggle="collapse" data-target="#collapsiblecontent">
      ≡
  </button>
  <ul class="nav navbar-nav navbar-toggleable-sm collapse"
id="collapsiblecontent">
    <li class="nav-item">
      <a class="nav-link active" href="#">Home <span class="sr-
only">(current)</span></a>
    </li>
    <li class="nav-item">
      <a class="nav-link" href="#">Features</a>
    </li>
    <li class="nav-item">
      <a class="nav-link" href="#">Pricing</a>
    </li>
    <li class="nav-item">
```

```
          <a class="nav-link" href="#">About</a>
      </li>
    </ul>
    </nav>
</header>
```

 The tag structure, class names, or data attributes may change with future versions of Bootstrap. If yours does not work as it should, be sure to check Bootstrap's own documentation. As a fallback option, you can start with the starting files provided with the sample code for this book.

The `.navbar-brand` and `.nav-link` classes have a `float:left` set by default. So that your navigation links should not float for the collapsed version of your navbar, you should undo the float. You can use the following SCSS code to remove the float for smaller viewports, and write it down at the end of the `scss/app.sccs` file:

```
.navbar {
  @include media-breakpoint-down(sm) {
    .navbar-brand,
    .nav-item {
      float: none;
    }
  }
}
```

If you run the bootstrap watch command your browser should automatically reload after saving the HTML or Sass code, if not, run the command again. Your browser should show the results at `http://localhost:8080/`. Click on and drag the edge of the browser window to make the window narrower than `768` pixels.

If all works as it should, you should see a collapsed version of the navbar, as shown in the following screenshot, with the site name or logo and a toggle button:

This is a good sign! Now click on the toggle button, and it should slide open, as shown in the following screenshot:

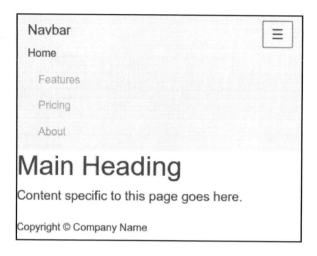

Success! Congratulations!

The new Reboot module and Normalize.css.

When talking about cascade in CSS, there will, no doubt, be a mention of the browser default settings getting a higher precedence than the author's preferred styling. In other words, anything that is not defined by the author will be assigned a default styling set by the browser. The default styling may differ for each browser and this behavior plays a major role in many cross-browser issues. To prevent these sorts of problems, you can perform a CSS reset CSS or HTML resets set a default author style for commonly used HTML elements to make sure that browser default styles do not mess up your pages or render your HTML elements to be different on other browsers.

Bootstrap uses Normalize.css written by Nicholas Galagher. Normalize.css is a modern, HTML5-ready alternative to CSS resets and can be downloaded from `http://necolas.git hub.io/normalize.css/`. It lets browsers render all elements more consistently and makes them adhere to modern standards. Together with some other styles, Normalize.css forms the new Reboot module of Bootstrap.

Box-sizing

The Reboot module also sets the globalbox-sizing value from `content-box` to `border-box`. The **box-sizing** property is the one that sets the CSS-box model used for calculating the dimensions of an element. In fact, box-sizing is not new in CSS, but nonetheless, switching your code to `box-sizing: border-box` will make your work a lot easier. When using the `border-box` settings, calculation of the width of an element includes border width and padding. So, changing the border width or padding of an element won't break your layouts.

Predefined CSS classes

Bootstrap ships with predefined CSS classes for everything. You can build a mobile first responsive grid for your project by only using div elements and the right grid classes. CSS classes for styling other elements and components are available too. Consider the styling of a button in the following HTML code:

```
<button class="btn btn-warning">Warning!</button>
```

Now your button will look like that shown in the preceding screenshot:

You should notice that Bootstrap uses two classes to style a single button. The first `.btn` class gives the button the general button layout styles. The second `.btn-warning` class sets the custom colors of the buttons.

 Partial attribute selectors in CSS give us the ability to make *partial* matches to attribute values. You can, for instance, match all elements having a class starting with `btn-`, so you may wonder why Bootstrap does not use the `[class^='btn-']` attribute selector instead of the `.btn` class to set the general button styles. Firstly, Bootstrap avoids partial attribute selectors, since some people claimed these selectors are slow. Secondly, `[class^='btn-']`does not match "not btn-".

You can also use these classes to style a hyperlink (`<a>`) like a button as follows:

```
<a class="btn btn-primary" href="#" role="button">Link</a>
```

Sass variables and mixins

You can change Bootstrap's default styles by changing the Sass variables in the `scss/_variabels.scss` file. Setting the `$brand-primary` variable to a different color value will change the look of the buttons with the btn-primary class in the preceding example.

You can reuse Bootstrap's Sass mixins to extend Bootstrap with your own custom classes. Sass mixins and variables are available to build your own (semantic) grid, but you can also create a custom button class by using the following SCSS code:

```scss
.btn-tomato {
  @include button-variant(white, tomato, white);
}
```

The preceding SCSS code compiles into the CSS code like the following:

```css
.btn-tomato {
  color: white;
  background-color: tomato;
  border-color: white;
}
.btn-tomato:hover {
  color: white;
  background-color: #ff3814;
  border-color: #e0e0e0;
}
.btn-tomato:focus, .btn-tomato.focus {
  color: white;
  background-color: #ff3814;
  border-color: #e0e0e0;
}
.btn-tomato:active, .btn-tomato.active,
.open > .btn-tomato.dropdown-toggle {
  color: white;
  background-color: #ff3814;
  border-color: #e0e0e0;
  background-image: none;
}
.btn-tomato:active:hover, .btn-tomato:active:focus, .btn-tomato:active.focus, .btn-tomato.active:hover, .btn-tomato.active:focus, .btn-tomato.active.focus,
  .open > .btn-tomato.dropdown-toggle:hover,
  .open > .btn-tomato.dropdown-toggle:focus,
  .open > .btn-tomato.dropdown-toggle.focus {
  color: white;
  background-color: #ef2400;
```

```
        border-color: #bfbfbf;
    }
    .btn-tomato.disabled:focus, .btn-tomato.disabled.focus, .btn-
tomato:disabled:focus, .btn-tomato:disabled.focus {
        background-color: tomato;
        border-color: white;
    }
    .btn-tomato.disabled:hover, .btn-tomato:disabled:hover {
        background-color: tomato;
        border-color: white;
    }
```

Bootstrap's Sass code avoids element and nested selectors; a motivation can be found at `http://markdotto.com/2015/07/20/css-nesting/`.

Bootstrap itself also avoids the `@extend` feature of Sass. The risk of using the `@extend` feature is creating complex unused CSS code. See also Hugo Giraudel's article at `https://www.sitepoint.com/avoid-sass-extend/`.

Using selector placeholders may reduce this risk, however Bootstrap does not use placeholder selectors. This does not forbid you from customizing and extending Bootstrap by using the `@extend` feature. You can, for instance, use the `@extend` feature to make your images responsive by default.

Images are not responsive by default in Bootstrap. To make an image responsive, you'll have to add the `.img-fluid` class to your `<img>` element.

You can use the `@extend` feature to make your images responsive by default by adding the following SCSS code at the end of the `scss/app.scss` file:

```
img {
    @extend .img-fluid;
}
```

Those who think using mixins is better than the `@extend` feature, should realize that Bootstrap's Sass code does not contain a mixin for making fluid images at all.

Browser support

As mentioned before, Bootstrap 4 does not support Internet Explorer version 8 and earlier. For projects that should support this browser I recommend you to use Bootstrap 3 instead. Bootstrap 4 also comes with optional Flexbox support. Only Internet explorer versions 11 and higher support the **CSS3 Flexible Box Layout Module**. You can read more about the pros and cons of the Flexbox module later on, in the *Flexible Boxes* section of this chapter. Besides Internet Explorer 8 and earlier, Bootstrap supports all major browsers, including many mobile browsers.

Vendor prefixes

CSS3 introduced **vendor-specific** rules, which offer you the possibility of writing some additional CSS, applicable for only one browser. At first sight, this seems the exact opposite of what we want. What we want is a set of standards and practicalities that work the same with every browser and a standard set of HTML and CSS which has the same effect and interpretation for every browser. These vendor-specific rules are intended to help us reach this utopia. Vendor-specific rules also provide us with early implementations of standard properties and alternative syntax. Last but not least, these rules allow browsers to implement proprietary **CSS** properties that would otherwise have no working standard (and may never actually become the standard).

For these reasons, vendor-specific rules play an important role in many new features of CSS3. For example, **animation properties, border-radius**, and **box-shadow**: all did depend on vendor-specific rules in past years. You can easily see that some properties may evolve from vendor prefixes to standard, because currently, most browsers support the **border-radius,** and **box-shadow** properties without any prefix.

Vendors use the following prefixes:

- **WebKit**: -webkit
- **Firefox**: -moz
- **Opera**: -o
- **Internet Explorer**: -ms

Consider the following CSS code:

```
transition: all .2s ease-in-out;
```

For full browser support, or to support at least the browser supported by Bootstrap, we'll have to write:

```
-webkit-transition: all .2s ease-in-out;
-o-transition: all .2s ease-in-out;
transition: all .2s ease-in-out;
```

More information about the transition property and browser support can also be found at the following URL: `http://caniuse.com/#feat=css-transitions`.

Because of different browsers and their different versions, browsers may use different vendor prefixes to support the same property in writing cross-browser CSS code which can become very complex.

Bootstrap's Sass code, which compiles into CSS code does not contain any prefixes. Instead of using prefixes, the **PostCSS autoprefixer** has been integrated into Bootstrap's build process. When you create your own build process you should also use the **PostCSS autoprefixer**. In `Chapter 2`, *Creating Your Own Build Process with Gulp,* you can read how to set up a build chain with Gulp.

Flexible boxes

Bootstrap 4 also comes with optional Flexbox support. The **Flexbox Layout** (also called flexible boxes) is a new feature of CSS3. It is extremely useful in creating responsive and flexible layouts. Flexbox provides the ability to dynamically change the layout for different screen resolutions. It does not use floats and contains margins that do not collapse with their content. The latest versions of all major browsers now support Flexbox layouts.

Information about browser support can also be found at `http://caniuse.com/#feat=flexbox`. Unfortunately, many older browsers do not have support for Flexbox layouts.

To enable Flexbox support, you will have to set the `$enable-flex` Sass variable to `true` and recompile Bootstrap. You do not have to change your HTML code after enabling Flexbox support.

The Yeoman workflow

Yeoman helps you to kickstart new projects, and you can use it as an alternative for Bootstrap CLI.

The Yeoman workflow comprises three types of tools for improving your productivity and satisfaction when building a web app: the scaffolding tool (`yo`), the build tool (Grunt, Gulp, and so on), and the package manager (like Bower and npm).

A Yeoman generator that scaffolds out a front-end Bootstrap 4 web app is available at `https://github.com/bassjobsen/generator-bootstrap4`. You can install it after installing Yeoman by running the following commands in your console:

- Install: `npm install -g generator-bootstrap4`
- Run: `yo bootstrap4`
- Run `grunt` for building and `grunt serve` for preview

The Yeoman generator for Bootstrap enables you to install your code with flexbox support. The generator can also install the Font Awesome and / or the Octicons icons fonts for direct usage in your app:

```
$ yo bootstrap4

     _-----_
    |       |    .--------------------------.
    |  (o)  |    |  'Allo 'allo! Out of the |
   `---------'   |  box I include Bootstrap |
   ( _'U'_ )     |     4, jQuery, and a     |
   /___A___\     |   Gruntfile to build your |
    |  ~  |      |           app.           |
  __'.___.'__    '--------------------------'
 ´   `  |° ´ Y `

? Would you like to enable flexbox (reduced browser and device support)? (y/N) █
```

Troubleshooting

If things are not running smoothly, you should ask yourself the following questions:

- Is your markup properly structured? Any unclosed, incomplete, or malformed tags, classes, and so on present?

You might find it helpful to do the following:

- Work back through the preceding steps, double-checking things along the way.
- Validate your HTML to ensure it's well formed.
- Compare the completed version of the exercise files with your own.
- Refer to the Bootstrap documentation for new updates to the relevant tag structures and attributes.
- Place your code in a snippet at `https://jsfiddle.net/` or `https://codepen.io/`, and share it with the good folks at `http://stackoverflow.com/` for help.

When we have so many moving parts to work with, things are bound to happen and these are some of our best survival methods!

Bootply is a playground for Bootstrap, CSS, JavaScript, and jQuery; you can use it to test your HTML code. You can also add your compiled CSS code, but Bootply cannot compile your CSS code.

Bootply can be found online at `http://www.bootply.com/`.

Our site template is almost complete. Let's pause to take stock before moving on.

Summary

If you've made it this far, you have everything you need ready to do some serious work. You have learned the basics of a new Bootstrap 4 project. You can easily set up a new project with Bootstrap CLI now and build a responsive navbar (navigation). The navbar uses the JavaScript Collapse plugin. You understand how to compile Bootstrap's Sass code into CSS now and finally got a better understanding of Bootstrap CSS and HTML code, including browser support.

This may be a good point to save a copy of these files so that they're ready for other future projects.

In the next chapter, you will learn how to set up your own build process with Gulp and automatically compile your projects.

2
Creating Your Own Build Process with Gulp

In this chapter, you will learn how to set up your own build process for your Bootstrap project. Bootstrap's CSS is written in Sass, so when you are not using the precompiled CSS code, you will have to compile the CSS code by yourself. You'll need a Sass compiler to compile the Sass code into CSS.

Also, Bootstrap JavaScript plugins should be bundled and minified before being taken into production.

After reading this chapter, you will have learned to:

- Set up a build process with Gulp
- Create different environments in your build processor
- Compile your Sass code into CSS
- Automatically add vendor prefixes to your CSS code
- Prepare the JavaScript plugin for your project
- Run a static web server
- Test your code
- Use standard Bootstrap components and tweak them to fit your needs
- Create a simple one-page marketing website with Bootstrap
- Publish your project on GitHub

What are we going to build?

In this chapter, you will create a build process for an example project. The process not only prepares your CSS and JavaScript code, but also runs a static web server, which automatically reloads on file changes in browser testing, runs some tests for your code, and more.

To demonstrate the different steps of the build process, you will create an example project. The example project is a simple one-page marketing layout powered by Bootstrap. At the end, you should have created an HTML page, which will look like that shown in the following screenshot:

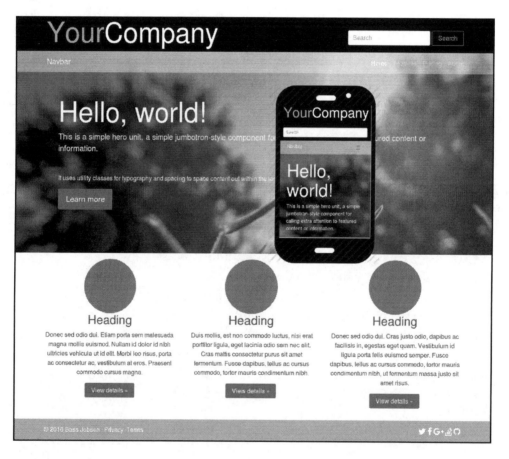

Requirements

Node.js is a JavaScript runtime environment built on **Chrome's V8 JavaScript engine**. Node.js uses an event-driven non-blocking input/output model and is very lightweight and efficient. To run the example code in this chapter, you should have installed Node.js on your system. Download the Node.js source code or a pre-built installer for your platform at `https://nodejs.org/en/download/`. Node.js is available for Linux, Mac OSX, and Windows.

npm is the package manager for Node.js, and it is installed automatically when installing Node.js.

After installing Node.js and npm, you should also install Gulp globally on your system. You can install Gulp by running the following command in your console:

```
npm install --global gulp-cli
```

What is Gulp and why should you use it?

Gulp is a task runner for Node.js. You can use it to create a build system. You can easily add automating tasks such as modification and copying to the build system. You can also use Gulp to create watch events. These events automatically rerun the tasks of the build system when a file changes. Bootstrap's CSS code is built with Sass, and you can use Gulp to compile your Sass code into static CSS code. After compiling your Sass code, you can build a task to post-process your CSS code.

Further on you will read that you can also use Gulp to test your code, run some linters, and get your code ready for production by minifying and optimizing it. Linting is the process of running a program that will analyze code for potential errors.

Bootstrap's build process

Bootstrap ships with its own build process. At the time of writing this book, Bootstrap's build process is written with **Grunt**. It enables you to compile and prepare a custom version of Bootstrap and run the documentation locally. Grunt is just like Gulp: it is a task runner for Node.js. Grunt does not use streams but saves the temporary code in file products.

The tasks for Bootstrap's Grunt build process can be found in the `Gruntfile.js` file included in the source files. You can use this file to understand which tasks you will have to run to get your code ready for testing in production.

In this chapter, we use Gulp instead of Grunt since Gulp is considered to be more intuitive and much easier to learn. Gulp is newer than Grunt, but its community is growing fast and new plugins are added every day.

Finally, you should note that task runners that link Gulp and Grunt will make your work easier but are not required to run your tasks on Node.js.

Installing Gulp in your project

Before we go any further, we must first initiate npm for our project by running the following command in our console:

```
npm init
```

Answer the questions like those shown in the following screenshot:

```
$ npm init
This utility will walk you through creating a package.json file.
It only covers the most common items, and tries to guess sensible defaults.

See `npm help json` for definitive documentation on these fields
and exactly what they do.

Use `npm install <pkg> --save` afterwards to install a package and
save it as a dependency in the package.json file.

Press ^C at any time to quit.
name: (tmp) bootstrap-one-page-marketing-design
version: (1.0.0)
description: Simple One Page Marketing Website Design powered by Bootstrap 4
entry point: (index.js) Gulpfile.js
test command: gulp test
git repository: https://github.com/bassjobsen/bootstrap-one-page-marketing-design/
keywords: bootstrap, panini, sass, gulp
author: Bass Jobsen
license: (ISC) MIT
```

The preceding command creates a new package.json file; this file holds various metadata relevant to the project, and it also contains the dependencies for the project. The Gulp plugins you will install later on are all (dev) dependencies of your project.

Now install Gulp in your project, devDependencies, by running the following command in your console:

```
npm install --save-dev gulp
```

The --save-dev flag writes down Gulp as a devDependency into the package.json file.

Creating the Gulpfile.js which holds your tasks

Create a new file called Gulpfile.js in your project directory and write down the following JavaScript code into it:

```
var gulp = require('gulp');

gulp.task('default', function() {
  // place code for your default task here
});
```

Later on you will add your Gulp task into this file. You can test it already by running the following command in your console:

```
gulp
```

The default task will run and do nothing.

Now you're ready to install not only Bootstrap but also the required Gulp plugins for your build process.

The clean task

Each time the build process runs, the clean task should remove the temporary _site directory and all of its contents:

```
// Erases the dist folder
gulp.task('clean', function() {
  rimraf('_site');
});
```

Notice that you'll have to install rimraf as follows:

```
npm install rimraf --save-dev
```

Setting up environments for development and production

Of course, you will need your build process to develop your project, but after that you will run different tasks to get your code ready for production. In the development stage, you need CSS code with **CSS sourcemaps** for easy debugging, and in the production stage, you probably will minify the CSS code without CSS sourcemaps.

The `gulp-environments` plugin makes it convenient to create separate environments, such as development and production, to run your tasks in. You can install this plugin by running the following command:

```
npm install --save-dev gulp-environments
```

Then add the plugin to your `Gulpfile.js` file, which should look like this:

```
var environments = require('gulp-environments');
```

Then assign the environments as follows:

```
var development = environments.development;
var production = environments.production;
```

Now you can pass a command line flag `--env` to set the environment:

```
gulp build --env development
```

You can also, conditionally assign a variable like:

```
var source = production() ? "source.min.js" : "source.js";
```

Or run sub tasks for only one environment:

```
.pipe(development(sourcemaps.init()))
```

 The full documentation and some examples of the gulp-environments plugin can be found at: `https://github.com/gunpowderlabs/gulp-envi ronments`.

Installing Bootstrap via Bower

Bower is a package management system for client-side programming. You can use Bower to install Bootstrap's source code and keep it up to date more easily. Initiate Bower by running the following command in your console:

```
bower init
```

Answer the questions like those shown in the following screenshot:

```
$ bower init
? name bootstrap-one-page-marketing-design
? description Simple One Page Marketing Website Design powered by Bootstrap 4
? main file Gulpfile.js
? what types of modules does this package expose?
? keywords bootstrap, panini, gulp, sass
? authors Bass Jobsen <bass@w3masters.nl>
? license MIT
? homepage https://github.com/bassjobsen/bootstrap-one-page-marketing-design/
? set currently installed components as dependencies? No
? add commonly ignored files to ignore list? Yes
? would you like to mark this package as private which prevents it from being ac
cidentally published to the registry? Yes
```

After the preceding steps, a `bower.json` file is created. Then run the following command in your console:

```
bower install bootstrap#4 --save-dev
```

The preceding command downloads Bootstrap to the `bower_components` folder. Notice that jQuery and Tether are also installed since Bootstrap depends on these libraries.

The `--save-dev` flag writes down Bootstrap as a `devDependency` into the `bower.json` file.

Creating a local Sass structure

Before we can start compiling Bootstrap's Sass code into CSS code, we have to create some local Sass or SCSS files. First, create a new `scss` subdirectory in your project directory. In the `scss` directory, create your main project file called `app.scss`.

Then create a new subdirectory in the new `scss` directory called `includes`. Now you will have to copy the `bootstrap.scss` and `_variables.scss` from the Bootstrap source code in the `bower_components` directory to the new `scss/includes` directory:

```
cp bower_components/bootstrap/scss/bootstrap.scss
scss/includes/_bootstrap.scss
cp bower_components/bootstrap/scss/_variables.scss scss/includes/
```

Notice that the `bootstrap.scss` file has been renamed as `_bootstrap.scss`, starting with an underscore, and has become a partial file now.

Import the files you have copied in the previous step into the `app.scss` file as follows:

```
@import "includes/variables";
@import "includes/bootstrap";
```

Then open the `scss/includes/_bootstrap.scss` file and change the import part for the Bootstrap partial files, so that the original code in the `bower_components` directory will be imported here. Notice that we set the include path for the Sass compiler to the `bower_components` directory later on. The `@import` statements should look like that shown in the following SCSS code:

```
// Core variables and mixins
@import "bootstrap/scss/variables";
@import "bootstrap/scss/mixins";
// Reset and dependencies
@import "bootstrap/scss/normalize";
.....
```

You're importing all of Bootstrap's SCSS code in your project now. When preparing your code for production, you can consider commenting out the partials you do not require for your project.

Modification of the `scss/includes/_variables.scss` is not required, but you can consider removing the `!default` declarations because the real default values are set in the original `_variables.scss` file which is imported after the local one.

Notice that the local `scss/includes/_variables.scss` file does not have to contain a copy of all Bootstrap's variables. Having them all makes it easier to modify them for customization; it also ensures that your default values do not change when updating Bootstrap.

Compiling Bootstrap's Sass code into CSS code

Now it's time to start compiling the Sass code into CSS code. Bootstrap's Sass code is written in the newer SCSS syntax. In this chapter, we do not discuss Sass in great detail. You should read Chapter 3, *Customizing Your Blog with Bootstrap and Sass*, to learn more about Sass itself.

Two Gulp plugins are available to compile Sass into CSS with Gulp. The first plugin is called gulp-ruby-sass and as its name already tells you, it compiles Sass to CSS with Ruby Sass. The second gulp-sass plugin uses node-sass to compile your Sass code with libSass. In this book, a gulp-sass plugin is used. Notice that Compass is not compatible with libSass.

You can install gulp-sass in your project by running the following command in your console:

```
npm install gulp-sass --save-dev
```

After installing the plugin, you can add the compile task to your Gulpfile.js as follows:

```
var sass = require('gulp-sass');
var bowerpath = process.env.BOWER_PATH || 'bower_components/';
var sassOptions = {
  errLogToConsole: true,
  outputStyle: 'expanded',
  includePaths: bowerpath
};

gulp.task('compile-sass', function () {
    return gulp.src('./scss/app.scss')
        .pipe(sass(sassOptions).on('error', sass.logError))
        .pipe(gulp.dest('./_site/css/'));
});
```

Notice that we set the includePaths option to the bowerpath variable as described previously; and also the development() condition is used to write CSS sourcemaps only in the development stage. You can read more about CSS sourcemaps in the next section.

CSS sourcemaps for debugging

The Sass compiler merges different Sass files to a single CSS file. This CSS file has been minified in most cases. When you are inspecting the source of HTML files with the developer tools of your browser, you cannot relate the style effects to your original Sass code. CSS Sourcemaps solve this problem by mapping the combined/minified file back to its unbuilt state.

CSS source maps were introduced to map minified JavaScript to its origin source. Since version 3 of the CSS source map protocol, it has also support for CSS. The Sass compiler (or better, the `gulp-sourcemap` plugin in this case) generates the CSS source map and adds a reference into the CSS file as follows:

```
/*# sourceMappingURL=app.css.map */
```

In the following screenshot, you will find an example of the style rules pointing to their Sass file of origin in the browser's developer's tools:

To use CSS sourcemaps, you have to install the `gulp-sourcemaps` plugin first:

```
npm install gulp-sourcemaps --save-dev
```

After that you can add the sourcemaps to your `compile-sass` task as follows:

```
gulp.task('compile-sass', function () {
    return gulp.src('./scss/app.scss')
```

```
        .pipe(development(sourcemaps.init()))
        .pipe(sass(sassOptions).on('error', sass.logError))
        .pipe(development(sourcemaps.write()))
        .pipe(gulp.dest('./_site/css/'));
});
```

Notice that the CSS sourcemaps are only generated in the development stage due to the `development()` wrapping and the `gulp-environments` plugin.

The `gulp-sourcemaps` plugin does also support the `gulp-postcss` and `gulp-cssnano` plugins as described later on. You should call these plugins between the `sourcemaps.init()` and `sourcemaps.write()` calls in the `compile-sass` task.

Running the postCSS autoprefixer

Since version 3.2, Bootstrap requires the autoprefixer plugin for vendor prefixing your CSS code. Running the postCSS autoprefixer plugin is easy and fully automated with Gulp.

The `gulp-postcss` plugin enables you to run other plugins to post-process your compiled CSS code.

Bootstrap requires the `postcss` autoprefixer which you can run with the `gulp-postcss` plugin. The autoprefixer automatically adds the required vendor prefixes to your CSS code, and it uses the data of the Can I Use database (`http://caniuse.com/`).

Notice that Bootstrap also requires the `mq4-hover-shim`, which is a shim for the Media Queries Level 4 hover @media feature.

See `https://www.npmjs.com/package/mq4-hover-shim` for more details about this shim.

Perform the following steps to install and configure both the `autoprefixer` and `mq4-hover-shim`. Start by running the following command in your console:

```
npm install gulp-postcss autoprefixer mq4-hover-shim --save-dev
```

Now you can declare a variable which contains your processors for the `gulp-postcss` plugin at the `Gulpfile.js`:

```
var processors = [
mq4HoverShim.postprocessorFor({ hoverSelectorPrefix: '.bs-true-hover ' }),
autoprefixer({
browsers: [
//
// Official browser support policy:
```

```
    //
    http://v4-alpha.getbootstrap.com/getting-started/browsers-devices/#supporte
    d-browsers
    //
    'Chrome >= 35',
    'Firefox >= 38',
    'Edge >= 12',
    'Explorer >= 9',
    'iOS >= 8',
    'Safari >= 8',
    'Android 2.3',
    'Android >= 4',
    'Opera >= 12'
    ]
    })
    ];
```

As you can see, the autoprefixer accepts a hash argument which sets which browser should be supported. You can copy this hash from the `bower_components/bootstrap/Grunt.js` file of Bootstrap's source files.

After setting your processors you can add the postcss plugin to your sass compile task as follows. Notice also that the `gulp-postcss` plugin supports the `gulp-sourcemaps` plugin:

```
gulp.task('compile-sass', function () {
    return gulp.src('./scss/app.scss')
        .pipe(development(sourcemaps.init()))
        .pipe(sass(sassOptions).on('error', sass.logError))
        .pipe(postcss(processors))
        .pipe(development(sourcemaps.write()))
        .pipe(gulp.dest('./_site/css/'));
});
```

Getting your CSS code ready for production

In the production stage of your project, you do not need CSS sourcemaps anymore. The `development()` wrapping in the `compile-sass` task already guarantees that CSS sourcemaps are not generated when the environment is set to production by the `gulp-environments` plugin.

The smaller your compiled CSS code, the faster it will load in your browser. So minifying the compiled CSS code will allow faster loading. CSSnano runs your CSS code through many focused optimizations, to ensure that the final result is as small as possible for a production environment.

A Gulp plugin for CSS nano is available too; you can install it by running the following command in your console:

```
npm install gulp-cssnano --save-dev
```

After installing the plugin, you can add it to your compile-sass task:

```
var cssnano = require('gulp-cssnano');
gulp.task('compile-sass', function () {
    return gulp.src('./scss/app.scss')
        .pipe(development(sourcemaps.init()))
        .pipe(sass(sassOptions).on('error', sass.logError))
        .pipe(postcss(processors))
        .pipe(production(cssnano()))
        .pipe(development(sourcemaps.write()))
        .pipe(gulp.dest('./_site/css/'));
});
```

The preceding code makes it clear that cssnano only runs when the environment is set to production. You can also run cssnano as a processor for the gulp-postcss plugin.

The most common issue for CSS performance is unused CSS code. You can comment out the CSS components and other code that you do not use in the scss/includes/_bootstrap.scss file to make your compiled CSS code smaller.

Linting your SCSS code

When you are using Sass to extend and modify Bootstrap's CSS code, it is important that you keep your code clean and readable. The SCSS-lint tool can help you to write clean and reusable SCSS code. A Gulp plugin is available for the SCSS-lint tool and you can install it by running the following command in your console:

```
npm install gulp-scss-lint --save-dev
```

Notice that the gulp-scss-lint plugin requires both Ruby and SCSS-lint installed already.

Now you can add the scss-lint task to your Gulpfile.js:

```
gulp.task('scss-lint', function() {
  return gulp.src('scss/**/*.scss')
    .pipe(scsslint());
});
```

Bootstrap has its own configuration file for the SCSS-lint tool. You can reuse this configuration for your custom code, and copy the configuration file from the Bootstrap source code to your local scss directory:

```
cp bower_components/bootstrap/scss/.scss-lint.yml scss/
```

Then modify your scss-lint task so that the configuration file is used:

```
gulp.task('scss-lint', function() {
  return gulp.src('scss/**/*.scss')
    .pipe(scsslint({'config': 'scss/.scss-lint.yml'}));
});
```

When running the linter over the current Sass files in the scss directory, include the local copies of the _variable.scss and _bootstrap.scss file. You will find that the comments in the _bootstrap.scss will give a warning.

In the .scss-lint.yml, you can enable this warning by changing the comments setting as follows:

```
Comment:
  enabled: true
  exclude: ['_bootstrap.scss']
```

Also in the example code, the following configuration has been changed:

```
ColorKeyword:
  enabled: false
```

Using keywords for colors, for instance orange instead of #ffa500 is mostly considered as a bad practice. In the example code in this book, color names are preferred because they're easier to read by humans.

You can read how to configure other settings in Chapter 3, *Customizing Your Blog with Bootstrap and Sass*.

Of course, you can add the scss-lint task to your default task, but you can also run it manually when needed. When adding the scss-lint task in the default task, you should consider using it together with the gulp-cached plugin to only lint the modified files:

```
var scsslint = require('gulp-scss-lint');
var cache = require('gulp-cached');
gulp.task('scss-lint', function() {
  return gulp.src('/scss/**/*.scss')
    .pipe(cache('scsslint'))
    .pipe(scsslint());
```

```
    });
```

You should also use the `gulp-cached` plugin as shown in the preceding code when linting your files via the watch task as described further on in this chapter.

Preparing the JavaScript plugins

Some of Bootstrap's components do not only require CSS but also JavaScript. Bootstrap comes with jQuery plugins for commonly used components. Similarly, the navbar requires the collapse plugin and the carousel component has its own plugin too.

Bootstrap's plugins require jQuery and the Tooltips and Popover components also require the Tether library.

In the build process, you can bundle jQuery, Tether, and the plugins into a single file by using the `gulp-concat` plugin.

You can install the `gulp-concat` plugin by running the following command in your console:

```
npm install gulp-concat --save-dev
```

After that the task that bundles the JavaScript files may look like:

```
gulp.task('compile-js', function() {
    return gulp.src([bowerpath+ 'jquery/dist/jquery.min.js', bowerpath+
'tether/dist/js/tether.min.js', bowerpath+
'bootstrap/dist/js/bootstrap.min.js','js/main.js'])
        .pipe(concat('app.js'))
        .pipe(gulp.dest('./_site/js/'));
});
```

The preceding `compile-js` task also bundles a local `js/main.js` file; you can put the plugin settings or your custom JavaScript code into this file.

Getting your JavaScript code ready for production

The preceding `compile-js` task only concatenates the JavaScript files which are already compiled and minified. These files are loaded from the `bower_components` directory.

The `bootstrap.min.js` file contains all the plugins. You will probably only use some of these plugins.

To create a smaller JavaScript file, you can only bundle the plugins you need and minify the code yourself in the build process.

You can minify your code with the `gulp-uglify` plugin that can be installed with the following command:

```
npm install --save-dev gulp-uglify
```

Your `compile-js` task may look like the following when using the `gulp-uglify` plugin:

```
gulp.task('compile-js', ['compress']);
```

After that the task that bundles the JavaScript files may look like this:

```
var uglify = require('gulp-uglify');
gulp.task('compress', function() {
  return gulp.src([
    bowerpath+ 'jquery/dist/jquery.js',
    bowerpath+ 'tether/dist/js/tether.js',
    bowerpath+ 'bootstrap/js/src/alert.js',
    bowerpath+ 'bootstrap/js/src/button.js',
    bowerpath+ 'bootstrap/js/src/carousel.js',
    bowerpath+ 'bootstrap/js/src/collapse.js',
    bowerpath+ 'bootstrap/js/src/dropdown.js',
    bowerpath+ 'bootstrap/js/src/modal.js',
    bowerpath+ 'bootstrap/js/src/popover.js',
    bowerpath+ 'bootstrap/js/src/scrollspy.js',
    bowerpath+ 'bootstrap/js/src/tab.js',
    bowerpath+ 'bootstrap/js/src/tooltip.js',
    bowerpath+ 'bootstrap/js/src/util.js',
    'js/main.js' // custom JavaScript code
    ])
    .pipe(uglify())
    .pipe(gulp.dest('dist/js/app.js'));
});
```

In the preceding code, leave out the JavaScript files you do not need for your project.

The preceding task also bundles the jQuery and Tether libraries, and you can also load these libraries via CDN. For this project, you can do this by using the following HTML in the `html/includes/footerjavascripts.html` template:

```
<!-- jQuery first, then Bootstrap JS. -->
<script
```

```
src="https://ajax.googleapis.com/ajax/libs/jquery/2.1.4/jquery.min.js"></sc
ript>
    <script
src="https://cdn.rawgit.com/HubSpot/tether/v1.2.0/dist/js/tether.min.js"></
script>
    <script src="{{ root }}js/app.js"></script>
```

Read more about the HTML templates in the coming sections.

Modularization of your HTML

Although we'll only create a one-page design in this chapter, using a template engine for your project is not a bad idea. Whenever you decide to extend your project with one or more other HTML pages, DRY coding your HTML will make your work more efficient and reusable. Many HTML template languages and engines are available. Bootstrap uses the *Jekyll* static site generator to enable you to run its documentation locally. Many templates for Bootstrap CLI use Nunjucks now. In this chapter, you will meet Panini for Gulp. Panini is a flat file compiler that uses the concepts of templates, pages, and partials powered by the Handlebars templating language.

For the marketing example project, you'll have to create the following file and directory structure, which holds your HTML templates:

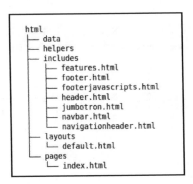

```
html
├── data
├── helpers
├── includes
│       ├── features.html
│       ├── footer.html
│       ├── footerjavascripts.html
│       ├── header.html
│       ├── jumbotron.html
│       ├── navbar.html
│       └── navigationheader.html
├── layouts
│   └── default.html
└── pages
    └── index.html
```

In the preceding file and directory structure, the `pages` directory contains your pages. Each page has a layout, which can be found in the `layouts` directory. Both pages and layouts may include the HTML partials from the `includes` directory.

You can read more about Panini at `http://foundation.zurb.com/sitesdocs/panini.html` and `https://github.com/zurb/panini/`.

Installing the Gulp task to compile the Panini HTML templates

Run the following command to install the Panini compiler in your project:

```
npm install panini --save-dev
```

After installing the Panini compiler, add your HTML compile task to your `Gulpfile.js` file as follows:

```
var panini = require('panini');
gulp.task('compile-html', function(cb) {
  gulp.src('html/pages/**/*.html')
    .pipe(panini({
      root: 'html/pages/',
      layouts: 'html/layouts/',
      partials: 'html/includes/',
      helpers: 'html/helpers/',
      data: 'html/data/'
    }))
    .pipe(gulp.dest('_site'));
    cb();
});
```

Now you can run the `Gulp compile-html` command in your console.

The `compile-html` task saves the compiled HTML templates to the `_site` directory. The CSS and JavaScript tasks also save their products into this directory.

Validating the compiled HTML code

Bootlint is a tool that checks for several common HTML mistakes in web pages which are built with Bootstrap. Bootstrap's components and widgets require their parts of the DOM to conform to certain structures. Bootlint checks the HTML structure of your pages and ensures that it is correct for these components. Bootlint also checks if the HTML document contains the required meta tags.

Notice that Bootlint requires a valid HTML5 page in the first place. To ensure your code is valid HTML we'll run another linter before we run Bootlint. Run the following command in your console to install the `gulp-html plugin`:

```
npm install gulp-html --save-dev
```

`gulp-html` is a Gulp plugin for HTML validation, using `vnu.jar`.

Then install the `gulp-bootlint` plugin:

```
npm install gulp-bootlint --save-dev
```

You can easily initiate a `html-validate` task now, as follows:

```
var validator = require('gulp-html');
var bootlint  = require('gulp-bootlint');
gulp.task('validate-html', [compile-html], function() {
  gulp.src('_site/**/*.html')
    .pipe(validator())
    .pipe(bootlint());
});
```

Then the `validate-html` task should run after the `compile-html` task has finished. That's why the second parameter of the `validate-html` task is set to `[compile-html]`.

Read more about asynchronous task support in Gulp at `https://github.com/gulpjs/gulp/blob/master/docs/API.md#async-task-support`.

You should choose whether or not you run the validators in your build process by yourself. You can easily remove the `validate-html` task from the HTML task:

```
gulp.task('html', ['compile-html','validate-html']);
```

Creating a static web server

Now that your tasks to compile your HTML, CSS, and JavaScript code are ready, it's time to show and inspect the result in your browser. **Browsersync** is a module that keeps your browser in sync when developing your code. Browsersync works by injecting an asynchronous script tag right after the `<body>` tag during initial request.

To use Browsersync with Gulp no special plugin is required; you can simply `require()` the module.

First install Browsersync by running the following command:

```
npm install browser-sync gulp --save-dev
```

Then create a task in your `Gulpfile.js` file which may look like the following:

```
var browser = require('browser-sync');
var port = process.env.SERVER_PORT || 8080;
// Starts a BrowerSync instance
gulp.task('server', ['build'], function(){
```

```
    browser.init({server: './_site', port: port});
  });
```

The server task depends on the build task (second argument `['build']` in the preceding code) which means that the build task should run before the server task.

The server task starts a static web server running on port 8080 serving the files in the temporary `_site` directory. The compiled files from the other tasks are saved in the `_site` directory.

Start watching your file changes

When your static webserver is up and running you can add a watch task to your build process. The watch task should trigger a task on file changes and reload the web browser.

Your watch task may look like the following:

```
// Watch files for changes
gulp.task('watch', function() {
  gulp.watch('scss/**/*', ['compile-sass', browser.reload]);
  gulp.watch('html/pages/**/*', ['compile-html']);
  gulp.watch(['html/{layouts,includes,helpers,data}/**/*'], ['compile-
html:reset','compile-html']);
});
```

The watch task watches your Sass files in the `scss` folder and your HTML templates in the `html` folder. The `compile-html` task calls `browser.reload` after finishing as follows:

```
.on ('finish', browser.reload);
```

Also notice that file changes in the Panini files, except from the `pages` directory. Run the `compile-html:reset` task before the `compile-html` task. The `compile-html:reset` task calls `panini.refresh()` because Panini loads layouts, partials, helpers, and data files once on the first run.

Copying and minifying your images

When your project uses images, you should copy them to the `_site` directory each time you run the build process, because when you run the build process, the clean task removes the temporary `_site` directory.

You can save the images and all other assets in an `asset` directory and run the following task to copy them to the _site directory:

```
// Copy assets
gulp.task('copy', function() {
  gulp.src(['assets/**/*']).pipe(gulp.dest('_site'));
});
```

In the case of images, you can consider to not only copy but also minify the images. You can do this with the `gulp-imagemin` plugin.

You can read more about this plugin at `https://github.com/sindresorhus/gulp-imagem in.`:

```
var gulp = require('gulp');
var imagemin = require('gulp-imagemin');
var pngquant = require('imagemin-pngquant');
gulp.task('default', () => {
    return gulp.src('assets/images/*')
        .pipe(imagemin({
            progressive: true,
            svgoPlugins: [
                {removeViewBox: false},
                {cleanupIDs: false}
            ],
            use: [pngquant()]
        }))
        .pipe(gulp.dest('_site/images'));
});
```

Putting it all together and creating the default task

At the end of the `Gulpfile.js` file we'll write down some tasks, including the default task, which runs a sequence of tasks of the build process. These tasks may look like the following:

```
gulp.task('set-development', development.task);
gulp.task('set-production', production.task);
gulp.task('test',['scss-lint','validate-html']);
gulp.task('build', ['clean','copy','compile-js','compile-sass','compile-html']);
gulp.task('default', ['set-development','server', 'watch']);
gulp.task('deploy', ['set-production','server', 'watch']);
```

The default task sets the environment to development by calling the set-development task first. Then it runs the server task, and starts the watch task after that. Because the server task depends on the build task, the build task always runs before the server task (Browsersync) starts. The deploys task does the same as the default task, but sets the environment to production in the first call.

The test task lints your SCSS code and checks the compiled HTML code. You can run the test task by running the gulp test command in your console. The result of the test task may look like the following:

```
[00:15:02] Starting 'scss-lint'...
[00:15:02] Starting 'compile-html'...
[00:15:12] Finished 'compile-html' after 9.25 s
[00:15:12] Starting 'validate-html'...
[00:15:12] Finished 'validate-html' after 22 ms
[00:15:45] 1 issues found in
/home/bass/testdrive/bootstrapbook/chapter2/scss/includes/_bootstrap.scss
[00:15:45] includes/_bootstrap.scss:1 [W] Comment: Use `//` comments
everywhere
[00:15:45] 2 issues found in
/home/bass/testdrive/bootstrapbook/chapter2/scss/includes/_page-header.scss
[00:15:45] includes/_page-header.scss:11 [W] PseudoElement: Begin
pseudo classes with a single colon: `:`
[00:15:45] includes/_page-header.scss:13 [W] TrailingWhitespace: Line
contains trailing whitespace
[00:15:45] Finished 'scss-lint' after 43 s
[00:15:45] Starting 'test'...
[00:15:45] Finished 'test' after 27 µs
[Wed Apr 27 2016 00:15:59 GMT+0200 (CEST)] ERROR
/home/bass/testdrive/bootstrapbook/chapter2/_site/index.html:58:13 E041
`.carousel` must have exactly one `.carousel-inner` child.
```

Now your build process is ready and you can start using it! To start your build process you'll have to run the following command in your console:

```
gulp
```

The gulp command runs the default tasks. It starts a static webserver and automatically watches for file changes.

Using the build process to finish your project

At the start of this chapter, I have shown you a screenshot of a responsive mobile-first one-page marketing site built with Bootstrap. In the rest of the chapter, I will guide you to build this site using the Gulp build process you have created in the preceding sections.

You will have to split up the HTML page into different parts in accordance with the HTML template structure you have already created.

The project will have a single breakpoint at 768 pixels. For viewports wider than 768 pixels, the navigation menu will become horizontal and other adoptions are made.

The layout template

As already mentioned, you'll use Panini to modularize your HTML code. Panini helps you to avoid code duplications in your HTML code.

Panini is powered by the `Handlebars` templating language. I highly recommend you to read Panini's documentation at the following URL: `http://foundation.zurb.com/sites/docs/panini.html`.

The `index.html` file, our main page, will only contain the following content :

```
---
layout: default
title: Home
---
{{> features}}
```

Apart from the `includes/features.html` page, included with the `{{> features}}` snippet, the `index.html` file loads all other HTML code from the default template (`layouts/default.html`). The default template is a common layout that every page in your design shares.

The code of the default template may look like the following:

```
<!DOCTYPE html>
<html lang="en">
  <head>
    <!-- Required meta tags always come first -->
    <meta charset="utf-8">
    <meta name="viewport" content="width=device-width, initial-scale=1,
```

```
shrink-to-fit=no">
    <meta http-equiv="x-ua-compatible" content="ie=edge">
    <title> Your Company :: {{title}}</title>
    <!--Bootstrap CSS -->
      <link rel="stylesheet" href="{{root}}css/app.css">
  </head>
  <body>
    {{> header}}
    {{> navigationheader}}
    {{> body}}
    {{> footer}}
    {{> footerjavascripts}}
  </body>
</html>
```

In this template the `{{> body}}` snippet includes the HTML code of the `index.html` file. The `index.html` file is the first page of your project. The layout default declaration tells Panini to use the default template found in the `html/layouts/default.html` file.

And the `{{> header}}` snippet includes a HTML partial in your page. The partial included with the `{{> header}}` declaration can be found in the `html/includes/header.html` file.

In the next section, you'll develop the page header. Before you start, run the `gulp` command, which runs the default task, and you will directly see the results of your work in your browser.

The page header

Resize your browser so that your viewport is smaller than 768px. The page header should look like that shown in the following screenshot:

Start writing the HTML code for your page header in the `html/includes/header.html` file.

The first version of the HTML code should look like the following:

```
<header class="page-header">
    <div class="container">
      <div class="row">
      <div class="col-xs-12"><h1
  class="display-4">Your<span>Company</span></h1></div>
          <div class="col-xs-12">
              <form class="form-inline">
              <input class="form-control" type="text" placeholder="Search">
              <button class="btn btn-outline-success"
  type="submit">Search</button>
              </form>
          </div>
        </div>
      </div>
    </header>
```

The HTML starts with a header element with a `page-header` class. After the `<header>` element follows a `<div>` element with the `container` class. Containers are the most basic layout element in Bootstrap and are required when using the grid system. The responsive grid system has 12 columns and four breakpoints. The breakpoint defines the five grids: the extra small grid, the small grid, the medium grid, the large grid and the extra large grid. Inside the container, we create a row as a `<div>` element with the `row` class. Columns inside the row are set with `col-{grid}-*` classes. You can read more about Bootstrap grids and responsive features in `Chapter 1`, *Getting Started with Bootstrap*.

In the row, we create two columns. The first column contains the company name, and the second column the search form. On small viewports this columns should span 100% of the viewport and be stacked. We'll use the `col-xs-12` class to accomplish that. The naming of the `col-xs-12` class means spanning 12 columns on the extra small (xs) grid. The `col-xs-12` class (although it sets `width:100%;` and `float: left;`) equals the default situation due to the `box-sizing: border-box` declaration. The box-sizing model is explained in more detail in `Chapter 1`, *Getting Started with Bootstrap*. In the border-box model, block-level elements occupy the entire space of its parent element (container). For this reason, the `col-xs-12` class can be considered as optional.

For the company name a `<h1>` element with a `display-3` class has been used. We'll also use a `<span>` element inside the `<h1>` to enable us to use two colors for the company name.

For the search form in the second column, a default inline form, set with the `form-inline` class and an outlined button, are used.

Now with your HTML code, you can start creating your custom CSS.

Custom CSS code for the page header

Of course, we'll use Sass to build our custom CSS code. For the page header create a new `scss/includes/_page-header.scss` Sass partial. This partial should be imported in the `scss/app.scss` file:

```
@import "includes/page-header";
```

Import the partial after Bootstrap so you can reuse Bootstrap mixins and extend the Bootstrap classes when needed. The SCSS code in the `scss/includes/_page-header.scss` file may look like the following:

```
.page-header {
  background-color: $page-header-background;
  .display-3 {
    color: $company-primary-color;
    span {
      color: $lightest-color;
    }
  }
  [class^="col-"]:last-child {
    margin-top: $spacer-y * 2;
  }
}
```

Instead of the `[class^="col-"]:last-child` selector in the preceding code, you can also use a new `selector/class`, for instance a `.search-form-column` class, and change your HTML code according to this new CSS class.

The color variables used in the preceding SCSS are declared in the `scss/includes/_variables.scss` file as follows:

```
$darkest-color: #000; // black;
$lighest-color: #fff; // white;
$company-primary-color: #f80; //orange;

// Page Header
$page-header-background: $darkest-color;
```

Fine tuning of your CSS and HTML code

When you resize your browser smaller than 544 pixels you'll find some issues.

First the search button wraps to the next line. Bootstrap's `inline-form` class only works for screens wider than 544 pixels. You can overwrite the Bootstrap default behavior and use the following SCSS code:

```
.page-header {
  .form-inline .form-control {
    display: inline-block;
    width: auto;
  }
}
```

Alternatively, you can remove the search button for the smallest screen by adding the `hidden-xs-down` class. The `hidden-xs-down` class makes elements invisible on only the extra small (xs) grid.

Secondly, you'll possibly find that the font size of the company name is too large to fit the smallest screens. You can use the `media-breakpoint-down()` mixins, as already described in Chapter 1, *Getting Started with Bootstrap*, to make the font size smaller for the narrowest screens:

```
.page-header {
  @include media-breakpoint-down(xs) {
    .display-3 {
      padding-bottom: $spacer-y;
      font-size: $display4-size;
      text-align: center;
    }
  }
}
```

Then you should switch to the larger screen, and resize your browser to a screen width wider than 768 pixels.

The columns should become horizontal with each having 50% (six columns) of the available space inside the container. On each grid, the container has a fixed width; for screens wider than 1200 pixels, the container always has a width of 1140 pixels.

You can accomplish this by adding the `col-md-6` class twice:

```
        <div class="col-xs-12 col-md-6"><h1
class="display-3">Your<span>Company</span></h1></div>
        <div class="col-xs-12 col-md-6">
```

The search box should float on the right side of the header. The right floating is done with the `pull-md-right` class as follows:

```
<form class="form-inline pull-md-right">
```

The `pull-md-right` helper class sets a float: right for the medium grid and up, so the compiled CSS code looks like this:

```
@media (min-width: 768px) {
  .pull-md-right {
    float: right !important;
  }
}
```

While building the page header, you have possibly noticed that the company name and search box may overlap on the medium grid for screen width between 768 and 992 pixels. You can solve this issue by replacing the `col-md-6` classes with the `col-lg-6` classes or alternatively modifying the CSS code so that the font size of the company name is smaller for a larger range of breakpoints. You can use the SCSS code, in the `scss/includes/_page-header.scss` file, as follows, to do this:

```
@include media-breakpoint-down(md) {
  .display-3 {
    padding-bottom: $spacer-y;
    font-size: $display4-size;
    text-align: center;
  }
}
```

And finally, you can do a last tweak in the `scss/includes/_page-header.scss` file to apply the `margin-top` for the search box that is set only for the larger screens:

```
@include media-breakpoint-up(md) {
  [class^="col-"]:last-child {
    margin-top: $spacer-y * 2;
  }
}
```

Styling the navbar and hero unit

The navbar and the hero unit are wrapped in a `<section>` element, which has the background image. The HTML code in the `html/includes/navigationheader.html` template looks as follows:

```
<section class="nature">

    <header>
    {{> navbar}}
    </header>

    {{> jumbotron}}
</section>
```

Create a new `scss/includes/_navigationheader.scss` Sass partial, which contains the following SCSS code:

```
// free photo from
https://www.pexels.com/photo/landscape-nature-sunset-trees-479/
.nature {
  background-image:url('/images/landscape-nature-sunset-trees.jpg');
}
```

Notice that you should save a copy of the `landscape-nature-sunset-trees.jpg` photo file in the `assets/images/` directory of your project. As already made clear, this image file is automatically copied to the temporary `_site/images` directory every time you run the build process.

For the navbar, we'll create a `html/includes/navbar.html` HTML template and an `scss/includes/_navbar.scss` Sass partial too. In these files, we reuse the code for the responsive navbar from Chapter 1, *Getting Started with Bootstrap*.

You should change the `scss/includes/_navbar.scss` file to set the background color of the navbar:

```
.navbar {
  //background: transparent;
  background: rgba(255,255,255,0.5);
  //@include gradient-horizontal(green, white);
}
```

Notice that in the preceding SCSS code two alternative backgrounds are commented out. You can try the alternative by removing the comment (and commenting out the others). If you have run the `gulp` command already you'll see the effects directly in your browser.

Consider saving the background value in a variable and save it in the `scss/includes/_variables.scss` file for code that can be more easily reused:

```
$navbar-background: rgba(255,255,255,0.5);
```

There is also nothing wrong with creating a new class for the navbar's background color:

```
.bg-nature {
 background: $navbar-background;
}
```

Then your HTML code should appear as follows:

```
<nav class="navbar navbar-dark bg-nature navbar-full" role="navigation">
```

For the hero unit, we'll use the HTML code for the Jumbotron component directly from Bootstrap's documentation. Save the HTML code into the `html/includes/jumbotron.html` file. Also now create a `scss/includes/_jumbotron.scss` Sass partial.

The HTML code in the `html/includes/jumbotron.html` file will look like the following:

```
<div class="container">
  <div class="jumbotron">
    <h1 class="display-3">Hello, world!</h1>
    <p class="lead">This is a simple hero unit, a simple jumbotron-
style component for calling extra attention to featured content or
information.</p>
    <hr class="m-y-2">
    <p>It uses utility classes for typography and spacing to space
content out within the larger container.</p>
    <p class="lead">
      <a class="btn btn-primary btn-lg" href="#" role="button">Learn
more</a>
    </p>
  </div>
</div>
```

Beside the `container`, `display-*` and `btn-*` classes you'll also find some new Bootstrap CSS classes. The `lead` class simply makes a paragraph stand out. The `<hr>` element has a `m-y-2` helper class, which sets the horizontal margins to two times the height of the `$spacer-y` value. The `m-y-2` helper class is an example of Bootstrap's utility classes, which enable you to set the spacing (padding and margin) of an element.

These utility classes are named using the format {property}-{sides}-{size}, where property is either p (padding) or m (margin), sides are l (left), r (right), t (top), b (bottom), x (left and right), or y (top and bottom), and the size is a value between 0 and 3, including 0 and 3, meaning {size} time $spacing-x or $spacing-y.

Then edit the following SCSS code in the scss/includes/_jumbotron.scss file:

```
.jumbotron {
  background-color: transparent;
  color: $lightest-color;
}
```

On smaller screens the navigation header should look like that shown in the following screenshot:

Now the navigation and hero units are ready and we can start styling the features as a part of our design.

Styling the features

Directly under the hero unit, the design shows three features. A single feature may look like that shown in the following screenshot. Each feature starts with a rounded image, which may contain a photo or icon followed by a heading and a text paragraph. At the end, you will find a button which is a **Call to action**.

On screens smaller than 768 pixels, the features should display under each other. On wider screens, the features become horizontal and form three equal width columns like those shown in the following screenshot:

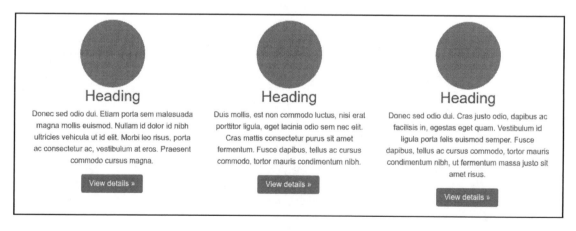

Again we create two files: the `html/includes/features.html` HTML template and a `scss/includes/_features.scss` Sass partial.

The structure of the HTML code in the `html/includes/features.html` HTML template may look like the following (notice that in the HTML code, the features are left out):

```html
<div class="container features">
  <div class="row">
    <div class="col-md-4">
      <!-- first feature -->
    </div><!-- /.col-md-4 -->
    <div class="col-md-4">
      <!-- second feature -->
    </div><!-- /.col-md-4 -->
    <div class="col-md-4">
      <!-- third feature -->
    </div><!-- /.col-md-4 -->
  </div><!-- /.row -->
</div>
```

As you can see, we'll use the Bootstrap grid again to display the features. You already know the container and row classes. The `col-md-4 class` creates a space spanning 4 of 12 grid columns on the medium (`md`) grid and up. The optional `col-xs-12` classes are left out here.

The HTML code for each feature may look like the following:

```html
<img class="img-circle"
src="data:image/gif;base64,R0lG...CRAEAOw==" alt="Generic placeholder
image" height="140" width="140">
        <h2>Heading</h2>
        <p>Donec sed odio dui. .....</p>
        <p><a class="btn btn-primary" href="#" role="button">View details
&raquo;</a></p>
```

The `img-circle` class automatically creates rounded views of your images. You can replace the `src="data:image/gif;base64,R0lG...CRAEAOw=="` image source with your own images.

 Read more about using the **data-URIs** for your images at `https://css-tr icks.com/data-uris/`.

Now you'll have to create some CSS code to tweak the features' look and feel. Write down the following SCSS code in the `scss/includes/_features.scss` file:

```scss
.features {
  padding-top: $spacer-y;

  [class^="col-"] {
```

```
    text-align: center;
  }
}
```

Instead of creating some new CSS code you can also consider to use Bootstrap's predefined CSS classes to accomplish the same.

You can use the utility classes to set the padding-top of the features as follows:

`<div class="container features p-t-1">`

And the `text-xs-center` class can be used to center the content of the features on all viewports:

`<div class="col-md-4 text-xs-center">`

Now the features are ready, too. Time to style the footer and finish your project.

Styling the footer of your page

Last but not least, we'll have to style the footer links to finalize our project. Again create an HTML template and a Sass partial to do this.

The `html/includes/footer.html` HTML template should contain HTML like the following:

```
<footer class="page-footer">
    <div class="container">
      <div class="pull-xs-right">
          <a href="https://twitter.com/bassjobsen"><i class="fa fa-
twitter fa-lg"></i></a>
          <a href="https://facebook.com/bassjobsen"><i class="fa fa-
facebook fa-lg"></i></a>
          <a href="http://google.com/+bassjobsen"><i class="fa fa-google-
plus fa-lg"></i></a>
          <a href="http://stackoverflow.com/users/1596547/bass-jobsen"><i
class="fa fa-stack-overflow fa-lg"></i></a>
          <a href="https://github.com/bassjobsen"><i class="fa fa-github
fa-lg"></i></a>
      </div>
      <div>&copy; 2016 Bass Jobsen &middot; <a href="#">Privacy</a>
&middot;<a href="#">Terms</a></div>
    </div>
</footer>
```

The footer of our page is simple and straightforward. It contains some copyright notes and a block of social links. The social links are floated on the right side of the footer by the `pull-xs-right` class. The icons of the social links are from the Font Awesome icon font. The `fa-*` CSS classes are not part of Bootstrap's CSS code.

In *Chapter 4, Bootstrappin' Your Portfolio,* you can read about how to compile Font Awesome's CSS code into your local CSS by using Sass. Simply load Font Awesome's CSS code from CDN by linking it in the `html/layouts/default.html` HTML template as follows:

```
<link rel="stylesheet"
href="https://maxcdn.bootstrapcdn.com/font-awesome/4.6.1/css/font-awesome.min.css">
```

All that remains to do is to give the background, links, and icons for the right colors and add some spacing. You can do this by entering the following SCSS code into the `scss/includes/_page-footer.scss` Sass partial:

```
.page-footer {
  background-color: $page-footer-background;
  color: $lightest-color;
  a {
    @include plain-hover-focus {
      color: $lightest-color;
    }
  }
  padding: $spacer-y 0;
  margin-top: $spacer-y;
}
```

The preceding code uses Bootstrap's `plain-hover-focus()` mixin which sets the plain, hovered, and focused states at once and uses the Media Queries Level 4 hover @media feature as discussed previously.

Again notice that the margin and padding can also be set by using Bootstrap's utility classes. Using `p-y-1` and `m-t-1` will have the same effect:

```
<footer class="page-footer p-y-1 m-t-1">
```

That's all! You did a great job till now!

Running your template with Bootstrap CLI

In this chapter, you have created a build process which builds and compiles your single page template by running the `gulp` command. In this book, you'll use Bootstrap CLI to set up your projects.

Bootstrap CLI enables you to choose your own starter templates. These starter templates also have a Gulp (or Grunt) build chain. For instance the source code of the Bootstrap material design template can be found at `https://github.com/bassjobsen/bootstrap-ma terial-design-styleguide`. Bootstrap CLI downloads the templates from GitHub and its commands call `npm` to run scripts.

To make your build process and template ready for Bootstrap CLI, you simply add the `npm` script calls to your `package.json` file as follows:

```
"scripts": {
  "build": "gulp deploy",
  "start": "gulp"
}
```

JavaScript task runners are not required

In this chapter, you have learned how to create a build process with Gulp. Both Gulp and Grunt are JavaScript task runners for Node.js. In the previous section you could see that Bootstrap CLI calls npm to run your scripts. For the same reason, some people claim that you can create a build process without Gulp or Grunt too.

 Read more about npm script objects at `http://blog.keithcirkel.co.uk /why-we-should-stop-using-grunt/`.

Publishing your work on GitHub

Since your template is ready to use, you may consider publishing it on GitHub. Other people may use your work, but on the other hand, they can also help you to improve it.

Read more about publishing your project on GitHub at `https://guides.g ithub.com/introduction/getting-your-project-on-github/`.

Since you have installed both the Bower packages and the Gulp plugins with the `--save-dev` option, your `bower.json` and `package.json` files contain an up-to-date list with the project dependencies. When publishing your project, you do not have to publish the dependencies too. People can download your project files and then install the dependencies by running the following commands:

```
bower install
npm install
```

After the running the `install` command, they can run your project with the `gulp` command; also the `bootstrap watch` command of Bootstrap CLI should work.

You can create a `.gitignore` file to ensure that only your project files are uploaded to GitHub. Your `.gitignore` file should contain the following lines of paths:

```
.DS_Store
bower_components
node_modules
npm-debug.log
_site
.sass-cache
```

Summary

In this chapter, you have learned how to create a build process for your Bootstrap projects with Gulp. You can reuse the build process for your newer projects. The build process compiles your Sass code into CSS code, prepares your JavaScript code, and runs a static web server to test the results. In the end, you built a single page marketing web page with most of Bootstrap's code and components, and some little tweaks. The build process you have created before compiles your code and enables you to test it.

Some tweaks require some knowledge about Sass. Hence, in the following chapter we will discuss Sass in more detail and use it to customize Bootstrap to create a design for your blog.

3
Customizing Your Blog with Bootstrap and Sass

In this chapter, you will study Sass in detail. Sass is a preprocessor for CSS. The Sass team says:

> *"Sass is the most mature, stable, and powerful professional grade CSS extension language in the world."*

The CSS code of Bootstrap is built with Sass. In this chapter, you will build a simple design with mostly Bootstrap components. You will use Sass to modify and extend Bootstrap's code. At the beginning of the chapter, you will read about the features Sass adds to CSS and how it helps you to code your CSS more efficiently and in a DRY manner.

After reading this chapter, you will:

- Understand the power of Sass
- Know how to modify Bootstrap's CSS
- Know how to extend Bootstrap's CSS code
- Know how to reuse Bootstrap's Sass mixin

Expected results and the process

You will deploy a design for your web blog with Bootstrap with the help of this chapter. The design is built with standard Bootstrap components and some little tweaks. After a short introduction to Sass, we'll start using Sass to modify and extend Bootstrap's CSS code to fit your requirements.

The end result of your efforts should look like that shown in the following screenshot:

The preceding screenshot shows the design for small screens, smaller than 768 pixels wide. We'll use a single breakpoint at 768 pixels. For screens wider than 768 pixels, the navigation becomes horizontal and new features will be added. For wider screens, the final result should look like that shown in the following screenshot:

Setting up your project and requirements

For this project, you'll use Bootstrap CLI again as it helps you to create a setup for your project comfortably. Bootstrap CLI requires you to have Node.js and Gulp already installed on your system.

Now create a new project by running the following command in your console:

```
bootstrap new
```

Enter the name of your project and choose the *An empty new Bootstrap project. Powered by Panini, Sass and Gulp* template. Now your project is ready to start with your design work. However, before you start, let's first go through the introduction to Sass and the strategies for customization.

The power of Sass in your project

Sass is a preprocessor for CSS code and is an extension of CSS3 which adds **nested rules**, variables, **mixins**, functions, **selector inheritance**, and more. In the following section, you can read how Sass extends the CSS syntax and helps you to **DRY code** your CSS.

Nested rules

Nested rules greatly enhance the efficiency of composing styles. For example, writing selectors in CSS can be highly repetitive:

```
.navbar-nav { ... }
.navbar-nav > li { ... }
.navbar-nav > li > a { ... }
.navbar-nav > li > a:hover,
.navbar-nav > li > a:focus { ... }
```

This same set of selectors and their styles can be written much more easily in Sass, by means of a simple nesting pattern as shown in the following SCSS code:

```
.navbar-nav { ...
  > li { ...
    > a { ...
      &:hover,
      &:focus { ... }
    }
  }
}
```

Once compiled, these rules come out as standard CSS. But, the nesting pattern makes the Sass styles much easier to write and maintain in some situations. Also notice that in the preceding code, the **& parent reference** has been used. The & parent reference refers to the *parent* selector when nesting. Consider the following SCSS code:

```
.link {
  &:hover {
    color: black;
  }
}
```

The preceding SCSS code compiles into CSS as follows:

```
.link:hover {
  color: black;
}
```

Without the & parent reference, there will be a space before the :hover selector.

Bootstrap's Sass code avoids child and element selectors. Nesting is mostly only used for states. When we take the preceding navbar example into account, you'll find that Bootstrap's SCSS may look similar to the following:

```
.navbar-nav {
  .nav-link {
    color: $navbar-dark-color;

    @include hover-focus {
      color: $navbar-dark-hover-color;
    }
  }
}
```

The states (:hover and :focus) are set with the hover-focus() mixin. This mixin also applies the **Media Queries Level 4 hover @media feature** when the $enable-hover-media-query variable has been set to true.

Consider the following SCSS code:

```
$enable-hover-media-query: true;
a {
  @include hover-focus {
    color: green;
  }
}
```

The preceding code compiles into CSS code as follows:

```
a:focus {
  color: green; }
@media (hover: hover) {
  a:hover {
    color: green; } }
```

You can read more about mixins further on in this chapter.

Notice that the hover-focus() mixin also uses the & parent reference to set the :hover and :focus selectors:

Variables

Variables make it possible to specify a value once (or revise it), and then use it automatically (or updated) throughout your entire style sheet. For example, we may use color variables, such as the following:

```
@off-white:    #e5e5e5;
@brand-primary:    #890000;
```

When we update the value of these variables, we can automatically update colors throughout the site. This is because we have used the variables throughout our SASS files in rules, such as the following:

```
a {
  color: @brand-primary;
}
.navbar {
  background-color: @brand-primary;
  .nav-link {
  color: @off-white;
  }
}
```

Every variable should be declared before using it. The !default declaration enables you to set default values, for instance:

```
@off-white:    #e5e5e5 !default;
```

The preceding code enables us to write Sass code which can be easily modified by changing the values of the default variables. Consider the following SCSS code:

```
$dark-color: darkblue;
$dark-color: darkgreen !default;

p {
  color: $dark-color;
}
```

The preceding CSS code compiles into CSS code as follows:

```
p {
  color: darkblue;
}
```

All of Bootstrap's variables can be found in a single and well documented partial file called `_variables.scss`. These variables are all declared with `!default`. As you have seen, you can easily overwrite these variables by putting a new declaration before the `@import` of the `_variables.scss` file into the project.

 Those who are used to Less instead of Sass should realize that Sass does not apply *lazy loading* and *the last declaration wins strategy* for variables. You can also not declare variables afterward in Sass.

Mixins

Mixins make it possible to generate an entire set of rules using concise and easy-to-manage formulations. For example, we can simplify the task of applying the different states to the `<a>` tag or other elements.

As an example, I will again show you Bootstrap `hover-focus()` mixin mentioned previously. These mixins will look like the following:

```
@mixin hover-focus {
  @if $enable-hover-media-query {
    &:focus { @content }
    @include hover { @content }
  }
  @else {
    &:focus,
    &:hover {
      @content
    }
  }
}
```

Then, we can use this mixin wherever needed:

```
.page-link {
  @include hover-focus() {
    color: tomato;
  }
}
```

When compiled, each element will get its essential lines of CSS. The previous compiled CSS code, with the `$enable-hover-media-query` variable has been set to false. It will look like the following:

```
.page-link:focus, .page-link:hover {
  color: tomato; }
```

Earlier versions of Bootstrap also had many mixins to add the vendor-prefixes to the compiled CSS code. This helped people to write single line declarations for properties that require one or more vendor prefixes for cross-browser support. Due to the usage of mixins one could also simply remove or add a prefix for a certain property in a single place.

Nowadays vendor prefixes are added automatically as already described in Chapter 2, *Creating Your Own Build Process with Gulp*.

Operations

Operations make it possible to do math, including math with variables. We can start with one color, and then lighten or darken it to get variations as follows:

```
a:hover { darken(@link-color, 15%); }
```

In the preceding SCSS code, `darken()` is a built-in color function of Sass. Sass contains many built-in functions for color, string, number, list, maps, and selector operations which you can use for your operations. You can even add your own functions to Sass.

 An overview of Sass's built-in functions can be found at http://sass-lan g.com/documentation/Sass/Script/Functions.html.

We can also calculate padding values for the grid. Thus, the following lines from Bootstrap's `mixins/_grid.scss` file sets the container class padding values to the amount of the `$gutter` value divided by two:

```
@mixin make-container($gutter: $grid-gutter-width) {
  margin-left: auto;
  margin-right: auto;
  padding-left:  ($gutter / 2);
  padding-right: ($gutter / 2);
  @if not $enable-flex {
    @include clearfix();
  }
}
```

The `mixins/_grid.scss` file in the preceding code is part of Bootstrap's source code and can be found in the bower_components folder.

Importing files

The Sass compiling process makes it possible to import and combine multiple files into a single, unified CSS file. We can specify the order of import, and organize the resulting style sheet precisely as needed for our desired cascade.

Thus, Bootstrap's import file, `bootstrap.scss`, begins with imports for essential variables and mixins. Then, it imports a Sass version of `normalize.css` (in place of a CSS reset), followed by basic styles for print media. Then, it moves to core styles, including the new reboot module (`_reboot.scss`), typographic fundamentals (`_type.scss`), and more specific details. Thus, the first several lines of the current `bootstrap.scss` file are given as follows:

```
// Core variables and mixins
@import "variables";
@import "mixins";

// Reset and dependencies
@import "normalize";
@import "print";
```

The resulting CSS file will be a single, unified whole, with styles cascading down from the general to the specific, from components to the utilities, just as they should.

The modular file organization

Because of the ability to import distinct files into a unified whole, we may easily organize our styles in coherent groupings and maintain them in distinct files. This is why Bootstrap comes with so many Sass files, one dedicated to navbar styles, another to buttons, another for alerts, one for carousel styles, and so on, all imported using the `bootstrap.scss` file.

For these reasons and others, Sass and its cousin preprocessors are more than a fad. They have become part of the standard practice for professional web development. Most developers agree that they point to the future of CSS.

Using the SCSS-linter for cleaner and more readable code

In `Chapter 2`, *Creating Your Own Build Process with Gulp*, you can read about how to integrate the SCSS-lint tool in your build process. You can also use this tool on the command line to check your code.

The SCSS-lint tool not only checks the syntax and code style but can also help you to write more reusable code. When you enable the `ColorVariable` check in your configuration file, you'll get a warning when you use hardcoded color values in your code. Assigning colors to variables is better in most cases because this enables you to reuse the color values and change them only in a single place.

Notice that you also should choose your variable names with care to write readable and reusable code.

 Some hints can be found at `http://webdesign.tutsplus.com/tutorials/quick-tip-name-your-sass-variables-modularly-webdesign-13364` and `http://sachagreif.com/sass-color-variables/`.

Bootstrap itself also uses the two-tier system, with both functional and descriptive variable names, as suggested by Sacha Greif.

Strategies for customization with Sass

Depending on your own experience and ideas, you can choose different strategies to reuse Bootstrap's Sass code to create your custom CSS code. Each strategy has its own cons and pros and depending on your needs you can use one or more of these strategies together to reach your targets.

In this book, I will demonstrate usages of each strategy and try to show you alternatives if applicable.

Using variables for customization

As you already know, variables enable you to define commonly used values at a single place. Bootstrap ships with a long list of variables, found in `scss/_variables.scss`.

These variables are well organized and documented. Let's take the $brand-primary variable as an example; it is used to assign some other variables too. In Bootstrap's scss/_variables.scss file, you will find:

```
$link-color:              $brand-primary !default;
$component-active-bg:     $brand-primary !default;
$btn-primary-bg:          $brand-primary !default;
$pagination-active-bg:    $brand-primary !default;
$pagination-active-border: $brand-primary !default;
$label-primary-bg:        $brand-primary !default;
$progress-bar-bg:         $brand-primary !default;
```

And also in some other Sass files, you can find usage of the $brand-primary variable:

```
scss/_utilities-background.scss: @include bg-variant('.bg-primary', $brand-
primary);
scss/_card.scss:   @include card-variant($brand-primary, $brand-primary);
scss/_utilities.scss: @include text-emphasis-variant('.text-primary',
$brand-primary);
```

All these variables in the preceding code are used to build Bootstrap's predefined CSS classes. You can use them to set the colors and styles of the components. You can style, for instance, the buttons and progress bars with the btn-primary and progress-primary classes respectively. And the bg-variant() mixin generates a contextual background in the color of the $brand-primary variable. The HTML code of a button may look like the following:

```
<button class="btn btn-primary">Button</button>
```

If your design is built with components having the *-primary classes set, you can simply change the look and feel of it by modifying the value of the $brand-primary variable.

In this chapter, we'll declare a new set of variables and keep Bootstrap's default values. Also, when you add some custom Sass code in the project, you can use Bootstrap's variables. The $spacer(-*) variables can be used to set margins and paddings. The following SCSS code will show you how to set the padding-top property using Bootstrap's variables:

```
main {
    article {
      padding-top: $spacer-y;
    }
}
```

Notice that the SCSS code uses the main selector. Bootstrap's Sass code avoids element selectors. Instead of the main selector, you can also create a main class or even a main-article class. Using classes instead of element selectors will make the CSS code easier to reuse, and on the other hand you will have to add extra CSS to your HTML.

Extending Bootstrap's predefined CSS classes

Sass has an @extend feature. The @extend feature makes it possible for one selector to extend the styles from the other one. The following example will show you how the @extend feature works:

```
$primary-color-dark:    #303F9F;

.selector1 {
  color: $primary-color-dark;
}

.selector2 {
  @extend .selector1;
}
```

The SCSS compiles into CSS code as follows:

```
.selector1, .selector2 {
  color: #303F9F; }
```

This can be very effective, but also complex when your code is nested. When you only use the new selector2 class in your HTML, it also will create some unused selectors in your CSS code.

Placeholder selectors can be used for reusable selectors which do not create unused CSS code. Placeholders look like normal selectors but start with a % sign and do not output the compiled CSS code:

```
$primary-color-dark:    #303F9F;

%selector1 {
  color: $primary-color-dark;
}

.selector2 {
  @extend %selector1;
}
```

The preceding SCSS code with the `%selector1` compiles into CSS code as follows:

```
.selector2 {
  color: #303F9F; }
```

 Bootstrap's Sass code avoids the `@extend` feature and for that reason also does not contain placeholder selectors.

In `Chapter 1`, *Getting Started with Bootstrap*, you can read how to make your images responsive, by default, by extending the `fluid-img` class.

(Re)Using Bootstrap's mixins

When creating custom CSS code for a project, you can reuse Bootstrap's mixins.

Instead of changing Bootstrap's variables to create a custom button, you can also create a custom button by using the following SCSS code:

```
.btn-accent-color {
  @include button-variant(#fff, $accent-color, #fff);
}
```

Now you can use the following HTML code to create a button in your custom `$accent-color` color:

```
<button class="btn btn-primary">Button</button>
```

When working with floating elements in your HTML by setting the `float` property you will also have to clear the float in some situations. A CSS clearfix enables you to clear the float(s) without having to use any additional markup.

 You can read more about floats at `https://css-tricks.com/all-about-floats/`.

Bootstrap has its own mixin to provide the clearfix; you can reuse this mixin in your custom SCSS code too:

```
.selector {
  @include clearfix();
}
```

Later on in this chapter, I will show you how to use Bootstrap's Sass mixins (and variables) to create a semantic grid yourself.

Bootstrap's mixins enable you to use Bootstrap's CSS in non-Bootstrap projects too. Of course, you can also use others Sass code in your Bootstrap projects as described in the following section.

Sass functions

In the preceding sections, you have read about Sass's built-in functions. You can also define custom functions in Sass. Functions do not set CSS properties such as mixins, but return a value. The following SCSS code will show you a simple example of a Sass function:

```
@function three-times($x) {
  @return 3 * $x;
}

p {
  margin: three-times(4)px;
}
```

In the preceding SCSS code, the `three-times()` function returns three times the input value, so the compiled CSS code will look like this:

```
p {
 margin: 12 px; }
```

Reusing others' code

Many other projects use Sass too. You can easily import files from other non-Bootstrap projects in your project. The preceding section enables you to use mixins already built by others in your project. Mixins do not generate output in the compiled CSS unless you call them.

In this chapter, you will use some mixins found on the Web to generate CSS triangles.

Compass

Compass is a CSS authoring framework that brings you various helpers to write CSS code. Compass requires **Ruby**, so to use Compass' helpers in your Bootstrap project, you will have to replace the `gulp-sass` plugin with the `gulp-ruby-sass` plugin in your Gulp build process. The `gulp-ruby-sass` plugin enables you to use Compass' helpers by setting the compass option to true.

 You can read more about the Compass framework at `http://compass-st yle.org`.

Writing your own custom SCSS code

Now that you know the basics of Sass, you are ready to start your own custom CSS code. Remember the blog website layout I showed you at the start of this chapter?

As you already have seen in `Chapter 2`, *Creating Your Own Build Process with Gulp*, we do not only modularize our CSS code but also the HTML code. The HTML templates are compiled with Panini and can be found in the `html` folder of our project.

The color scheme

You will start your project with a color scheme. Open the `scss/includes/_variables.scss` file. This file contains a copy of Bootstrap's variables. You can remove these variables since we'll use Bootstrap's defaults with a few exceptions.

Now write the following SCSS code in the `scss/includes/_variables.scss` file:

```
$primary-color-dark:    #303f9f;
$primary-color:         #3f51b5;
$primary-color-light:   #c5cae9;
$accent-color:          #ff5722;
$accent-color-light:    #ffab91;
$dark-color:            #000;
$light-color:           #fff;
```

You can run the `gulp` or `bootstrap watch` command in your console to start a browser at `http://localhost:8080` to see your work in progress.

After adding the color scheme, your project is still empty. Time to start your first tweak. Add the following SCSS code to the end of the file:

```
$body-bg:    $gray-lighter;
$body-color: $dark-color;
$link-color: $accent-color;
```

The `$gray-lighter` variable in the preceding code is part of Bootstrap's default variables. You can't use it without copying the default Bootstrap color values to the beginning of the local _variables.scss file, since the local _variables.scss file is imported before the original Bootstrap file.

The preceding code overwrites Bootstrap's default color values for the background and font colors of the <body> element and changes the colors of the hyperlinks.

At the end the content of the `scss/includes/_variables.scss` file may look like the following:

```scss
// Colors
//
// Grayscale and brand colors for use across Bootstrap.

$gray-dark:                 #373a3c;
$gray:                      #55595c;
$gray-light:                #818a91;
$gray-lighter:              #eceeef;
$gray-lightest:             #f7f7f9;

$brand-primary:             #0275d8;
$brand-success:             #5cb85c;
$brand-info:                #5bc0de;
$brand-warning:             #f0ad4e;
$brand-danger:              #d9534f;

// Theme colors
$primary-color-dark:        #303f9f;
$primary-color:             #3f51b5;
$primary-color-light:       #c5cae9;
$accent-color:              #ff5722;
$accent-color-light:        #ffab91 !default;
$dark-color:                #000 !default;
$light-color:               #fff !default;

$body-bg:    $gray-lighter !default;
$body-color: $dark-color !default;
$link-color: $accent-color !default;
```

Preparing the HTML templates

Firstly, change the default layout so that it will meet our requirements. Edit the html/layouts/default.html file and change the <body> section to use some partials. The <body> section should look like the HTML code shown here:

```
<body>
    {{> page-header}}
    {{> navbar}}
    <div class="main-content container bg-dark">
        <div class="row">
            <main class="col-md-9" role="content">
                {{> body}}
            </main>
            <aside class="col-md-3">
                {{> sidebar}}
            </aside>
        </div>
    </div>
    {{> footer}}
    {{> footerjavascripts}}
</body>
```

Then create the `page-header.html`, `navbar.html`, `sidebar.html` and `footer.html` templates in the `html/includes` directory according to the structure in the preceding HTML code. Since we also modularize our Sass code, you can also create the following Sass partials in the `scss/includes/` directory: `_page-header.scss`, `_navbar.scss`, `_sidebar.scss`, and `_footer.scss`.

The `{{> body}}` snippet in the layout will be replaced with the content of the files in the `html/pages` directory. In this example, the `html/pages` directory only contains an `index.html` file. Since we're creating a blog layout, we also create a `scss/includes/_blog.scss` partial for the styles of the main content which contains blog entries.

And last but not least, these new Sass partials should be imported in the `scss/app.scss` file:

```scss
@import "includes/variables";
@import "includes/bootstrap";

// page elements
@import "includes/page-header";
@import "includes/navbar";
@import "includes/sidebar";
@import "includes/footer";

// pages
@import "includes/blog";
```

Now your file structure is ready too and you can start styling the page header.

Styling the page header

The HTML code for the page header, in the `html/includes/page-header.html` file, may look like the following:

```
<header class="container bg-primary-color-dark">
  <div class="row">
      <div class="col-xs-12">
        <h1 class="display-3">Your blog</h1>
      </div>
  </div>
</header>
```

Apart from the `bg-primary-color-dark` class, all CSS classes in the preceding HTML code are predefined Bootstrap CSS classes.

The SCSS code for the the `bg-primary-color-dark` class in the `scss/includes/_page-header.scss` file may simply look like that shown here:

```
.bg-primary-color-dark {
  color: $light-color;
  background-color: $primary-color-dark;
}
```

Instead of the custom SCSS code, you can also use Bootstrap's `bg-variant()` mixin for contextual backgrounds:

```
@include bg-variant('.bg-primary-color-dark', $primary-color-dark);
```

 Notice that the `bg-variant()` mixin sets the font color to white always and declares the colors with the `!important` declaration.

The preceding solution requires modifications of the SCSS and HTML because you have to add the CSS classes to your HTML code. You can accomplish this in the `html/includes/page-header.html` file, without any CSS class in the HTML:

```
<header>
  <div>
      <div>
        <h1>Your blog</h1>
      </div>
  </div>
</header>
```

You can use the following SCSS code, in the `scss/includes/_page-header.scss` file, to style the preceding HTML code:

```scss
body {
    header:first-of-type {
    @include make-container();
    @include make-container-max-widths();
    background-color: $primary-color-dark;
    color: $light-color;
    > div {
      @include make-row();
      > div {
        @include make-col-ready();
        @include make-col(12);
        h1 {
          @extend .display-3;
        }
      }
    }
  }
}
```

The SCSS has a nesting of four levels deep. When you change the structure of your HTML code, your CSS code may easily become broken. The preceding also makes your CSS code less reusable.

You do not generate any CSS classes, which also means you cannot reuse them in your HTML code.

The `@extend .display-3;` still generates a `.display-3` selector in the compiled CSS code which is unused forever. But on the other hand, you do not need the precompiled CSS classes for the grid anymore, due to the usage of Bootstrap's Sass grid mixins. These grid mixins: `make-container()`, `make-container-max-widths()`, `make-row()`, and `make-col-span()`, do not enable you to use only semantic HTML. Bootstrap's CSS solution for the grid requires containers and rows which do not fit pure semantic code. Even when you switch to the optional flexbox mode, you still need these wrappers.

When you're using Bootstrap's Sass grid mixins, you can easily compile Bootstrap without the predefined grid classes. Setting the `$enable-grid-classes` Sass variable to `false`, compiles Bootstrap without these grid classes.

It's not easy to say that the first solution with CSS classes is better than the second more semantic solution or vice versa. The solution to choose depends on your requirements and personal favorites. The smallest code is not always the most reusable code and the cleanest HTML is always the most maintainable code.

Whatever solution you choose, try to be consistent and do not use different solutions for the same project.

The page header is ready now and should look like that shown in the following screenshot:

Let's go and style the navbar in the following section.

Styling the navbar

Now it is time to style our navbar. We use the HTML code from the responsive navbar from `Chapter 1`, *Getting Started with Bootstrap*. Copy the HTML code into the `html/includes/navbar.html` file. The navbar HTML should be wrapped inside a container with the `bg-primary-color` class as follows:

```
<div class="container bg-primary-color">
    <button class="navbar-toggler hidden-md-up pull-xs-right" type="button"
data-toggle="collapse" data-target="#collapsiblecontent">
        ≡
    </button>
  <nav class="navbar navbar-dark navbar-full" role="navigation">
    <ul class="nav navbar-nav navbar-toggleable-sm collapse"
id="collapsiblecontent">
      <li class="nav-item">
        <a class="nav-link active" href="#">Home <span class="sr-
only">(current)</span></a>
      </li>
      <li class="nav-item">
        <a class="nav-link" href="#">Features</a>
      </li>
      <li class="nav-item">
        <a class="nav-link" href="#">Pricing</a>
      </li>
      <li class="nav-item">
        <a class="nav-link" href="#">About</a>
      </li>
    </ul>
  </nav>
</div>
```

As you can see in the preceding code, we'll have to create a new `bg-primary-color` class. Edit the following SCSS code in the `scss/include/_navbar.scss` file:

```scss
.bg-primary-color {
  background-color: $primary-color;
  color: $light-color;
}
```

The navbar should look like that shown in the following screenshot:

When inspecting the results in a browser window smaller than 768 pixels wide, the navbar should collapse and look like that shown in the following screenshot:

The responsive navbar requires the **JavaScript Collapse** plugin. In the next step, we'll justify the navbar links. In the `scss/include/_navbar.scss` file, you can edit the following SCSS code to justify the links:

```scss
.navbar {
  @include nav-justified;
}
```

The `nav-justified` mixin is not part of Bootstrap. You can find this mixin in the `includes/mixins/_nav-justified.scss` file. You can also find the latest version of this mixin at the following URL: `https://github.com/bassjobsen/214792f5543b6b551befaea81178acf7/`. More information can be found at `http://bassjobsen.weblogs.fm/bootstrap-4s-responsive -navbars/`. The mixin is imported via the `includes/_mixins.scss` partial. Later on, we'll import other mixins in the same way.

The `nav-justified` mixins sets the break point at 768 pixels by default. The preceding code shows that reusing mixins written by others is a piece of cake.

Since the links are justified now, you can set the `active` and `hover` colors for the `nav` links in the `scss/include/_navbar.scss` file as follows:

```
.navbar {
  .nav-link {
    &.active,
    &:hover {
      background-color: $accent-color;
    }
  }
}
```

Inspect the results in your browser. You'll find that your page should look like the following screenshot:

When you resize your browser window so that the viewport is smaller than 768 pixels, you'll see that some small tweaks are required.

First the initial nav link overlaps the *hamburger* button. Clicking the *hamburger* button should make the collapsed menu visible, but you cannot click it due to the overlapping. You can solve this by moving the HTML code of the button to the page header. The HTML code in your `html/includes/page-header-html` file should look like the following:

```
<header class="container bg-primary-color-dark">
<div class="row">
    <div class="col-xs-12 bg-primary-color-dark">
        <button class="navbar-toggler hidden-md-up pull-xs-right"
type="button" data-toggle="collapse" data-target="#collapsiblecontent">
            ≡
        </button>
        <h1 class="display-3">Your blog</h1>
    </div>
</div>
</header>
```

And finally, add the following SCSS code into the file to set the color of the button to white:

```
.navbar-toggler {
  color: $light-color;
}
```

The nav links, apart from the first one, have a `margin-left` property set, as can been seen in the following screenshot:

This left margin is useful on large screens, but on smaller screens we want to remove it. You can use Bootstrap's media query ranges, as already described in Chapter 1, *Getting Started with Bootstrap*, to remove this margin. Edit the following SCSS code in the `scss/includes/_navbar.scss` file to remove the margins:

```
.navbar {
  @include media-breakpoint-down(sm) {
    .nav-item + .nav-item {
      margin-left: 0;
    }
  }
}
```

After these final tweaks, it is time to resize your browser window again. Make your viewport wider than 768 pixels. The navbar will become horizontal now.

First add the following SCSS code to accomplish that the links fill the full height of the navbar:

```
.navbar {
  padding-top: 0;
  padding-bottom: 0;
}
```

Now we'll add a CSS triangle under the active navbar link. Bootstrap does not provide a mixin for CSS triangles, but these Sass mixins can be found on the Web. In this example, we'll use the triangle helper mixin from `https://css-tricks.com/snippets/sass/css-triangle-mixin/`. The triangle helper mixin requires the `opposite-direction()` mixin by Hugo Giraudel. You'll find both mixins in the `scss/includes/mixins/_triangle.scss` file.

Again we shall reuse some useful mixins already written and tested by others. Adding the triangle to the active navbar link is now as simple as editing the following SCSS code into the file:

```scss
.nav-link {
  position: relative;
  @include media-breakpoint-up(md) {
    &.active {
      &::before {
        @include triangle(bottom, $accent-color);
        position: absolute;
        margin-left: -1em;
        left: 50%;
        top: 100%;
      }
    }
  }
}
```

Notice that you also have to set `position: relative` for the `nav-link` class. Since we only want to have triangles on the large viewport, the code has been wrapped inside the `@include media-breakpoint-up(md) {}` mixin call.

At the end, your navbar should look like that shown in the following screenshot:

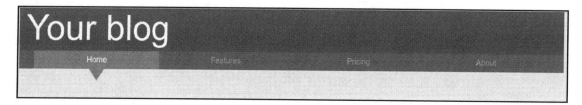

Your navbar already will look pretty good now, but as a bonus you're going to add your photo in the middle of it.

First add the required HTML code to the `html/includes/navbar.html` template:

```html
    ...
  <li class="nav-item">
    <a class="nav-link" href="#">Features</a>
  </li>
  <li class="nav-item">
    <img class="your-photo img-circle" src="{{root}}images/you.png"
alt="Your photo" height="140" width="140">
  </li>
  <li class="nav-item">
```

```
        <a class="nav-link" href="#">Pricing</a>
    </li>
    ...
```

Save your photo in the `assets/images` directory of your project to ensure it is copied to the temporary `_site` directory every time you rebuild your project.

The only thing left to do now is coding the SCSS code for the photo. We'll set the display property to none by default to ensure that the photo is not visible in the small viewports and use Bootstrap's media query ranges again to show it on larger viewports:

```
.navbar {
  .your-photo {
    display: none;
    @include media-breakpoint-up(md) {
      display: block;
      position: absolute;
      top: -100%;
    }
  }
}
```

Bootstrap's `img-circle` class ensures that your photo is displayed as a circle. Also the navbar is ready now and will look like that shown in the following screenshot:

In the next section, you will style the main part of your blog page, including the side bar.

A navbar without Bootstrap's predefined CSS classes

Due to Bootstrap's predefined CSS classes, you can easily add a navbar to your project. Your HTML markup is the same for each project and you only have to add the CSS classes to your HTML to style it.

Of course, you can also remove the CSS classes and use only Sass to style your navbar.

Instead of the `navbar`, `navbar-dark` classes you can also use the following SCSS code:

```
nav[role="navigation"] {
  @extend .navbar;
  @extend .navbar-dark;
  @include nav-justified;
  padding-top: 0;
  padding-bottom: 0;
}
```

Your photo does not require the `your-photo` and `img-circle` classes. You can also extend the `img-circle` class as follows:

```
nav[role="navigation"] {
  li > img {
    display: none;
    @extend .img-circle;
    @include media-breakpoint-up(md) {
      display: block;
      position: absolute;
      top: -100%;
     z-index: 1;
    }
  }
}
```

 Notice that in the SCSS code, the `img-cicle` class is extended outside the media query range. Sass does not allow you to extend an outer selector from within `@media`. The `z-index` is set to ensure that the photo is not overlapped by other content.

In the SCSS, each `nav-item` selector can be replaced with a `nav[role="navigation"] > ul > li` selector and each `nav-link` selector with a `nav[role="navigation"] > ul > li` selector, and so on. Notice that you also have to replace the `nav-item` and `nav-link` selectors in the `justify-nav` mixin.

The main part of your blog page

On small viewports, the sidebar is under the main content. On large viewports the side bar floats on the right side of the main content.

On large viewports the main content gets ¾ of the available space, the rest ¼ part is left for the side bar. We can accomplish this by using the `col-md-9` and `col-md-3` classes in our HTML.

The layout columns are set in the default layout template in the `html/layouts/default.html` file:

```
<div class="main-content container">
    <div class="row">
        <main class="col-md-9" role="content">
            {{> body}}
        </main>
        <aside class="col-md-3">
            {{> sidebar}}
        </aside>
    </div>
</div>
```

Again the `col-md-*` classes are not required. You can accomplish the same by editing the following SCSS code in the `scss/includes/_blog.scss` file:

```
main[role="content"] {
  @include make-col();
  @include media-breakpoint-up(md) {
    @include make-col-span(9);
  }
  + aside {
    @include make-col();
    @include media-breakpoint-up(md) {
      @include make-col-span(3);
    }
  }
}
```

Or even remove the container and row classes too, as follows:

```
.main-content {
  @include make-container();
  @include make-container-max-widths();
  > div {
    @include make-row();
    main[role="content"] {
      @include make-col();
      @include media-breakpoint-up(md) {
        @include make-col-span(9);
      }
      + aside {
        @include make-col();
        @include media-breakpoint-up(md) {
          @include make-col-span(3);
        }
      }
```

```
        }
      }
   }
```

You can disable the predefined grid classes with the `$enable-grid-classes` variable when using Sass mixins for the grid. Skipping the predefined grid classes and using mixins instead will make the compiled CSS code smaller. Smaller CSS code will load faster.

 Bootstrap's source code also contains a special Sass partial called `bootstrap-grid.scss`. You can compile the `bootstrap-grid.scss` file instead of the `bootstrap.scss` file to get the CSS code for the grid only.

The preceding code enables you to use only Bootstrap's grid for your project without the overhead of the other components. The grid requires the `box-sizing: border-box` setting which is not included in the SCSS code of the `bootstrap-grid.scss` file.

Styling the blog posts

Your page can contain a list of blog posts, each post starting with a relevant photo. In the example we'll show only one blog post. The blog post may look like that shown in the following screenshot:

The HTML code for each blog post, saved in the `html/pages/index.html` file, will look like the following:

```
<article>
    <img src="{{root}}images/blog1.png" class="img-fluid">
    <div class="blog-post">
    <header><h1>Blog post 1</h1><time>16:00:00
01/01/2018</time></header>
        <p>Lorem ipsum dolor sit amet, consectetuer adipiscing
elit. Aenean commodo ligula eget dolor. Aenean massa. Cum sociis natoque
penatibus et magnis dis parturient montes, nascetur ridiculus mus. Donec
quam felis, ultricies nec, pellentesque eu, pretium quis, sem. Nulla
consequat massa quis enim. Donec pede justo, fringilla vel, aliquet nec,
vulputate eget, arcu. In enim justo, rhoncus ut, imperdiet a, venenatis
vitae, justo. Nullam dictum felis eu pede mollis pretium.</p>
        <p><a href="">Read more ...</a>
        <footer></footer>
        </div>
</article>
```

The images have the `img-fluid` class to make them responsive. Now the blog post will look like that shown in the following screenshot:

Edit the SCSS code in the `scss/includes/_blog.scss` partial. First give the heading tags the desired color:

```scss
.main-content {
  h1,
  h2,
  h3 {
    color: $primary-color;
  }
}
```

Alternatively, for the preceding code, we can also set `$headings-color: $primary-color;` in the `scss/includes/_variables.sccs` file. When setting the `$heading-color` variable, you'll have to explicitly add the color for the `<h1>` element in the page header, in the `scss/includes/_page-header.scss` file as follows:

```scss
.bg-primary-color-dark {
  background-color: $primary-color-dark;
  color: $light-color;
  h1 {
    color: $page-header-heading-color;
  }
}
```

To use the preceding SCSS, you'll also have to set `$page-header-heading-color: $light-color !default;` in the `scss/includes/_variables.sccs` file.

Then for the finishing touch give each article a `padding-top`:

```scss
main {
    article {
        padding-top: $spacer-y;
    }
}
```

You can also add the `p-t-1` class to your HTML code. The `p-t-1` class is one of the new spacing classes from Bootstrap 4. These utility classes enable you to set the spacing (padding and margin) of an element. You can read more about them in the *Styling of the navbar and hero unit* section of Chapter 2, *Creating Your Own Build Process with Gulp*.

And finally, we have to style the blog post itself. For that, first set the background color and the border of the blog post by editing the following SCSS code into the `scss/includes/_blog.scss` file:

```scss
.blog-post {
    padding: $spacer-y $spacer-x;
```

```
        margin-top: $spacer-y;
        background-color: $light-color;
        border: 1px solid $gray;
    }
```

Again the padding and margin can also be set by adding the `m-t-1` and `p-a-1` CSS classes to your HTML code.

When inspecting the result in your browser, it should look like that shown in the following screenshot:

In the end, we add a CSS triangle pointing to the photo to the top of our blog post for aesthetic reasons.

Since we'll need a triangle having a border, we add two triangles. The second triangle, which is a little smaller, overlays the first one. The dark background color of the first triangle looks like a border. The SCSS code for the triangles can be edited in the file, and should look like this:

```
    .blog-post {
      position: relative;
      &::before {
```

```
        @include triangle(top,$gray,1.1em);
        position: absolute;
        left: 29px;
        bottom: 100%;
      }
      &::after {
        @include triangle(top,$light-color);
        position: absolute;
        left: 30px;
        bottom: 100%;
      }
    }
  }
```

The triangles look like those shown in the following screenshot:

The blog posts are ready now. Let's go on and style the side bar of our page.

Styling the side bar

The side bar of the blog page is built with a Bootstrap list group and will look like that shown in the following screenshot:

You can simply turn a `<ul>` list into a list group with Bootstrap and the predefined `list-group` and `list-group-item` CSS classes. Now you can see the flexibility and re-usability of Bootstrap's CSS classes in practice. With ease we can replace the `<ul>` element with a `<div>` element and a list of `<a>` tags. The HTML code for the side menu in the `html/includes/sidebar.html` file may look like the following:

```
<aside>
  <h2>Archive</h2>
  <!-- list -->
  <div class="list-group">
    <a href="#" class="list-group-item">Cras justo odio</a>
    <a href="#" class="list-group-item">Dapibus ac facilisis in</a>
    <a href="#" class="list-group-item">Morbi leo risus</a>
    <a href="#" class="list-group-item">Porta ac consectetur ac</a>
    <a href="#" class="list-group-item">Vestibulum at eros</a>
  </div>
</aside>
```

The SCSS code to set the basic styles of the side bar can be edited in the `scss/includes/_sidebar.scss` file as follows:

```
aside {
  margin-top: $spacer-y;
  padding: $spacer-y $spacer-x ($spacer-y / 3) $spacer-x;
  background-color: $light-color;
  border: 1px solid $gray-dark;
}
```

And finally, set the color accents of the mouse hovers of the list by overwriting Bootstrap's variables in the local `sccs/includes/_variables.scss` file as shown in the following SCSS code:

```
$list-group-hover-bg: $accent-color;
$list-group-link-hover-color: $light-color;
```

Your blog page is nearly ready to start blogging. The only thing left to do now is building the footer for the page.

The page footer

The page footer should look like that shown in the following screenshot:

The page footer has two equal sized columns on the larger viewport. These columns stack when the viewport become narrower than 768 pixels.

The main HTML in the `html/includes/footer.html` HTML template may look like the following:

```
<footer class="container page-footer bg-dark">
    <div class="row">
        <div class="col-md-6">
            <!-- left -->
        </div>
        <div class="col-md-6">
            <!-- right -->
        </div>
    </div>
</footer>
```

The footer is split into two equal sized columns by using the `col-md-6` classes. These columns get 50% (6 of 12 columns) of the space on the medium (md) and larger grids. As already mentioned, you can also choose to use Bootstrap's Sass mixins to build your grid.

The background and font colors are set with the `bg-dark` class. The following SCSS code in the `scss/includes/_footer.scss` compiles into the `bg-dark` class:

```
.bg-dark {
  color: $light-color;
  background-color: $dark-color;
}
```

The `bg-dark` class can also be generated with the following mixin call:

```
@include bg-variant('.bg-dark', $dark-color);
```

To create the social media button later on we'll also need a `bg-accent-color` class. To make the `bg-*` classes more easy to reuse, you may remove them to a new Sass partial. The `scss/includes/_backgrounds.scss` may contain the following SCSS code:

```
@include bg-variant('.bg-primary-color-dark', $primary-color-dark);
@include bg-variant('.bg-primary-color', $primary-color);
@include bg-variant('.bg-accent-color', $accent-color);
@include bg-variant('.bg-dark', $dark-color);
```

Now that the background and font colors are set, we'll create some style for the footer itself. Also the footer gets a CSS triangle pointing upward. You can edit the following SCSS code into the `scss/includes_footer.scss` file to set the main styles for the footer:

```
.page-footer {
  position: relative;
  padding: $spacer;
  margin-top: $spacer-y;
```

```
  &::after {
    @include triangle(top,$dark-color);
    position: absolute;
    bottom: 100%;
    left: 10%;
  }
}
```

Of course, you can also set the paddings and margin with Bootstrap's m-t-1 and p-x-1 classes.

The left footer column

The left column of the footer contains a small footer text and a row of social media buttons:

```
        <p class="page-foooter-text">Lorem ipsum dolor sit
amet, consectetuer adipiscing elit. Aenean commodo ligula eget dolor.
Aenean massa. Cum sociis natoque penatibus et magnis dis parturient montes,
nascetur ridiculus mus.</p>
        <div class="social-buttons">
            <ul>
                <li>FB</li>
                <li>TW</li>
                <li>G+</li>
            </ul>
        </div>
```

The footer text does not require any additional styles. Use the following SCSS code in the scss/includes/_footer.scss file to style the social media buttons:

```
.social-buttons {
  ul {
    padding: 0;
    margin: 0;
    list-style: none;
    li {
      padding: 10px;
      border: 1px solid $accent-color-light;
    }
  }
  .page-footer & {
    li {
      float: left;
      @extend .bg-accent-color;
    }
  }
}
```

```
    @include clearfix();
  }
```

Notice the usage of the & parent reference in the preceding code:

```
  .page-footer & {
    li {
      @extend .bg-accent-color;
      float: left;
    }
  }
```

The & parent reference is used to reverse the selector order. The preceding SCSS code will compile into CSS code as follows:

```
  .page-footer .social-buttons li {
    float: left;
  }
```

This means that the float: left is only set for the .social-buttons li selector when it is a child of the .page-footer selector. So in our project, the social media buttons will only have a float: left when they are inside the .page-footer selector. We use this method to reuse our social media button SCSS code later on to build a fixed list of social media buttons on the side of our page.

Because of the floating of the list elements in the preceding code, you cannot set the background color on the <ul> tag. You can solve this with the @extend .bg-accent-color; declaration.

The right footer column

The right column contains a form to subscribe to your newsletter. The form is built with Bootstrap's input group component. The HTML code of the form should look like the following:

```
          <h3>Join our Newsletter</h3>
          <div class="input-group">
            <input type="text" class="form-control"
placeholder="Your e-mail">
            <span class="input-group-btn">
              <button class="btn btn-accent-color"
type="button">Subscribe</button>
            </span>
          </div>
```

You can use the following SCSS code to compile the `btn-accent-color` class:

```scss
.btn-accent-color {
  @include button-variant(#fff, $accent-color, #fff);
}
```

The preceding code for the `btn-accent-color` class is saved in the `scss/includes/_footer.scss` file now. Saving buttons in a separated partial called `_buttons.scss` will make your code easier to reuse.

Of course you do not have to create the `btn-accent-color` class at all. The following SCSS code will style your button exactly the same:

```scss
.page-footer {
  button {
    @extend .btn;
    @include button-variant(#fff, $accent-color, #fff);
  }
}
```

And finally, we should give the `<h3>` element the right color with the following SCSS code:

```scss
.page-foter {
  h3 {
    color: $accent-color;
  }
}
```

Reusing the SCSS code of the social buttons

As a bonus, we'll add a fixed list of social media buttons at the left side of our page, which will look like that shown in the following screenshot:

First add the following HTML snippets at the end of the `html/includes/footer.html` file:

```
<div class="social-buttons fixed-media bg-accent-color">
<ul>
    <li>FB</li>
    <li>TW</li>
    <li>G+</li>
</ul>
</div>
```

Notice that the `bg-accent-color` is added to the wrapping `<div>` element.

The only SCSS code we have to edit to the `scss/includes/_footer.scss` is as follows:

```
.social-buttons {
  &.fixed-media {
    display: none;
    @include media-breakpoint-up(md) {
      position: fixed;
      top: 150px;
      display: block;
    }
  }
}
```

As you can see, Sass enables you to reuse most of the SCSS code you have coded before to style the social media buttons in the page footer. You can consider saving the social media buttons code in a separate HTML template and Sass partial for easier reuse.

At the time of writing this book, all modern browsers except Opera Mini support the `position: fixed;` declaration from keeping an element in a fixed location regardless of the scroll position.

 To learn more about this, go to: `http://caniuse.com/#feat=css-fixed`.

Source code of this chapter

You can download the source code of this chapter at the download section of Packt Publishing website at `http://www.packtpub.com/support`. Run the following commands in your console to start:

```
bower install
npm install
bootstrap watch
```

Those who do not have Bootstrap CLI installed can run the `gulp` or `npm start` command instead of the `bootstrap watch` command.

> The source code is also available at GitHub: `https://github.com/bassjo bsen/bootstrap-weblog`.

Using the CLI and running the code from GithHub

Install the Bootstrap CLI using the following commands in your console:

```
[sudo] npm install -g gulp bower
npm install bootstrap-cli --global
```

Then use the following command to set up a web log for a Bootstrap 4 project:

```
bootstrap new --repo https://github.com/bassjobsen/bootstrap-weblog.git
```

Summary

In this chapter, you have got a grip on Sass. You now know how to use Sass to customize Bootstrap's components. You built a web page for your web log and applied different strategies to style it with Sass. In further chapters, you can apply your new Sass knowledge to build amazing web designs with Bootstrap and Sass.

In the next chapter, we'll create a WordPress theme with Bootstrap 4.

4
Bootstrappin' a WordPress Theme

WordPress is a very popular **Content Management System (CMS)** system. It now powers 25 percent of all sites across the web. WordPress is free, open-source, and based on PHP. To learn more about WordPress, you can also visit Packt's WordPress Tech page at `https://www.packtpub.com/tech/wordpress`.

Now, let's turn our design from the Chapter 3, *Customizing Your Blog with Bootstrap and Sass*, into a WordPress theme. There are many Bootstrap-based themes that we could choose. We've taken care to integrate Bootstrap's powerful Sass styles and JavaScript plugins with the best practices found for HTML5. It will be to our advantage to use a theme that does the same. We'll use the JBST4 theme for this exercise. JBST4 is a blank WordPress theme built with Bootstrap 4.

The JBST 4 theme has established itself as a starter theme that leverages the power of Bootstrap while hewing to the implementation of best practices at every turn.

In this chapter, we will perform the following:

- Install WordPress and the JBST 4 theme
- Integrate our customized Sass and JavaScript files with the JBST 4 theme
- Customize the theme template files to deliver the markup we need for our design
- Configure the Grid and navbar
- Build the page header and footer
- Customize the side-bar and use the off-canvas menu template

- Style the buttons and comments
- Use Font Awesome to create social links
- Create an image slider with Bootstrap's Carousel Component
- Build a masonry grid

Installing WordPress and other requirements

You will need a (local) web server with **PHP** and **MySQL** to run WordPress.

AMPPS is an easy to install software stack of , MySQL, PHP, **Perl, Python,** and **Softaculous** Apache, Mysql, PHP, Perl, Python, and Softaculous auto-installer that can be used on desktops and office servers. AMPPS is available for free, and you can run it on Linux, Mac OS X, and Windows. You can download AMPPS at `http://ampps.com/downloads`.

An app for WordPress is available at `http://ampps.com/apps/blogs/WordPress`.

Windows users can also use **WampServer**. WampServer is a Windows web development environment. It allows you to create web applications with Apache2, PHP, and a MySQL database. Alongside **PhpMyAdmin**, WampServer allows you to manage easily your databases. More information about WampServer can be found at `http://www.wampserver.com/en/`.

Installing WordPress

After installing your web server you can install WordPress. Installation of WordPress is very easy and takes on average about 5 minutes to complete. If we are already comfortable with performing such installations, you should try their famous 5-minute install. Detailed instructions are available too at `https://codex.wordpress.org/Installing_WordPress`.

Node.js, Gulp, and Bower

The **JBST 4 WordPress theme** is built with Gulp and it's frontend libraries and their dependencies are managed with Bower. You should install Node.js on your system to run Gulp. Node.js is a JavaScript runtime built on Chrome's V8 JavaScript engine. More information about how to install Node.js can be found at `https://nodejs.org/en/`.

Node.js comes with npm installed. npm is a Node.js package manager. After installing Node.js, you can simply install both Gulp and Bower by running the following commands in your console:

```
npm install --global gulp-cli
npm install --global bower
```

Read more about Bower at http://bower.io/. In Chapter 2, *Creating Your Own Build Process with Gulp,* you can read more about Gulp and learn how to set up your own build process.

Installing the JBST 4 theme

Let's get started by downloading the JBST theme. Navigate to your wordpress/wp-content/themes/ directory and run the following command in your console:

```
git clone https://github.com/bassjobsen/jbst-4-sass.git jbst-weblog-theme
```

Then navigate to the new jbst-weblog-theme directory and run the following command to confirm everything is working:

```
npm install
gulp
```

When all works as expected you can perform the following steps to create a custom theme:

1. Navigate inside the jbst-weblog-theme directory to the style.css file and open it in your favorite text editor. Once you've opened the file, you'll notice that it only contains some basic styles required for WordPress styles. Site styles are provided by a styles.css style sheet file located inside the assets/css directory, which is compiled by Bootstrap. We'll follow this approach as well. The style.css file then serves primarily to name our theme, give appropriate credits, declare the license, and so on. So, let's do that.

2. Change the comments to reflect your new theme information. Here's what I've done with some hints for you:

```
/*
JBST Weblog Theme, Copyright 2016 Bass Jobsen
JBST Weblog Theme is distributed under the terms of the GPLv2
Theme Name: JBST Weblog Theme
Theme URI: https://github.com/bassjobsen/jbst-weblog-theme
Description: A custom Weblog theme based on the JBST 4 Theme
(https://github.com/bassjobsen/jbst4-sass).
```

```
Author: Bass Jobsen
Author URI: http://bassjobsen.weblogs.fm/
Version: 1.0.0
License: GNU General Public License & MIT
License URI: license.txt
Tags: one-column,two-columns,three-columns,left-sidebar,
right-sidebar,responsive-layout
Text Domain: jbst-4
*/
```

3. Save the file.

4. Now let's add a custom screenshot so that we can recognize the theme in the WordPress Dashboard. You should replace the `screenshot.png` file.

5. Grab a screenshot from our results in `Chapter 3`, *Customizing Your Blog with Bootstrap and Sass*. The screenshot should accurately show the theme design and be saved in PNG format. The recommended image size is 1200 x 900 pixels.

6. Replace the default JBST screenshot with our new custom screenshot.

We now have our own copy of the JBST theme setup.

Let's install it!

Installing the theme

Be prepared. The changes that we made earlier have temporarily severed connections to Bootstrap styles, JavaScript, and so on. We're going to update these connections in the following steps. We're simply going to make the process more enjoyable by having the theme installed and running so that we can test our progress along the way!

From your WordPress Dashboard, navigate to **Appearance** | **Themes** and activate the theme. If you've renamed it and provided the new screenshot (or used the provided theme-starter files), you'll see something like the following screenshot:

1. Click on the **Active** button now. Activation will reveal a new **Customize** button.
2. Then click on the **Customize** button.
3. You'll be taken to a page where you can set up several basic options quickly as follows:

   - **Site Identity**: Update your tagline
   - **Colors**: Noting to set
   - **Background Image**: Nothing to set
   - **Menus**: You'll add a new menu here in the next section
   - **Widgets**: The side bar is already set
   - **Static Front page**: Your latest posts

4. In the right-hand side pane, you should see the default Bootstrap navbar, a side bar, and the first **Hello World** post installed by default:

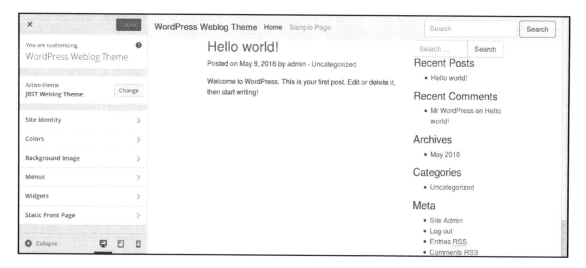

Congratulations! You've got the JBST theme installed.

 If you do not see the default Bootstrap styles applied to the navbar or text, you probably have forgotten to run the `gulp` command first. And you have to run the bower install `npm` install commands before you can run the `gulp` command.

Let's set up our page components.

Reusing the Sass code

You've already coded the Sass code for our theme in `Chapter 3`, *Customizing Your Blog with Bootstrap and Sass*. To reuse this code you can copy the Sass files and directory from the `scss/includes` directory of `Chapter 3`, *Customizing Your Blog with Bootstrap and Sass* into the folder `assets/scss/includes` directory of your `jbst-weblog-theme` theme directory. You may overwrite the `_navbar.scss` Sass partial that already exists and remove the `_bootstrap.scss` Sass partial. You should end up with a file and directory structure like that shown in the following image:

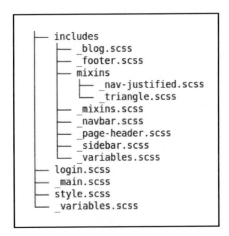

Now edit the `assets/scss/styles.scss` file. First import the
`includes/variables.scss` file just before the import of the custom variables and import
the other partials at the end of the `assets/scss/styles.scss` file after the `// Import
Customizations` comment. After your changes, the SCSS code in the
`assets/scss/styles.scss` file should look like the following:

```
/****************************************************************
Stylesheet: Main Stylesheet

Here's where the magic happens. Here is where you import
all of your Sass files so they can compile into one
CSS file.

/****************************************************************

Stylesheet: Main Stylesheet

Here's where the magic happens. Here is where you import
all of your Sass files so they can compile into one
CSS file.

****************************************************************/
@import "includes/variables";
@import "variables"; // custom variables

// Core variables and mixins
@import "../../vendor/bootstrap/scss/custom";
@import "../../vendor/bootstrap/scss/variables";
@import "../../vendor/bootstrap/scss/mixins";

// Reset and dependencies
```

```scss
@import "../../vendor/bootstrap/scss/normalize";
@import "../../vendor/bootstrap/scss/print";

// Core CSS
@import "../../vendor/bootstrap/scss/reboot";
@import "../../vendor/bootstrap/scss/type";
@import "../../vendor/bootstrap/scss/images";
@import "../../vendor/bootstrap/scss/code";
@import "../../vendor/bootstrap/scss/grid";
@import "../../vendor/bootstrap/scss/tables";
@import "../../vendor/bootstrap/scss/forms";
@import "../../vendor/bootstrap/scss/buttons";

// Components
@import "../../vendor/bootstrap/scss/animation";
@import "../../vendor/bootstrap/scss/dropdown";
@import "../../vendor/bootstrap/scss/button-group";
@import "../../vendor/bootstrap/scss/input-group";
@import "../../vendor/bootstrap/scss/custom-forms";
@import "../../vendor/bootstrap/scss/nav";
@import "../../vendor/bootstrap/scss/navbar";
@import "../../vendor/bootstrap/scss/card";
@import "../../vendor/bootstrap/scss/breadcrumb";
@import "../../vendor/bootstrap/scss/pagination";
@import "../../vendor/bootstrap/scss/tags";
@import "../../vendor/bootstrap/scss/jumbotron";
@import "../../vendor/bootstrap/scss/alert";
@import "../../vendor/bootstrap/scss/progress";
@import "../../vendor/bootstrap/scss/media";
@import "../../vendor/bootstrap/scss/list-group";
@import "../../vendor/bootstrap/scss/responsive-embed";
@import "../../vendor/bootstrap/scss/close";

// Components w/ JavaScript
@import "../../vendor/bootstrap/scss/modal";
@import "../../vendor/bootstrap/scss/tooltip";
@import "../../vendor/bootstrap/scss/popover";
@import "../../vendor/bootstrap/scss/carousel";

// Utility classes
@import "../../vendor/bootstrap/scss/utilities";

// Import Customizations
// mixins
@import "includes/mixins";

// page elements
@import "includes/page-header";
```

```
@import "includes/navbar";
@import "includes/sidebar";
@import "includes/footer";

// pages
@import "includes/blog";

// Import your custom styles
@import "main";
```

Run the `gulp styles` command in your console to test your effort and compile the CSS code.

Conflicts between WordPress and Bootstrap – predefined classes

The HTML pages of WordPress contain a lot of CSS classes to style them by default. Themes such as JBST 4 can overwrite WordPres's default HTML code and enable you to change the HTML structure of elements of your WordPress website.

You can read more about the WordPress template hierarchy at https://developer.wordpress.org/themes/basics/template-hierarchy/. Let's take the search form as an example. To display a site search form on your website you can call the WordPress `get_search_form()` PHP function. This function returns a search form built with the HTML code as shown in the following:

```
<form role="search" method="get" id="searchform"
    class="searchform" action="<?php echo esc_url( home_url( '/' ) ); ?>">
    <div>
        <label class="screen-reader-text" for="s"><?php _x( 'Search for:',
'label' ); ?></label>
        <input type="text" value="<?php echo get_search_query(); ?>"
name="s" id="s" />
        <input type="submit" id="searchsubmit"
            value="<?php echo esc_attr_x( 'Search', 'submit button' ); ?>"
/>
    </div>
</form>
```

Of course, you can write some SCSS code to compile the CSS code to style the preceding form. Bootstrap's CSS code for the input-group requires a different HTML structure. Instead of writing SCSS code, you can also create a searchform.php file in your theme directory. The searchform.php file contains the HTML code for the search form and overwrites WordPres's default search form. The HTML code in the searchform.php file of the JBST theme looks as follows:

```
<form role="search" method="get" class="search-form" action="<?php echo
home_url( '/' ); ?>">
    <div class="input-group">
        <input type="search" class="form-control" placeholder="<?php echo
esc_attr_x( 'Search...', 'search', 'jbst-4' ) ?>" value="<?php echo
get_search_query() ?>" name="s"  />
        <span class="input-group-btn">
            <button class="btn btn-secondary" type="button"><?php echo
esc_attr_x( 'Search', 'search', 'jbst-4' ) ?></button>
        </span>
    </div>
</form>
```

As you can see, the HTML for the preceding search form already contains the HTML structure and the required CSS classes for Bootstrap.

You will also have to edit the following SCSS code into the scss/includes_navbar.scss file:

```
.navbar {
  .search-form {
    @extend .pull-md-right;
    @include media-breakpoint-up(md) {
      .input-group {
        max-width: 300px;
      }
    }
  }
}
```

Later on, you'll create a WordPress menu for your main navigation and turn it into a Bootstrap navbar.

Turn the navigation into a Bootstrap navbar

Item and links in Bootstrap's navbar requires special CSS classes. Because menus are dynamically created by calling the `wp_nav_menu()` custom PHP function, adding the right CSS classes for each menu item is not that simple. The `wp_nav_menu()` function can be called with an array of arguments. The `walker` parameter enables you to assign an instance of a custom `walker` class. The `walker` class provides developers with a means to traverse tree-like data structures for the purpose of rendering HTML. The menu `walker` class enables you to generate a custom menu in combination with the `wp_nav_menu()` call.

The JBST theme also uses a custom walker PHP class and the HTML code of the menu in the `parts/nav-topbar.php` file may look like the following code:

```
<nav class="navbar navbar-light bg-faded navbar-full" role="navigation">
  <div class="navbar-toggleable-sm collapse"
    id="CollapsingNavbar">
    <a class="navbar-brand" href="http://wordpress">
    WordPress Weblog Theme</a>
    <ul class="nav navbar-nav">
      <li class="nav-item">
        <a href="http://wordpress" class="nav-link active">Home  <span
class="sr-only">(current)</span></a>
      </li>
      <li class="nav-item">
        <a href="http://wordpress/?page_id=2" class="nav-link">Sample
Page</a>
      </li>
      <li class="nav-item"><a class="nav-link"><img class="your-photo img-
circle" src="/wp-content/themes/jbst-weblog-theme/assets/images/you.png"
alt="Your photo" height="140" width="140"></a></li>
      <li class="nav-item"><a href="http://wordpress/?page_id=6"
class="nav-link">Page 3</a></li>
      <li class="nav-item"><a href="http://wordpress/?page_id=9"
class="nav-link">Page 4</a></li>
    </ul>
    <form class="form-inline pull-md-right search-form" ac-
tion="http://wordpress/">
      <input class="form-control" type="text" placeholder="Search">
      <button class="btn btn-primary-outline" type="button">Search</button>
    </form>
  </div>
</nav>
```

So the JBST theme turns WordPress HTML code into standard Bootstrap HTML code including the required CSS classes. The preceding HTML structure for the navigation enables us to reuse the SCSS code we created in Chapter 3, *Customizing Your Blog with Bootstrap and Sass* already.

On the other hand, without the PHP `walker` class, the HTML code of the main navigation may look like the following:

```
<div class="menu-main-navigation-container">
<ul id="menu-main-navigation" class="menu">
  <li id="menu-item-4" class="menu-item menu-item-type-custom menu-item-
object-custom menu-item-home menu-item-4">
<a href="http://wordpress">Home</a></li>
  <li id="menu-item-5" class="menu-item menu-item-type-post_type menu-item-
object-page menu-item-5">
<a href="http://wordpress/?page_id=2">Sample Page</a></li>
  <li id="menu-item-12" class="menu-item menu-item-type-custom menu-item-
object-custom menu-item-12">
<a><img class="your-photo img-circle" src="/wp-content/themes/jbst-weblog-
theme/assets/images/you.png" alt="Your photo" height="140"
width="140"></a></li>
  <li id="menu-item-7" class="menu-item menu-item-type-post_type menu-item-
object-page menu-item-7">
<a href="http://wordpress/?page_id=6">Page 3</a></li>
  <li id="menu-item-10" class="menu-item menu-item-type-post_type menu-
item-object-page menu-item-10">
<a href="http://wordpress/?page_id=9">Page 4</a></li>
</ul>
</div>
```

You can style the preceding HTML code by adding the following SCSS code at the end of the `scss/includes/_navbar.scss` Sass partial:

```
.menu-main-navigation-container {
  @extend .navbar-toggleable-sm;
  @extend .collapse;
  ul {
    @extend .nav;
    @extend .navbar-nav;
    li {
      @extend .nav-item;
      a {
        @extend .nav-link;
      }
    }
  }
}
```

With the search form and navbar examples, you've seen that you can apply different strategies to use WordPress with Bootstrap: You can change the HTML output of WordPress to fit Bootstrap's coding standards or write SCSS code which extends Bootstrap's CSS classes with WordPress CSS classes. Both strategies can be useful, but in the case where you cannot simply extend Bootstrap's CSS classes and have to write new complex SCSS code to fit WordPress' HTML code you, should probably prefer to change the HTML output.

About the grid

The default page has a main content area and a side bar. In our original design from Chapter 3, *Customizing Your Blog with Bootstrap and Sass*, the side bar has a width of 25% (col-md-3). The JBST 4 theme has a side bar of 33.3% (col-md-4). And so the design requires a width of 75% (col-md-9) whilst the theme sets 66.6% (col-md-8) for the main content area. You can change the CSS grid classes in the index.php, page.php, and sidebar.php pages in the theme directory to fix this issue.

As already described in Chapter 1, *Getting Started with Bootstrap*, you can also accomplish the same by using Bootstrap's Sass mixins and variables for the grid. For instance, create a new Sass partial (_grid.scss) and edit the following SCSS code into it:

```
main[role="main"] {
  @include make-col();
  @include media-breakpoint-up(md) {
    @include make-col-span(9);
  }
  + .sidebar {
    @include make-col();
    @include media-breakpoint-up(md) {
      @include make-col-span(3);
    }
  }
}
```

The preceding SCSS code will break the full page width layout in the template-full-width.php file because the main[role="main"] selector is not unique and is used for different layouts of the JBST 4 theme.

Notice that you also will have to set the `$enable-grid-classes` Sass variable to false in the `assets/scss/_variables.scss` file to compile Bootstrap without grid classes.

Configuring the navbar

In this section, we'll set up the navbar items for our site pages, and we'll also go ahead and add the markup for the navbar.

Click on the **Customize** button on the theme page again. Under **Menus** create a new menu called **Main navigation**, Check both **The main menu** as location and **Automatically add new top-level pages to this menu** under menu options:

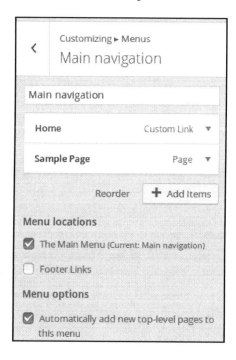

Then add some items under the menu. Select both the **Home** and **Sample Page** under the
Pages option:

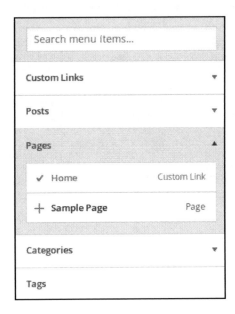

Now press the **Save & Publish** button and close the customizer after that.

The main navigation of our example template has four menu links and a photo in the
middle, so we'll have to add two more pages. We'll add the photo later on.

In your WordPress Dashboard, navigate to **Pages** | **Add new** and add two new pages.

Finally, the Navigation bar should look like that shown in the following screenshot:

In the next section, you will reuse the HTML and Sass code from Chapter 3, *Customizing
Your Blog with Bootstrap and Sass*.

Updating the HTML code

Now edit the nav-topbar.php file in the parts directory of the theme directory. You can take the `html/includes/navbar.html` file from Chapter 3, *Customizing Your Blog with Bootstrap and Sass*, as an example. You should remove both the navbar-brand and the search form. At the end, the HTML and PHP code should look like this:

```
<div class="container bg-primary-color">
  <nav class="navbar navbar-dark" role="navigation">
  <div class="nav navbar-nav navbar-toggleable-sm collapse"
id="CollapsingNavbar">
    <a class="navbar-brand" href="<?php echo home_url(); ?>"><?php
bloginfo('name'); ?></a>
    <?php jbst4_top_nav(); ?>
  </div>
  </nav>
</div>
```

In the preceding code, notice that we have wrapped the navbar code inside a `<div class="container bg-primary-color"></div>` container. The `<nav>` tag has got a `navbar` and `navbar-dark` class.

Adding your photo to the middle of the navbar

First copy your photo to the `assets/images` directory in your theme directory. Then open the customizer or navigate to **Appearance** | **Menus** in your WordPress Dashboard, and add a new item to the menu:

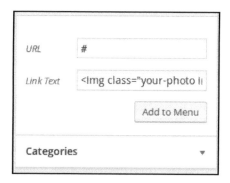

Enter the following HTML code in the **Navigation label** field:

```
<img class="your-photo img-circle" src="/wp-content/themes/jbst-weblog-
theme/assets/images/you.png" alt="Your photo" height="140" width="140">
field should contain the # sign, you will remove it in the next step to
ensure <a> tag around the image does not have a href attribute.
```

As you can see, the photo is still wrapped in an <a> tag. The <a> tag does not have a href attribute, but it still has a mouse hover and changes the position of the image. You can solve these issues by replacing the styles for your-photo selector in the assets/styles/scss/includes/_navbar.scss file with the following SCSS code:

The URL field should contain the # sign. You will remove it in the next step to ensure the <a> tag around the image does not have a href attribute.

 If you have installed WordPress in a sub-directory such as /wordpress/, you have to change the link to the image. Also, the jbst-weblog-theme should correspondence with the name of your theme directory.

Save the new menu item by pressing the **Add to menu** button. Drag the new menu item to the third and most central position in the menu structure and click the arrow on the right of the item to configure it. Remove the # sign in the **URL** field.

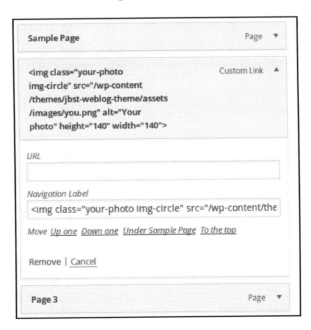

Press the **Save menu** button when you are finished. Navigate to your website and inspect the results of your efforts.

As you can see, the photo is still wrapped in an <a> tag. The <a> tag does not have a href attribute, but it still has a mouse hover and changes the position of the image. You can solve these issues by replacing the styles for your-photo selector in the assets/styles/scss/includes/_navbar.scss file with the following SCSS code:

```scss
.nav-item:nth-child(3) .nav-link {
  display: none;
  @include media-breakpoint-up(md) {
    position: absolute;
    top: -100%;
    z-index: 1;
    display: block;
    &.active,
    &:hover {
      background-color: transparent;
    }
  }
}
```

Run the gulp command after you are done with the changes. You will find that your navbar now looks like that shown in the following screenshot:

Giving your blog a page header

Open and edit the header.php file in the theme directory. Add the following line of PHP just before the topbar template part including:

```php
<?php get_template_part( 'parts/page', 'header' ); ?>
```

In the create a new template part in the parts directory called `page-header.php`, edit the following HTML and PHP code into it:

```
<header class="container bg-primary-color-dark">
  <div class="row">
      <div class="col-xs-12 bg-primary-color-dark">
          <button class="navbar-toggler hidden-md-up pull-xs-right"
type="button" data-toggle="collapse" data-target="#CollapsingNavbar">
              ≡
          </button>
          <h1 class="display-3"><?php bloginfo('name'); ?></h1>
      </div>
  </div>
</header>
```

The `<?php bloginfo('name'); ?>` PHP code automatically shows the name of your blog in the page header. Notice that the **hamburger** menu to toggle the visibility of the menu on smaller viewports is also part of the page header.

Don't forget the page footer

Adding the page footer is as simple as adding the page header. Edit the `footer.php` file in your theme directory. Again you can take the `html/includes/page-footer.html` HTML partial from Chapter 3, *Customizing Your Blog with Bootstrap and Sass,* as an example.

At the end, the HTML and PHP code in the `footer.php` file should look as follows:

```
<footer class="container page-footer bg-dark">
  <div class="row">
    <div class="col-md-6">
        <p class="page-foooter-text">Lorem ipsum dolor sit amet,
consectetuer adipiscing elit. Aenean commodo ligula eget dolor. Aenean
massa. Cum sociis natoque penatibus et magnis dis parturient montes,
nascetur ridiculus mus.</p>
            <nav role="navigation">
              <?php jbst4_footer_links(); ?>
            </nav>
            <div class="social-buttons">
              <ul>
                <li>FB</li>
                <li>TW</li>
                <li>G+</li>
              </ul>
            </div>
        </div>
```

```
            <div class="col-md-6">
              <h3>Join our Newsletter</h3>
                <div class="input-group">
                  <input type="text" class="form-control" placeholder="Your
e-mail">
                    <span class="input-group-btn">
                      <button class="btn btn-accent-color"
type="button">Subscribe</button>
                    </span>
                </div>
            </div>
            <div class="col-xs-12 text-xs-center">
              &copy; <?php echo date('Y'); ?> <?php bloginfo('name'); ?>.
            </div>
        </div>
      </footer>
      <?php wp_footer(); ?>
    </body>
</html> <!-- end page -->
```

The additional `<nav>` element with the `<?php jbst4_footer_links(); ?>` PHP code can be used to display a link menu in the footer. Choose the **Footer Links** menu location when configuring the menu.

You have to add the SCSS code to style the Footer Links menu to the `assets/scss/includes/_footer.scss` file yourself. This SCSS code may look like the following:

```
page-footer {
    nav[role="navigation"] {
      ul {
        list-style: none;
        margin: 0;
        padding: 0;
        li {
          float: left;
          padding: 10px;
        }
      }
      @include clearfix;
    }
}
```

Also notice that we've added an extra grid row to the footer which holds the copyrights notes:

```
<div class="col-xs-12 text-xs-center">
  &copy; <?php echo date('Y'); ?> <?php bloginfo('name'); ?>.
</div>
```

The code for the social media link block on the left side of our page is also added to the `footer.php` file:

```
<div class="social-buttons fixed-media bg-accent-color">
  <ul>
    <li>FB</li>
    <li>TW</li>
    <li>G+</li>
  </ul>
</div>
```

Styling your blog posts

First add an image to the **hello world** blog post. Edit the blog post in the WordPress Dashboard and add a **Featured Image**, as shown in the following screenshot:

Featured Image ▲

Click the image to edit or update

Remove featured image

 Make sure that your WordPress installation has a writable `wp-content/uploads` directory to store the uploaded media. Also see `https://codex.wordpress.org/Changing_File_Permissions` for more information about file permissions.

Now edit the `loop-archive.php` file so that the HTML and PHP code looks like that shown here:

```
<article id="post-<?php the_ID(); ?>" <?php post_class(''); ?>
role="article">
<?php the_post_thumbnail('full'); ?>
<div class="blog-post">
    <header class="article-header">
        <h2><a href="<?php the_permalink() ?>" rel="bookmark" ><?php
the_title(); ?></a></h2>
        <?php get_template_part( 'parts/content', 'byline' ); ?>
    </header> <!-- end article header -->

    <section class="entry-content" itemprop="articleBody">

        <?php the_content('<button class="btn btn-accent-color">Read
more...</button>'); ?>
    </section> <!-- end article section -->

    <footer class="article-footer">
        <p class="tags"><?php the_tags('<small class="text-
muted">' . __('Tags:', 'jbst-4') . '</small> ', ', ', ''); ?></p>
    </footer> <!-- end article footer -->
</div>
</article> <!-- end article -->
```

In the preceding code, the `the_post_thumbnail('full');` PHP function call is moved to the top. This code displays the featured image. A `<div class="blog-post"></div>` wrapper is added too. The wrapper adds the blog-post CSS class according the SCSS code in the `scss/includes/_blog.scss` file.

The side bar of your blog

The HTML and PHP code for the side bar can be found in the `sidebar.php` file in your theme directory. The side bar loads WordPress Widgets. You can manage your widgets in the WordPress Dashboard. Navigate to **Appearance** | **Widget** and configure the widgets.

Each widget has a built-in HTML structure with CSS classes. You can change or modify the HTML and CSS structure when you register your side bar. The JBST 4 theme's side bars are registered in the `assets/functions/sidebar.php` file of the theme as follows:

```
register_sidebar(array(
    'id' => 'sidebar1',
    'name' => __('Sidebar 1', 'jbst-4'),
```

```
    'description' => __('The first (primary) sidebar.',
        'jbst-4'),
    'before_widget' => '<div id="%1$s" class="widget %2$s">',
    'after_widget' => '</div>',
    'before_title' => '<h4 class="widgettitle">',
    'after_title' => '</h4>',
));
```

 More information about registering and configuring side bars can be found at https://codex.wordpress.org/Function_Reference/registe r_sidebar and https://codex.wordpress.org/Function_Reference/th e_widget.

When writing the SCSS for the side bar and its widgets, you can choose whether to style the side bar in one go or to create style rules for each widget.

To style the side bar all at once, you can edit the SCSS code in the assets/scss/includes/_sidebar.scss as follows:

```
.sidebar {
  padding: $spacer-y $spacer-x ($spacer-y / 3);
  margin-top: $spacer-y;
  background-color: $light-color;
  border: 1px solid $gray-dark;
}
```

Notice that we've applied the style rules on the sidebar selector. The sidebar selector is not unique and is probably also used for other side bases in the theme.

After running the `gulp` command, your side bar may look like that shown in the following screenshot:

From here I'll show you how to style the side bar per widget. First change the SCSS code in the `assets/scss/includes/_sidebar.scss` file as follows:

```scss
.sidebar {
  .widget {
    padding: $spacer-y $spacer-x ($spacer-y / 3);
    margin-top: $spacer-y;
    background-color: $light-color;
    border: 1px solid $gray-dark;
  }
}
```

After running the `gulp` command each widget will look like that shown in the following screenshot:

Now we should turn the lists inside the widget into Bootstrap's list groups. You can do this by extending Bootstrap's list-group CSS selectors in your SCSS code. Consider the following SCSS code:

```scss
sidebar {
  widget {
    ul {
      @extend .list-group;
      li {
        @extend .list-group-item;
      }
    }
  }
}
```

Run the `gulp` command again unless you have run the gulp watch command already. You'll find that the lists are styled like Bootstrap's list groups now. Bootstrap's list groups do not change the background color on mouse hovers as required by our design. You can extend the SCSS code to fix the preceding problem. At the end, the SCSS should look like this:

```scss
sidebar {
  widget {
    ul {
      @extend .list-group;
      li {
        @extend .list-group-item;
        padding: 0;
        a {
          display: block;
          padding: .75rem 1.25rem;
          text-decoration: none;
          @include hover-focus-active {
            color: $list-group-link-hover-color;
            background-color: $list-group-hover-bg;
          }
        }
      }
    }
  }
}
```

The preceding SCSS code removes the padding from the `li` selectors and applies it on the `a` selectors. The `a` selectors also got a display: block; declaration to ensure that the links fill the available space just like other block level elements.

The widgets should look like that shown in the following screenshot:

Notice that the preceding breaks the mark up and styling of the recent comments due to each list item containing two links (`<a>` tags). Be prepared to create special style rules for only the `ul.recentcomments` selector to fix this issue.

As you have seen, the list group does not handle hovered links by default. The Bootstrap Navs component does support hovered links. Especially, the Stacked pills variant of the Navs component seems to fit our requirements. You can use the widget list into stacked pills Navs components by replacing the SCSS code with the following SCSS code into the `assets/scss/includes/_sidebar.scss` file:

```scss
.widget {
  padding: $spacer-y $spacer-x ($spacer-y / 3);
  margin-top: $spacer-y;
  background-color: $light-color;
  border: 1px solid $gray-dark;
  ul {
    @extend .nav;
    @extend .nav-pills;
    @extend .nav-stacked;
    li {
      @extend .nav-item;
      // Place the border on the list items and negative margin up for
better styling
      margin-bottom: -$list-group-border-width;
      background-color: $list-group-bg;
      border: $list-group-border-width solid $list-group-border-color;
      a {
        @extend .nav-link;
        border-radius: 0;
        @include hover-focus-active {
          color: $list-group-link-hover-color;
          background-color: $list-group-hover-bg;
        }
      }
    }
  }
}
```

Now your widget may look like that shown in the following screenshot:

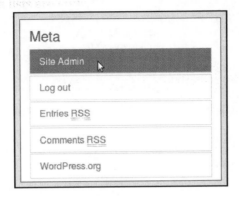

The off-canvas side bar

On the official Bootstrap website at `http://getbootstrap.com/examples`, you can find an off-canvas example. The example will show you how to build a toggle able off-canvas navigation menu for use with Bootstrap. You can use an off-canvas side bar in your theme too. On the smaller viewports, a page with the off-canvas menu will look like that shown in the following screenshot:

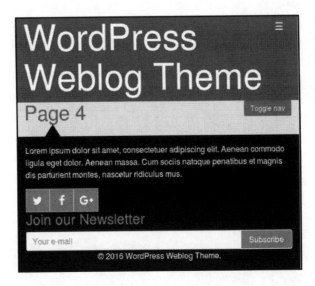

When you click the **Toggle nav** button in the preceding page, the page content slides to the left and the side bar becomes visible.

The off-canvas menu use the template called `template-offcanvas.php` in the `theme directory/` It should contain the following HTML and PHP code:

```php
<?php
/*
Template Name: Off-canvas Side bar
*/
?>

<?php get_header(); ?>
    <div class="container" id="content">
        <div id="inner-content" class="row row-offcanvas row-offcanvas-
right">
            <main id="main" class="col-xs-12 col-md-8"
                role="main">

            <p class="pull-xs-right hidden-md-up">
                <button type="button" class=
                    "btn btn-primary btn-sm" data-toggle="offcanvas">
<?php _e('Toggle nav', 'jbst-4') ?>
</button>
            </p>

                <?php if (have_posts()) :
                    while (have_posts()) : the_post(); ?>

                    <?php get_template_part
                        ( 'parts/loop', 'page' ); ?>

                    <?php endwhile; endif;
            </main> <!-- end #main -->

            <?php get_sidebar('offcanvas'); ?>
            <div class="clearfix hidden-xs-up"></div>
        </div> <!-- end #inner-content -->
    </div> <!-- end #content -->

<?php get_footer(); ?>
```

You should notice that the `template-offcanvas.php` file is very similar to the `page.php` and `index.php` files. At the beginning of the file, you'll find the templates comments, including the **Template name**. The `<div id="inner-content">` element got two additional CSS classes, both the `row-offcanvas` and `row-offcanvas-right` classes are added. The `row-offcanvas` class sets a CSS transition for the sliding of the content section, whilst the `row-offcanvas-right` class sets the position of the content section for the menu on the right side of the page. The main element gets an optional `col-xs-12` CSS class. And a toggle button is added:

```
<div class="pull-xs-right hidden-md-up">
  <button type="button" class="btn btn-primary btn-sm" data-
toggle="offcanvas"><?php _e('Toggle nav', 'jbst-4') ?></button>
</div>
```

The `hidden-md-up` class guarantees that the button is only visible on the small viewports. And finally, the side bar is rendered with the `<?php get_sidebar('offcanvas'); ?>` PHP call. Due to the `offcanvas` parameter, not the `default sidebar.php` template, the `sidebar-offcanvas.php` template is loaded.

The `sidebar-offcanvas.php` template is similar to the sidebar.php template. Its content should look like the following:

```
<div class="col-xs-6 col-md-4 sidebar sidebar-offcanvas" id="sidebar">
    <?php if ( is_active_sidebar( 'offcanvas' ) ) : ?>

        <?php dynamic_sidebar( 'offcanvas' ); ?>

    <?php else : ?>

    <!-- This content shows up if there are no widgets defined in the
backend. -->

    <div class="alert help">
    <p><?php _e("Please activate some Widgets.", "jbst-4");  ?>
</p>
    </div>

    <?php endif; ?>

</div>
```

The preceding HTML and PHP code got an additional `col-xs-6` CSS class and loads the `offcanvas` side bar.

The HTML code is ready now. Let's evaluate the SCSS and JavaScript code to finish the `offcanvas` menu.

The SCSS code can be found in the Sass partial called `_offcanvas.scss` in the `assests/scss/includes` directory. Make sure that the `_offcanvas.scss` file is imported into the `styles.scss` file as follows:

```
// templates
@import "includes/offcanvas";
```

The `_offcanvas.scss` file itself contains the following SCSS code:

```
html,
body {
  overflow-x: hidden; /* Prevent scroll on narrow devices */
}

/*
 * Off Canvas
 * --------------------------------------------------
 */
@include media-breakpoint-down(sm) {
  .row-offcanvas {
    position: relative;
    transition: all .25s ease-out;
  }
  .row-offcanvas-right {
    right: 0;
  }
  .row-offcanvas-left {
    left: 0;
  }
  .row-offcanvas-right
  .sidebar-offcanvas {
    right: -100%; /* 12 columns */
  }
  .row-offcanvas-right.active
  .sidebar-offcanvas {
    right: -50%; /* 6 columns */
  }
  .row-offcanvas-left
  .sidebar-offcanvas {
    left: -100%; /* 12 columns */
  }
  .row-offcanvas-left.active
  .sidebar-offcanvas {
    left: -50%; /* 6 columns */
```

```
    }
    .row-offcanvas-right.active {
      right: 50%; /* 6 columns */
    }
    .row-offcanvas-left.active {
      left: 50%; /* 6 columns */
    }
    .sidebar-offcanvas {
      position: absolute;
      top: 0;
      width: 50%; /* 6 columns */
    }
  }
```

Last, but not least, we require some JavaScript code to handle the toggle button. In the `assets/scripts/wp-jbst.js` we find the following lines of JavaScript code, between the `jQuery(document).ready(function() {});` code:

```
    // offcanvas menu
    jQuery('[data-toggle="offcanvas"]').click(function () {
      jQuery('.row-offcanvas').toggleClass('active');
    });
```

In the WordPress Dashboard, navigate to **Pages** and edit a page. Select the new `offcanvas` template under templates as shown in the following screenshot:

Save the page and inspect the results in your browser. When resizing your browser window to a viewport below 768 pixels you will find that the `offcanvas` menu works and looks like that shown in the following screenshot:

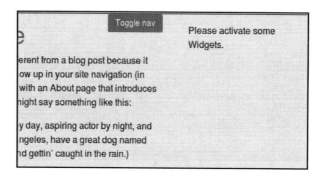

Now you can navigate to **Appearance** | **Widgets** in the WordPress Dashboard and add some widgets to the off-canvas side menu. Notice that when your menu become taller than the content, it will overlap the footer due to the position: absolute; declaration for the off-canvas menu. You can set a z-index property for the off-canvas menu to fix the overlapping issue.

To use the new off-canvas template for your front page, you'll have to set a static page as your front page. Navigate to **Settings** | **Reading** in the WordPress Dashboard and select your page. On the selected page, you'll have to select the template as shown before:

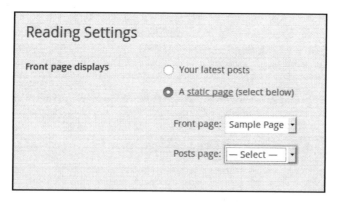

Instead of changing the front page setting you can also copy the `template-offcanvas.php` file to a new `home.php` or `front-page.php`. Read the `https://developer.wordpress.org/themes/basics/template-hierarchy/` page to learn more about WordPress' template system.

Applying style to the buttons

Our design contains several buttons now: the button in the footer, the search button, the toggle button for the off-canvas menu, and also the button of the comment form. Let's find a better solution to style the button of our theme.

Remember that you can apply Bootstrap's `btn` and `btn-*` CSS classes on the `<button>` tag and also use them on `<a>` and `<input>` tags.

First, create a new Sass partial called `assets/scss/includes/_buttons.scss` and then move the `btn-accent-color selector` into it. The `assets/scss/includes/_buttons.scss` file should contain the following SCSS code:

```
.btn-accent-color {
  @include button-variant(#fff, $accent-color, #fff);
}
```

Again we'll have two strategies to style the buttons of the theme. We can adopt the HTML code and make sure that every button has the required `btn` and `btn-*` CSS classes. Or alternatively create some generic CSS selectors to style the buttons.

When using generic selectors in the `assets/scss/includes/_buttons.scss` file, the SCSS code may look as follows:

```
button,
input[type="submit"],
.button {
 @extend .btn;
 @include button-variant(#fff, $accent-color, #fff);
}
```

Although the preceding selectors are generic, do not style the search button nor the toggle button of the off-canvas menu. Both the search button and the off-canvas have `btn-primary` classes with a higher specificity in the HTML code. On the other hand, the selector does style the toggle button of the navbar.

Compiling the `btn-accent-color` CSS class and changing the HTML according to it seems a more firm strategy in this situation.

Edit the `searchform.php` file to add the required CSS classes for the search button as follows:

```
<button class="btn btn-accent-color " type="button"><?php echo esc_attr_x(
'Search', 'search', 'jbst-4' ) ?></button>
```

The toggle button for the off-canvas menu can be found in the template-offcanvas.php file file as seen before. And finally, the button for the comment form is found in the `comments.php` in the theme directory. Notice that you should use the PHP function call here to set the CSS classes as follows:

```
<?php comment_form(array('class_submit'=>'btn btn-accent-color')); ?>
```

In the next section, we'll look at the comments in more detail. You can read more about WordPress' `comment_form()` PHP function at `https://codex.wordpress.org/Function_Reference/comment_form`.

Other tweaks in your Sass

When adding more content, pages, and plugins to your WordPress project you'll find more elements to style. This chapter provides you with the knowledge and strategies to do it yourself. The following hints to style the pagination and search form button may help you to understand how to approach this in the right manner.

The pagination

You probably would have found out that the active links of the navigation did not get the right background color. You can fix this issue by adding the following lines of SCSS code to the `scss/includes/_variables.scss` file:

```
// pagination
$pagination-active-color: $light-color;
$pagination-active-bg: $accent-color;
$pagination-active-border: #ddd; // $pagination-border-color;
```

Search form button

You may have also discovered that the border color of the search button in the side bar does not look good on a white background. You can use the following SCSS code in the `_main.scss` file to fix this:

```scss
// search form button
.search-form {
  .input-group-btn {
    .btn {
      border: $input-btn-border-width solid $input-group-addon-border-color;
    }
  }
}
```

Before the preceding tweak, you should know that the search button looks like that shown in the following screenshot:

After the tweak, the button looks as follows:

Styling the user comments on your pages

WordPress enables your users to comment on your blogs. The JBST theme uses Bootstraps' Media object to display the comments. The media object is an abstract element used as the basis for building more complex and repetitive components. You can use it to style a HTML list too. HTML lists are useful to display comments threads.

In the JBST 4 theme, the `comments.php` file in the main theme folder contains the HTML and PHP code for the comments. The `comments.php` file is part of WordPress template system as described before. It contains the following PHP snippet:

```
<ol class="commentlist">
    <?php wp_list_comments
        ('type=comment&callback=jbst4_comments'); ?>
</ol>
```

The `jbst4_comments` callback function to display the comment list can be found in the `assets/functions/comments.php` file, it contains the following HTML and PHP code:

```
<?php
// Comment Layout
function jbst4_comments($comment, $args, $depth) {
    $GLOBALS['comment'] = $comment; ?>
     <li <?php comment_class('media'); ?>>
            <div class="media-left">
                <?php echo get_avatar
                    ( $comment, 75, '', sprintf
                        ( esc_html__( 'Avatar of %s', 'jbst-4' ),
get_comment_author() ),
                            array('class' => 'media-object')); ?>
            </div>
            <div class="media-body">
                <article id="comment-<?php comment_ID(); ?>
" class="clearfix col-lg-12">
                    <header class="comment-author">
                        <?php
                            // create variable
                            $bgauthemail = get_comment_author_email();
                        ?>
                        <?php printf(__('%s', 'jbst-4'),
get_comment_author_link()) ?> on
                        <time datetime="<?php echo comment_time('Y-m-j');
?>">
<a href="<?php echo htmlspecialchars
    ( esc_url(get_comment_link( $comment->comment_ID )) ) ?>">
<?php comment_time(__(' F jS, Y - g:ia', 'jbst-4')); ?> </a></time>
                        <?php edit_comment_link
(__('(Edit)', 'jbst-4'),' ','') ?>
                    </header>
                    <?php if ($comment->comment_approved == '0') : ?>
                        <div class="alert alert-info">
                            <p>
<?php _e('Your comment is awaiting moderation.', 'jbst-4') ?></p>
                        </div>
```

```php
            <?php endif; ?>
            <section class="comment_content clearfix">
                <?php comment_text() ?>
            </section>
            <?php comment_reply_link
                (array_merge( $args, array
                ('depth' => $depth, 'max_depth' => $args
                ['max_depth']))) ?>
        </article>
    </div>
<!-- </li> is added by WordPress automatically -->
<?php
}
```

The preceding code will wrap the comments into a HTML list using the Bootstrap Media object as follows:

```html
<ul class="media-list">
  <li class="media">
    <div class="media-left">
      <!-- avatar -->
    </div>
    <div class="media-body">
        <!-- comment -->
    </div>
  </li>
  ...
</ul>
```

 You can read more about Bootstrap's Media object at `http://v4-alpha.g` `etbootstrap.com/layout/media-object/`.

By default, the comments in the JBST 4 theme look like that shown in the following screenshot:

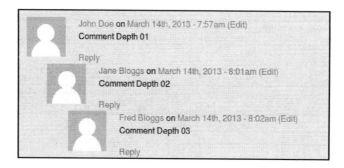

Now let's style the comments to be consistent with our design. First add a black color and border in accordance with the color scheme. Edit the `assets/scss/includes/_comments.scss` file and add the following SCSS code to it:

```
.comments-area {
  .media-body {
    padding: $spacer-y $spacer-x;
    margin-top: $spacer-y;
    background-color: $light-color;
    border: 1px solid $gray;
  }
}
```

Secondly, style the date and author name with the following SCSS code:

```
.comments-area {
  .comment-author {
    font-size: $font-size-sm
    @extend .text-muted;
  }
}
```

Instead of the preceding SCSS rules, you can also modify the HTML code in the file. The HTML code may then look as follows:

```
<small class="text-muted">
  <time datetime="<?php echo comment_time('Y-m-j'); ?>">
    <a href="<?php echo htmlspecialchars( esc_url(get_comment_link(
$comment->comment_ID )) ) ?>"><?php comment_time(__(' F jS, Y - g:ia',
'jbst-4')); ?> </a>
  </time>
</small>
```

After that you may style the reply button. You can use the following SCSS code to style the buttons:

```
.comments-area {
.comment-reply-link {
  @extend .btn;
  @extend .btn-accent-color;
  }
}
```

Finally, run the `gulp` command if you haven't run the gulp watch command already, and inspect the result in your browser. The comments should now look like that shown in the following screenshot:

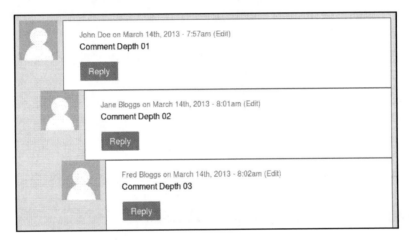

Adding a carousel to your page

Bootstrap's Carousel component enables you to create a slideshow for cycling through images or slides of text. Of course, you can also add a carousel to your theme.

First you should upload your image to the `assets/images/slides` directory of your theme. All images should have the same width and height.

As an example, we have added three images into the assets/images/slides directory called slide1.jpg, slide2.jpg and slide3.jpg. These images are released in the CC0 Public Domain and you can find them on Pixabay (https://pixabay.com/).

In the next section, we'll use PHP to create the desired HTML output of our template files. If you are not familiar with PHP yet, the official website can be found at the following URL: http://php.net/. To learn the basics of PHP you can visit Packt's PHP Tech Page at https://www.packtpub.com/tech/php.

Now you can create a new template in the parts directory. You may call it component-carousel.php.

In the component-carousel.php, you'll have to link the images in the assets/images directory in the HTML / PHP code as follows:

```
    <div class="carousel-inner" role="listbox">
    <?php for ($i=1; $i<=3; $i++){?>
      <div class="carousel-item<?php echo ($i==1) ? ' active' : ''?>">
        <img src="<?php echo get_template_directory_uri();
  ?>/assets/images/slides/slide<?php echo $i ?>.jpg" alt="First slide">
      </div>
    <?php } ?>
    </div>
```

Bootstrap's carousel markup structure can be found in its documentation pages at the following URL: http://getbootstrap.com/components/carousel/.

The complete HTML and PHP code should look like this:

```
<div id="carousel-example-generic" class="carousel slide" data-
ride="carousel">
  <ol class="carousel-indicators">
    <li data-target="#carousel-example-generic" data-slide-to="0"
class="active"></li>
    <li data-target="#carousel-example-generic"
          data-slide-to="1"></li>
    <li data-target="#carousel-example-generic"
          data-slide-to="2"></li>
  </ol>
  <div class="carousel-inner" role="listbox">
  <?php for ($i=1; $i<=3; $i++){?>
    <div class="carousel-item
          <?php echo ($i==1) ? ' active' : ''?>">
      <img src=
          "<?php echo get_template_directory_uri();
            ?>/assets/images/slides/slide
```

```
          <?php echo $i ?>.jpg" alt="First slide">
    </div>
  <?php } ?>
  </div>
  <a class="left carousel-control"
        href="#carousel-example-generic" role="button"
        data-slide="prev">
    <span class="icon-prev" aria-hidden="true"></span>
    <span class="sr-only">Previous</span>
  </a>
  <a class="right carousel-control"
        href="#carousel-example-generic"
        role="button" data-slide="next">
    <span class="icon-next" aria-hidden="true"></span>
    <span class="sr-only">Next</span>
  </a>
</div>
```

Finally, you should load the carousel on your front page. Edit the `index.php` file in the theme directory and the following PHP snippet to it:

```
...
<?php if(is_home()){ get_template_part
      ( 'parts/component', 'carousel' ); } ?>
<?php if (have_posts()) : while
      (have_posts()) : the_post(); ?>
...
```

The `if(is_home())` conditional ensures that the carousal is only displayed on the front page.

In `Chapter 5`, *Bootstrappin' Your Portfolio*, you can read more about marking up the carousel. You can reuse the SCSS code for the carousel from `Chapter 5`, *Bootstrappin' Your Portfolio*, to style the carousel in the WordPress theme too by simply copying the `_carousel.scss` partial into the `assets/scss/includes` directory and importing it in the `styles.scss` file.

As you have seen, the carousel works very well. When you want to use other images in the slider, you'll have to replace the images in the `assets/images/slides` directory. Replacing the images is no problem when you are the maintainer of the project yourself. In the case that you distribute the website and theme to someone else you probably would prefer that they could replace the slider images in the Dashboard.

The WordPress' plugin directory contains many useful plugins to extend your Dashboard. Plugins for Bootstrap's slider are available too. The plugin directory can be found at `https://wordpress.org/plugins/`. The plugin at `https://wordpress.org/plugins/twitter-bootstrap-slider/` can be used to add a Bootstrap carousel to your WordPress project.

Using Font Awesome in your theme

In `Chapter 5`, *Bootstrappin' Your Portfolio*, you can read how to compile the Font Awesome CSS code into your local style sheet with Sass. You can also run Font Awesome from CDN, as described in `Chapter 2`, *Creating Your Own Build Process with Gulp*.

To run Font Awesome from CDN in your WordPress theme, you can enqueue the CDN URL. Edit and add the following line of PHP code to activate Font Awesome:

```
//enqueues the external font awesome stylesheet
wp_enqueue_style('font-awesome', '//maxcdn.bootstrapcdn.com/font-awesome/4.6.3/css/font-awesome.min.css');
```

Building the social links with Font Awesome

The theme contains two blocks with social links; one fixed on the left side of the page and the other one in the footer. The HTML code for both blocks can be found in the `footer.php` file. To prevent code duplication you can create a new template called `parts/components-social-links.php`. Then edit the following HTML code into the new `parts/components-social-links.php` file:

```html
<ul>
  <li><a href="https://twitter.com/bassjobsen">
    <i class="fa fa-twitter fa-fs fa-lg"></i></a></li>
  <li>
    <a href="https://facebook.com/bassjobsen">
    <i class="fa  fa-facebook fa-fs fa-lg"></i></a></li>
  <li>
    <a href="http://google.com/+bassjobsen">
    <i class="fa fa-google-plus fa-fs fa-lg"></i></a>
  </li>
</ul>
```

In the preceding HTML code, the fa-fs CSS class guarantees that each icon gets the same width and height. Then in the footer.php file replace both the <ul> list with the following PHP code:

```php
<?php get_template_part( 'parts/component', 'social-links' ); ?>
```

Finally, you'll have to make some small change in your SCSS code for the social media blocks. First move the SCSS code for the social media block from _includes/_footer.scss to a new file called _includes/_social-button.scss. *Don't forget to import this new file in the styles.scss file by adding the following SCSS code snippet:*

```scss
// Components
@import "includes/social-buttons";
```

The SCSS code in the _includes/_social-button.scss file should look like this:

```scss
.social-buttons {
  &.fixed-media {
    display: none;
    @include media-breakpoint-up(md) {
      position: fixed;
      top: 150px;
      display: block;
    }
  }
  ul {
    padding: 0;
    margin: 0;
    list-style: none;
    li {
      padding: 10px;
      border: 1px solid $accent-color-light;
      a {
        color: $light-color;
      }
    }
  }
  .page-footer & {
    li {
      float: left;
      @extend .bg-accent-color;
    }
  }
  @include clearfix();
}
```

At the end, your social buttons should like that shown in the following screenshot:

Using the masonry template

A masonry grid layout works by placing elements in an optimal position based on available vertical space, sort of like a mason fitting stones in a wall. The Cards module of Bootstrap enables you to organize elements (cards) into masonry-like columns with just CSS. The Card module is a flexible and extensible content container. It replaces the panels, thumbnails, and wells used in earlier versions of Bootstrap.

The JBST 4 theme already contains a template for you, which organizes your post into masonry-like columns.

You can test the masonry template on your front page by copying the template-masonry file to the `front-page.php` file. Or select a page using this template as your front page.

The CSS code to display the masonry items in the right manner is compiled from the SCSS in the `assets/sccs/includes/_masonry.scss` file. The SCSS code in this file looks as follows:

```
.masonary {
  .card-columns {
    padding-top: $spacer-y;
  }
}
.mansory-blog-post {
  position: relative;
  padding: $spacer-y $spacer-x;
  background-color: $light-color;
  border: 1px solid $gray;
}
```

The masonry grid layout is not available in IE9 and below as they have no support for the `column-*` CSS properties.

If you're looking for test data for your theme, you can import the `data.xml` found in the download section of this chapter. In the Dashboard, navigate to **Tool | Import**. Then choose to install the WordPress importer to import posts, pages, comments, custom fields, categories, and tags from a WordPress export file. We use **import** to import the data.xml file. You do not have to reassign any author, but you should check the **Download and import file attachments** option. More information about testing your WordPress themes can be found at `https://codex.wordpress.org/Theme_Unit_Test`.

The end result of your efforts may look like that shown in the following screenshot:

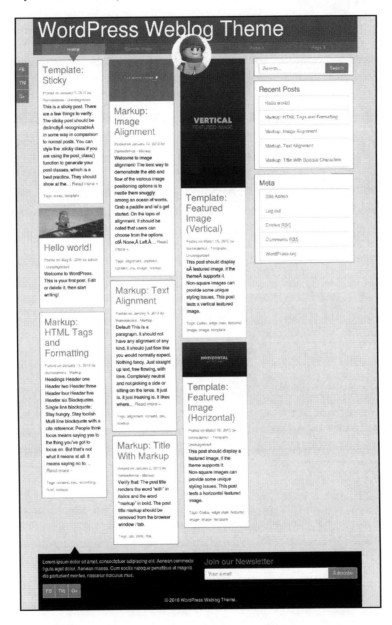

Child theming

JBST is a start theme and not a framework. WordPress has a structure to build child themes. The main purpose of child theming is its ability to upgrade the parent theme easily. JBST 4 is intended to be used as a starter theme, not as a parent or theme framework. In almost all instances, it is recommended you just hack away and customize JBST 4 itself as described in this chapter.

You can run Bower to keep Bootstrap's code and its dependencies up to date.

Download at GitHub

You can download the newest and updated version of this theme at GitHub too. You will find it at the following URL: `https://github.com/bassjobsen/jbst-weblog-theme`.

Summary

In the chapter, you could see that we could easily reuse the SCSS from `Chapter 3`, *Customizing Your Blog with Bootstrap and Sass*, by using a WordPress Bootstrap theme which turns WordPress' HTML code into standard Bootstrap code. Both the SCSS code and the JBST theme use and reuse Bootstrap's predefined CSS classes whenever possible. This strategy enables us to write clear code which can be easily reused.

In this chapter, we've built a custom WordPress theme with Bootstrap. Because we began with the excellent JBST 4 theme as our starter theme, we did not have to build from scratch. We asserted control over the markup structure by customizing the template files and created some custom template files. After that we styled buttons and comments using Bootstrap's styles.

And finally we integrated Bootstrap's carousel component to create an image slider on our front page and build an off-canvas menu and masonry grid layout for the theme.

Congratulations! That's quite an accomplishment.

The process we've used in this chapter can be used to transform any Bootstrap design into a WordPress theme.

So, let's turn back to designing with Bootstrap. Next, we are going to design a portfolio site.

5
Bootstrappin' Your Portfolio

Let's imagine we're ready for a fresh design of our online portfolio. As always, time is scarce. We need to be efficient, but the portfolio has to look great. And of course, it has to be responsive. It should work across devices of various form factors, since this is a key selling point for our prospective clients. This project will enable us to leverage a number of Bootstrap's built-in features, even as we customize Bootstrap to suit our needs.

What we'll build

We've thrown together a couple of home page mock-ups. Though we have in mind what we want for large screens, we've begun with a handheld screen size to force ourselves to focus on the essentials.

You'll notice the following features:

- A collapsed responsive navbar with logo
- A sliding carousel with four images of featured portfolio items
- A single-column layout with three blocks of content, each with a heading, a short paragraph, and a nice big button with an invitation to read further
- A footer with social media links

Here is the design mock-up as shown in the following screenshot:

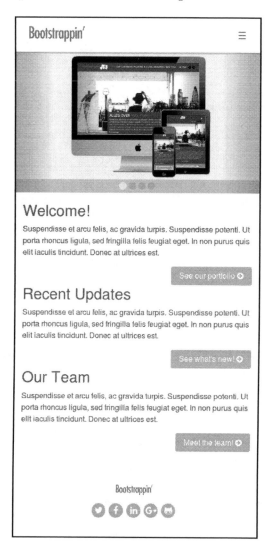

Altogether, this should provide a good introduction to our work. The carousel is tall enough to give a good amount of visual space to our portfolio images. It is not difficult to navigate quickly to the content below, where a user can efficiently scan key options for taking the next step inside. By presenting key links as nice big buttons, we will establish a helpful visual hierarchy for the key action items, and we will ensure that visitors do not have problems because of fat fingers.

For ease of maintenance, we've elected to have only two major breakpoints in this design. We'll use the single-column layout for screen sizes narrower than 768 px. Then, we'll shift to a three-column layout:

You'll note the following features in the mock-up for tablets and higher versions:

- A navigation bar at the top, which is enhanced with icons
- A widescreen version of the home page carousel, with images stretching to fill the full width of the browser
- A three-column layout for our textual content blocks
- A footer with content at the center

The color scheme is fairly simple: Shades of gray, plus a golden-green color for links and highlights.

With these design goals in mind, we'll can move on and get our content in place.

Surveying the exercise files

Let's look at the first few files for this exercise. Create a new project by using Bootstrap CLI, as already described in *Chapter 1, Getting Started with Bootstrap*.

You can install Bootstrap CLI by running the following command in your console:

```
npm install -g bootstrap-cli
```

Then you can set up your project by running the following command:

```
bootstrap new
```

Again, choose a new empty Bootstrap project. When prompted, select Panini, Sass, and Gulp option.

You'll see files similar to the template we set up in *Chapter 1, Getting Started with Bootstrap*:

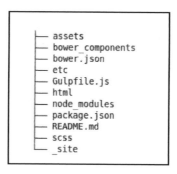

There are a few additions you will have to make now:

- Create a new assets/images folder.
- Copy the files of the img folder to the new assets/images folder. It contains five images:
  - One logo image, named logo.png
  - Four portfolio item images
- Add a new task to the `Gulpfile.js` file:

```
// Copy assets
gulp.task('copy', function() {
    gulp.src(['assets/**/*']).pipe(gulp.dest('_site'));
});
```

- And finally, add the preceding task to the default task at the end of the file:

```
gulp.task('build', ['clean','copy','compile-js','compile
sass','compile-html']);
```

The `html` folder that contains your Panini HTML templates should have the following file and folder structure:

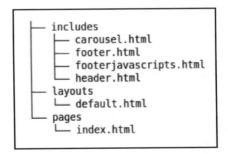

You can read more about Panini at `https://github.com/zurb/panini`.

Here are some of the details of the files shown in the preceding screenshot:

- The `html/pages/index.html` file contains the following HTML and template code:
  - The `{{> carousel}}` snippet which includes the carousel (`includes/carousel.html`)

- Content blocks, like that shown beneath:

```
<h2>Welcome!</h2>
<p>Suspendisse et a.....</p>
<p><a href="#">See our portfolio</a></p>
```

- The `includes/header.html` file, included in `layouts/default.html`, contains our navbar and has the following new touches:
    - Navbar items have been updated to reflect our new site architecture:

```
<header role="banner">
  <nav class="navbar navbar-light bg-faded" role="navigation">
  <a class="navbar-brand" href="index.html">Bootstrappin'</a>
   <button class="navbar-toggler hidden-md-up pull-xs-right"
  type="button" data-toggle="collapse"
data-target="#collapsiblecontent">
      ≡
  </button>
  <ul class="nav navbar-nav navbar-toggleable-sm collapse"
id="collapsiblecontent">
     <li class="nav-item">
       <a class="nav-link active" href="#">Home <span class="sr-
only">
    (current)</span></a>
     </li>
     <li class="nav-item">
       <a class="nav-link" href="#">Portfolio</a>
     </li>
      <li class="nav-item">
       <a class="nav-link" href="#">Team</a>
     </li>
     <li class="nav-item">
       <a class="nav-link" href="#">Contact</a>
     </li>
  </ul>
  </nav>
</header>
```

- The `includes/footer.html` file, included in `layouts/default.html`, contains the following items:
  - A logo in the footer
  - Social links:

```
<footer role="contentinfo">

  <p><a href="{{root}}index.html"><img
      src="{{root}}images/logo.png"
      width="80" alt="Bootstrappin'"></a></p>

  <ul class="social">
    <li><a href="#" >Twitter</a></li>
    <li><a href="#" >Facebook</a></li>
    <li><a href="#" >LinkedIn</a></li>
    <li><a href="#" >Google+</a></li>
    <li><a href="#" >GitHub</a></li>
  </ul>

</footer>
```

Other than the navbar, which we set up in *Chapter 1*, *Getting Started with Bootstrap*, no Bootstrap classes have been added to style the carousel, columns, or icons yet.

Further on, we'll discuss how to use Sass to customize your project. Now you can see that the `app.scss` file imports the `includes/_navbar.scss` file. The SCSS in the file removes the floats for the navigation links for smaller screens, as already discussed in *Chapter 1*, *Getting Started with Bootstrap*.

Instead of the preceding modifications, you can also start with the files found in the `chapter5/start` folder. In this folder, run the `npm install and bower install` commands first. After running `npm` and bower commands, you can run the `bootstrap` *watch* or `gulp` command to view the results in your browser.

You'll see the navbar, followed by the portfolio images:

The blocks of text and the footer, with a list of social links, follow after the images:

```
Welcome!

Suspendisse et arcu felis, ac gravida turpis. Suspendisse potenti. Ut porta rhoncus ligula, sed fringilla felis feugiat
eget. In non purus quis elit iaculis tincidunt. Donec at ultrices est.

See our portfolio

Recent Updates

Suspendisse et arcu felis, ac gravida turpis. Suspendisse potenti. Ut porta rhoncus ligula, sed fringilla felis feugiat
eget. In non purus quis elit iaculis tincidunt. Donec at ultrices est.

See what's new!

Our Team

Suspendisse et arcu felis, ac gravida turpis. Suspendisse potenti. Ut porta rhoncus ligula, sed fringilla felis feugiat
eget. In non purus quis elit iaculis tincidunt. Donec at ultrices est.

Meet the team!

Bootstrappin'

    • Twitter
    • Facebook
    • LinkedIn
    • Google+
    • GitHub
```

It's not much to speak of yet. Let the transformation begin.

We'll start by applying the Bootstrap classes, allowing us to quickly and efficiently establish the fundamentals for our interface elements using Bootstrap's default CSS styles and JavaScript behaviors.

Marking up the carousel

Let's get started with our carousel, which will rotate between four featured images from our portfolio.

Bootstrap's carousel markup structure can be found in its documentation pages at `http://g etbootstrap.com/components/carousel/`.

Following the pattern used in the example, we'll begin with this structure to set up the fundamental element. This will contain all parts of the carousel, followed by the progress indicators:

```
<div id="carousel-feature" class="carousel slide" data-ride="carousel">
  <ol class="carousel-indicators">
    <li data-target="#carousel-feature" data-slide-to="0"
class="active"></li>
    <li data-target="#carousel-feature" data-slide-to="1"></li>
    <li data-target="#carousel-feature" data-slide-to="2"></li>
  </ol>
</div>
```

Note that I've used a `div` tag with an ID (`id="carousel-feature"`) to establish the fundamental context of `carousel`. The `carousel` class applies the Bootstrap's carousel CSS to the carousel elements, adding appropriate styles to the carousel indicators, the carousel items, and the next and previous controls.

The `carousel-feature` ID must be used in the `data-target` attributes of the progress indicators. This signals the JavaScript plugin to update the indicator for the active carousel item with the `active` class. We've provided that class for the first indicator to get things started. From there, the JavaScript takes over. It removes the class, and adds it to the appropriate indicator as the carousel cycles.

Also, note that the `data-slide-to` values begin counting from 0. This is the standard behavior for JavaScript and other programming languages. Just remember: Start counting at zero, not one.

After the indicators, the element of the class `carousel-inner` follows. This serves as the wrapper to contain all of the carousel items—in this case, our images.

The carousel items come within `carousel-inner`. They are a group of `div` tags, each with `class="item"`. Modify the first item to have both the classes `item` and `active`, to make it visible from the outset.

Thus, the markup structure works as follows:

```
<!-- Wrapper for slides -->

<div class="carousel-inner" role="listbox">
    <div class="carousel-item active">
        <img src="{{root}}images/project1.png" alt="Streetart.com
Homepage">
    </div>
    <div class="carousel-item">
```

```
        <img src="{{root}}images/project2.png" alt="Your bussiness">
    </div>
    <div class="carousel-item">
        <img src="{{root}}images/project3.png" alt="Your blog">
    </div>
    <div class="carousel-item">
        <img src="{{root}}images/project4.png" alt="Menstrualcups.eu
Homepage">
    </div>
</div><!-- /.carousel-inner -->
```

After the carousel items, we need to add the carousel controls. These will provide the next and previous buttons at the left and right edges of the carousel. After the controls, we'll close up our entire markup structure with the closing `div` tag:

```
<!-- Controls -->
  <a class="left carousel-control" href="#carousel-feature" role="button"
data-slide="prev">
    <span class="icon-prev" aria-hidden="true"></span>
    <span class="sr-only">Previous</span>
  </a>
  <a class="right carousel-control" href="#carousel-feature" role="button"
data-slide="next">
    <span class="icon-next" aria-hidden="true"></span>
    <span class="sr-only">Next</span>
  </a>
</div><!-- /#homepage-feature.carousel -->
```

> The carousel controls need to have the ID of the fundamental carousel element (`#carousel-feature`) for their `href` value. The code, then, looks like this:
> ```
> <a class="left carousel-control" href="#carousel-feature"
> role="button" data-slide="prev">
> ```
> Now you can write down the complete code for the carousel in the file. Once this code is in place, run the `gulp` command if you didn't run the `bootstrap watch` already. Bootstrap's styles and JavaScript should start working. Your images should now work as a sliding carousel!

Notice that the carousel component requires both jQuery and the JavaScript plugin. The Gulp build process merges jQuery and all plugin code into a single `app.js` file.

By default, the carousel will slide every 5 seconds. Let's set the interval to 2 seconds to give our users time to appreciate the full beauty of our work:

1. Create a new file called `js/main.js`.

2. Add the following lines. We'll begin with the jQuery method of checking to ensure page elements are ready, and then initialize the carousel with an interval of 2,000 milliseconds:

```
$( document ).ready(function() {
  $('.carousel').carousel({
    interval: 2000
  });
});
```

3. Notice that you should automatically copy the `js/main.js` file from the assets folder and link it in the file, or add it to the `compile-js` task in your `Gulpfile.js` file:

```
gulp.task('compile-js', function() {
  return gulp.src([bowerpath+
  'jquery/dist/jquery.min.js', bowerpath+
  'tether/dist/js/tether.min.js', bowerpath+
  'bootstrap/dist/js/bootstrap.min.js','js/main.js'])
.pipe(concat('app.js'))
.pipe(gulp.dest('./_site/js/'));
});
```

 You should also consider adding the `js/main.js` file to the Gulp `watch` task. You can read more about Gulp and the Gulp tasks in `Chapter 2`, *Creating Your Own Build Process with Gulp*.

4. Save and restart your application. You will see that the interval has increased to 2 seconds.

Instead of passing the options via JavaScript as we did just now, you can also pass them via data attributes. The interval of the carousel can be set via the `data-interval` attribute:

```
<div id="carousel-feature" class="carousel slide" data-ride="carousel"
data-interval="2000">
```

For this and other options, see the Bootstrap carousel documentation at `http://getbootstr ap.com/javascript/#carousel`.

We'll return to customize the styling of the carousel, its indicators, and its icons later in the chapter. In the next section, you will learn how to use both JavaScript and CSS (SCSS) to modify the working of the carousel.

How does the carousel work?

The jQuery plugin changes the CSS classes of the items of the carousel. When the page loads, the first item already has the `active` class; when the interval has passed, the plugin moves the `active` class to the next item, and so on. The plugin not only changes the position of the `active` class, but also temporally adds the `next` and `left` classes. Together with the CSS3 animations on these classes, the sliding effect is created. You can read more about CSS3 animations at the following URL:

`https://developer.mozilla.org/en-US/docs/Web/CSS/CSS_Animations/Using_CSS_an imations`.

The `transition` is set on the `carousel-inner` class as follows:

```
transition: transform .6s ease-in-out;
```

In this declaration, the `ease-in-out` value sets the transition-timing-function of the animation (transition effect); for more information, see `https://developer.mozilla.org/en/docs/Web/CSS/transition-timing-function`. In essence, it lets you establish an acceleration curve, so that the speed of the transition can vary over its duration. Later on, we'll see that you can also use keyframes to describe the different states of the transition.

The transformations performed are **translate3ds**. The `translate3d()` CSS function moves the position of the element in the 3D space. More information can be found at `https://developer.mozilla.org/en-US/docs/Web/CSS/transform-function/translate3d`. The carousel moves the carousel items over the X-axis as follows:

```
&.next,
&.active.right {
  left: 0;
  transform: translate3d(100%, 0, 0);
}
```

Changing the carousel by adding new animations

When we replace the CSS animation as described in the previous section with another animation, the carousel's slider effect changes.

The `Animate.css` project by Daniel Ede contains a lot of CSS animations for you to use in your projects. You can use these animations for our carousel too. You can find the library at `http://daneden.github.io/animate.css/`.

We can create the new animation with SCSS code. Because our build process already runs the `autoprefixer`, you don't need to take the vendor prefixes into account. In our example, we'll use the `flipInX` animation of the `Animate.css` library, which rotates the images over the x axis.

Now add the following SCSS code at the end of the `scss/includes/_carousel.scss` file:

```
@keyframes flipInX {
  from {
    transform: perspective(400px) rotate3d(1, 0, 0, 90deg);
    animation-timing-function: ease-in;
    opacity: 0;
  }
  40% {
    transform: perspective(400px) rotate3d(1, 0, 0, -20deg);
    animation-timing-function: ease-in;
  }
  60% {
    transform: perspective(400px) rotate3d(1, 0, 0, 10deg);
    opacity: 1;
  }
  80% {
    transform: perspective(400px) rotate3d(1, 0, 0, -5deg);
  }
  to {
    transform: perspective(400px);
  }
}
.flipInX {
  backface-visibility: visible !important;
  animation-name: flipInX;
}
.carousel-inner {
  position: relative;
  width: 100%;
  overflow: hidden;

  > .carousel-item {
    position: relative;
    display: none;
    transition: none;
    backface-visibility: visible !important;
    animation-name: flipInX;
    animation-duration: 0.6s;

    // Account for jankitude on images
    > img,
```

```scss
    > a > img {
      @extend .img-fluid;
      line-height: 1;
    }
  }
  > .active,
  > .next,
  > .prev {
    display: block;
  }
  > .active {
    top: 0;
  }
  > .next,
  > .prev {
    position: absolute;
    left: 0;
    width: 100%;
  }
  > .next {
    top: 100%;
  }
  > .prev {
    top: -100%;
  }
  > .next.left,
  > .prev.right {
    top: 0;
  }
  > .active.left {
    top: -100%;
  }
  > .active.right {
    top: 100%;
  }
}
@keyframes flipInX {
  from {
    transform: perspective(400px) rotate3d(1, 0, 0, 90deg);
    animation-timing-function: ease-in;
    opacity: 0;
  }
  40% {
    transform: perspective(400px) rotate3d(1, 0, 0, -20deg);
    animation-timing-function: ease-in;
  }
  60% {
    transform: perspective(400px) rotate3d(1, 0, 0, 10deg);
```

```scss
      opacity: 1;
    }

    80% {
      transform: perspective(400px) rotate3d(1, 0, 0, -5deg);
    }
    to {
      transform: perspective(400px);
    }
}
.flipInX {
  backface-visibility: visible !important;
  animation-name: flipInX;
}
.carousel-inner {
  position: relative;
  width: 100%;
  overflow: hidden;

  > .carousel-item {
    position: relative;
    display: none;
    transition: none;
    backface-visibility: visible !important;
    animation-name: flipInX;
    animation-duration: 0.6s;
    // Account for jankitude on images
    > img,
    > a > img {
      @extend .img-fluid;
      line-height: 1;
    }
  }
  > .active,
  > .next,
  > .prev {
    display: block;
  }
  > .active {
    top: 0;
  }
  > .next,
  > .prev {
    position: absolute;
    left: 0;
    width: 100%;
  }
  > .next {
```

```
        top: 100%;
    }
    > .prev {
      top: -100%;
    }
    > .next.left,
    > .prev.right {
      top: 0;
    }
    > .active.left {
      top: -100%;
    }
    > .active.right {
      top: 100%;
    }
  }
}
```

If ran the `bootstrap watch` or `gulp` command already, you can inspect the results in the browser. You'll find that the images rotate over the *x*-axis now.

JavaScript events of the Carousel plugin

Bootstrap provides custom events for most plugins' unique actions. The Carousel plugin fires the `slide.bs.carousel` (at the beginning of the slide transition) and `slid.bs.carousel` (at the end of the slide transition) events. You can use these events to add custom JavaScript code. You can, for instance, change the background color of the body on the events by adding the following JavaScript into the `js/main.js` file:

```
$('.carousel').on('slide.bs.carousel', function () {
  $('body').css('background-
color','#'+(Math.random()*0xFFFFFF<<0).toString(16));
});
```

Note that the `gulp watch` task is not set for the `js/main.js` file, so you have to run the `gulp` or `bootstrap watch` command manually after you are done with the changes.

For more advanced changes to the plugin's behavior, you can overwrite its methods by using, for instance, the following JavaScript code:

```
!function($) {
var number = 0;
    var tmp = $.fn.carousel.Constructor.prototype.cycle;
    $.fn.carousel.Constructor.prototype.cycle = function (relatedTarget) {
        // custom JavaScript code here
        number = (number % 4) + 1;
        $('body').css('transform','rotate('+ number * 90 +'deg)');
```

```
            tmp.call(this); // call the original function
    };

}(jQuery);
```

This code sets the `transform` CSS property without vendor prefixes. The autoprefixer only prefixes your static CSS code. For full browser compatibility, you should add the vendor prefixes in the JavaScript code yourself.

> Bootstrap exclusively uses CSS3 for its animations, but Internet Explorer 9 doesn't support the necessary CSS properties.

Let's continue leveraging the power of Bootstrap's default styles and set up a responsive grid for the content below the carousel.

Creating responsive columns

We have three blocks of text, each with a heading, a short paragraph, and a link. In screen sizes of approximately tablet width or more, we would like this content to be laid out in three columns. In narrower screen widths, the content will organize itself in one full-width column.

Take a moment to visit and read the documentation for Bootstrap's mobile-first responsive grid. You can find it at `http://getbootstrap.com/css/#grid`.

In short, the grid is based on a 12-column system. The basic class structure allows us to use a class of `col-12` for full width, `col-6` for half width, `col-4` for one-third width, and so on.

Thanks to the creative use of media queries, Bootstrap's grid can be very adept at responding to different screen sizes. Recall that we want our welcome message to have a single-column layout up for screens to tablet-size, and then adapt a three-column layout at approximately 768 px for larger screens. Conveniently, Bootstrap has a built-in breakpoint at 768 px, which is the default value defined in the `$grid-breakpoints` Sass variable. Above 768 px is the large range, beginning at 992 px, also defined in the `$grid-breakpoints` Sass variable, then the extra-large screen, measured at 1,200 px and higher. I'll refer to these as Bootstrap's extra-small, small, medium, large, and extra-large breakpoints.

With the medium breakpoint, there is a special column class that uses the formulation `col-md-`. Because we want three columns after the small breakpoint, we'll use `class="col-md-4"`. Below the medium breakpoint, the elements will remain full-width. Above it, they will shift to one-third width and line up side by side. Notice that the navbar also collapses at 768 px. The full structure is given here, with paragraph contents abbreviated for clarity:

```
<div class="container">
  <div class="row">
    <div class="col-sm-4">
    <h2>Welcome!</h2>
    <p>Suspendisse et arcu felis ...</p>
    <p><a href="#">See our portfolio</a></p>
  </div>
  <div class="col-sm-4">
    <h2>Recent Updates</h2>
    <p>Suspendisse et arcu felis ...</p>
    <p><a href="#">See what's new!</a></p>
  </div>
  <div class="col-sm-4">
    <h2>Our Team</h2>
    <p>Suspendisse et arcu felis ...</p>
    <p><a href="#">Meet the team!</a></p>
  </div>
  </div><!-- /.row -->
</div><!-- /.container →
```

 You should edit the preceding code in the `html/pages/index.html` file.

If you're unfamiliar with the `container` and `row` classes, here is what they do:

- The `container` class constrains the width of the content and keeps it centered within the page
- The `row` class provides the wrapper for our columns, allowing extra left and right margins for the column gutters
- Both the `container` class and the `row` class are `clearfixed` so that they contain floating elements and clear any previous floating elements

Now, save the file and run the `bootstrap watch` or `gulp` command if you have not already done so. With your browser width above 768 px, you should see the following three-column layout take shape:

Welcome!

Suspendisse et arcu felis, ac gravida turpis. Suspendisse potenti. Ut porta rhoncus ligula, sed fringilla felis feugiat eget. In non purus quis elit iaculis tincidunt. Donec at ultrices est.

See our portfolio

Recent Updates

Suspendisse et arcu felis, ac gravida turpis. Suspendisse potenti. Ut porta rhoncus ligula, sed fringilla felis feugiat eget. In non purus quis elit iaculis tincidunt. Donec at ultrices est.

See what's new!

Our Team

Suspendisse et arcu felis, ac gravida turpis. Suspendisse potenti. Ut porta rhoncus ligula, sed fringilla felis feugiat eget. In non purus quis elit iaculis tincidunt. Donec at ultrices est.

Meet the team!

Resize your browser window below 768 px, and you'll see it revert to a single column:

Welcome!

Suspendisse et arcu felis, ac gravida turpis. Suspendisse potenti. Ut porta rhoncus ligula, sed fringilla felis feugiat eget. In non purus quis elit iaculis tincidunt. Donec at ultrices est.

See our portfolio

Recent Updates

Suspendisse et arcu felis, ac gravida turpis. Suspendisse potenti. Ut porta rhoncus ligula, sed fringilla felis feugiat eget. In non purus quis elit iaculis tincidunt. Donec at ultrices est.

See what's new!

Our Team

Suspendisse et arcu felis, ac gravida turpis. Suspendisse potenti. Ut porta rhoncus ligula, sed fringilla felis feugiat eget. In non purus quis elit iaculis tincidunt. Donec at ultrices est.

Meet the team!

With our responsive grid in place, let's turn those links into clearly visible calls to action by utilizing Bootstrap's button styles.

Turning links into buttons

Turning our key content links into visually effective buttons is straightforward. The key classes we'll employ are as follows:

- The `btn` class will style a link as a button.
- The `btn-primary` class will assign a button the color of our primary brand color.
- The `pull-xs-right` class will float the link to the right, moving it into wider space to make it a more appealing target. The `xs` part of the class name means that it should be applied on every viewport wider than the extra-small breakpoint of 0 pixels. The `pull-md-right` class only floats the elements on viewports wider than 768 px.

Add these classes to the link at the end of each of our three content blocks:

```
<p><a class="btn btn-primary pull-xs-right" href="#">See our
portfolio</a></p>
```

Save. You should see the following result:

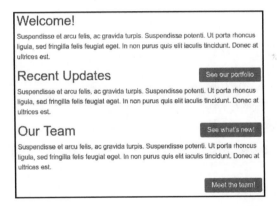

We've made great progress. Our key elements are taking shape.

With our fundamental markup structure in place, we can start working on the finer details. Getting there will require some custom CSS. We're going to approach this by leveraging the power of Bootstrap's Sass files. If you're new to Sass, no worries! I'll walk you through it step by step and you can also read *Chapter 3, Customizing Your Blog with Bootstrap and Sass* for the same.

Understanding the power of Sass

In the following sections, we will be organizing, editing, customizing, and creating SCSS files in order to generate the desired CSS for our designs.

 If you are unfamiliar with Sass and would like to learn more about it, I would recommend reading my *Sass and Compass Designer's Cookbook* book (`https://www.packtpub.com/web-development/sass-and-compass-des igners-cookbook`) or the documentation at `https://www.sass-lang.com /`.

In a nutshell, we may say that generating CSS using the Sass preprocessor is an exciting and freeing experience. The key benefits of working with Sass are discussed in the following sections.

Customizing Bootstrap's Sass according to our needs

As we work with Bootstrap's Sass files, we'll exert considerable control over them by doing the following:

- Organizing our `scss` folder to give us the flexibility and freedom to accomplish what we need while making future maintenance easier
- Customizing Bootstrap's Sass variables
- Creating a few custom Sass files of our own
- Incorporating a set of font-based icons in our site assets, providing the icons that we need for our social media links

In other words, we'll be doing more than merely learning and applying Bootstrap's conventions. We'll be bending them to our will.

In this chapter's exercise files, open the `scss` directory. Inside, you should see the following structure:

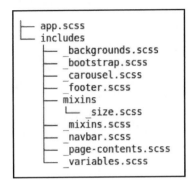

To prepare for what's ahead, I've given you a head start by explaining the new layer of organization. All of Bootstrap's Sass files are saved in the `bower_components/bootstrap/scss/` folder. You should not modify these files; you can (re)use them as described in the next sections. Keeping the original files untouched enables you to update Bootstrap without undoing your modifications.

First, the `app.scss` file imports two partial files:

```
@import "includes/variables";
@import "includes/bootstrap";
```

The file `includes/_bootstrap.scss` is a modified copy of the original `bootstrap.scss` file. This file imports all other original Bootstrap files, and it is used in the compiling process to create one unified style sheet from all of our imported Sass files. The `includes/_variables.scss` file is a modified copy of the original `_variables.scss` file. This file contains the declaration of all Bootstrap's Sass variables. Because the `includes/_variables.scss` file is imported before the original `_variables.scss` file, the variables in it can be used to overwrite Bootstrap's default settings.

Why go through this trouble? Because we'll soon be modifying Bootstrap's default settings and creating custom Sass files of our own. When we do that, we can leave the `Bootstrap` folder and its files as they are while making adjustments in the custom files that we will create.

Let's begin the customization! We'll start by customizing Bootstrap's variables and adding a few new variables of our own.

Customizing variables

Next, we'll create a copy of Bootstrap's variables file and customize it to our needs:

1. Find the `includes/_variables.scss` file in the `scss` folder and open it in your editor.
2. Scanning through the lines of this file, you'll see the variables used to set the CSS values for everything from basic colors to the body background, font-families, navbar height and background, and so on. It's beautiful to behold. It's even more fun to meddle with. Before we meddle, let's create our own copy of this file, allowing us to leave Bootstrap's default variables intact in case we ever want to revert back to them.

Next, let's implement our new color scheme:

1. In the topmost section of our new `includes/_variables.scss` file, you'll see the default Bootstrap variables for grays and brand colors:

   ```
   $gray-dark:              #373a3c;
   $gray:                   #55595c;
   $gray-light:             #818a91;
   $gray-lighter:           #eceeef;
   $gray-lightest:          #f7f7f9;
   ```

2. We have the specific values that we're after. So, let's simply substitute our desired values (feel free to do the math if you prefer!). Then, we'll add an additional two variables to encompass the full range that we need. The result is as follows:

   ```
   $gray-dark:              #454545;
   $gray:                   #777;
   $gray-light:             #aeaeae;
   $gray-lighter:           #ccc;
   $gray-lightest:          #ededed;
   ```

3. Next, we'll update the `$brand-primary` variable under `Brand colors`. We'll adjust this to our golden hue:

   ```
   // Brand colors
   // ------------------------
   $brand-primary:          #c1ba62;
   ```

4. When you run the bootstrap watch (or gulp) command already, your browser automatically reloads after saving the `includes/_variables.scss file`.

If this is successful, the most noticeable changes will be in the link color and buttons with the `btn-primary` class, which will both take the new `$brand-primary` color.

Customizing the navbar

Now, let's edit the variables that set the navbar height, colors, and hover effects.

Let's start by changing the height. The navbar has a padding of `$spacer / 2` by default, and the total height is set by the font size and the vertical padding.

In the local `includes/_variables.scss` file, search for the `$navbar-padding-vertical` variable and update it as follows. This will expand the navbar height:

```
$navbar-padding-vertical: $spacer;
```

Now we can set the background color of the navbar. The original HTML code in the `html/includes/headers.html` file had a `bg-faded` class. Because we want a white background color for our navbar, we can simply remove this class; the body already has a white background, and not setting the background property for the navbar will color the navbar white too.

You can also use Sass and Bootstrap's mixins to generate a new `bg-white` class. Create a new file `scss/includes/_backgrounds.scss` and edit the following SCSS into it:

```
@include bg-variant('.bg-white', #fff);
```

Note that the `bg-variant` mixin declares the `background-color` and `color` properties with `!important`. Because the `color` property is set to `#fff` (white) by default, using the `bg-variant` mixin does not seem to be the most flexible solution. Setting the `background-color` property for the navbar selector in the `scss/includes/_navbar.scss` file is a better solution. You can set the `background-color` property as follows:

```
.navbar {
 background-color: #fff;
}
```

The color of the navbar links is set by the `.navbar-light` or `.navbar-dark` classes. You should use the `.navbar-dark` class for navbars with a dark background and `.navbar-light` for light background. Our navbar in the `html/includes/header.html` file has got the `.navbar-light` class, so in order to change the link colors, you'll have to modify the `$navbar-light-*` variables in the `includes_variables.scss` file as follows:

```
$navbar-light-color:              $gray;
$navbar-light-hover-color:        $link-hover-color;
$navbar-light-active-color:       $link-hover-color;
$navbar-light-disabled-color:     $gray-lighter;
```

Note that we've already changed the `$gray` and `$gray-lighter` variables before, and the `$link-hover-color` variable has got the same value as the `$brand-primary` variable which we have set to the `#c1ba62;` color value.

If you like having a different background color for the hovered and active links, you can open the `scss/includes/_navbar.scss` file with your favorite text editor and perform the following steps:

1. First, remove the vertical padding with the following SCSS code:

```scss
.navbar {
  padding-top: 0;
  padding-bottom: 0;
}
```

2. Now apply the padding on the `.nav-link` selectors and set the background color for the hover and active states:

```scss
.navbar {
  .nav-link
  {
    padding: $spacer;
    &:hover,
    &.active {
      background-color: $gray-lightest;
    }
  }
}
```

3. Because the `.navbar-brand` has a larger font size, you will have to correct the padding for this selector:

```scss
.navbar {
  .navbar-brand {
    padding: ($spacer - ((($font-size-lg - $font-
```

```
size-base) * $line-height) / 2));
    }
}
```

If you did not run the `bootstrap watch` command already, run it now and you should see the following new features in your navbar:

- It should grow about 16px (2 x 1em) taller
- Its background color should turn white
- The nav item backgrounds change on hover and active states
- Link text should activate our brand-primary color on hover and when active, as shown in the following screenshot:

Now, let's put our logo image in place.

Adding the logo image

Find the `logo.png` file in the assets/images folder. You may notice that its dimensions are large, 900 px wide. In our final design, it will be only 120 px wide. Because the pixels will be compressed into a smaller space, this is a relatively easy way to ensure that the image will look good on all devices, including retina displays. Meanwhile, the file size of the image, which has already been optimized for the Web, is only 19 KB.

So, let's put it in place and constrain its width:

1. Open the `html/includes/header.html` file in your text editor.
2. Search for this line within the navbar markup:

   ```
   <a class="navbar-brand"
     href="index.html">Bootstrappin'</a>
   ```

3. Replace the HTML from the previous step with the following image tag, including its `alt` and `width` attributes:

   ```
   <a class="navbar-brand" href="index.html"><img src="
   {{root}}/images/logo.png" alt="Bootstrappin'"
     width="120"></a>
   ```

Be sure to include the width attribute, setting its width to 120 px. Otherwise, it will appear very large on the page.

If you didn't run the bootstrap watch command already, run it now. You should see the logo in place:

You may notice that the navbar height has expanded, and that its bottom edge no longer lines up with the bottom edge of the active nav item. This is due to the padding placed around the `bar-brand` class earlier. We need to adjust the appropriate padding values. We can do that in a few quick steps:

1. Use your text editor to open the `scss/includes/_navbar.scss` file again. Change the padding of the `bar-brand` class as follows:

   1. `padding: ($spacer - ((2.16rem - ($font-size-base * $line-height)) / 2));`

2. When resizing the width of the image to 120 px, its height becomes around 34.51 pixels, 34.51 / 16 = 2.16 rem.

The powers of Sass continue to impress. Of course, we should also take care of the collapsed responsive navigation, so resize your browser to a viewport smaller than 768 px.

The navigation should now look like that shown in the following screenshot:

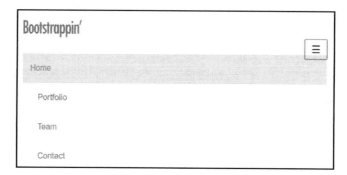

You will see that there is not enough padding around the logo and that the toggle button is not in line with the logo. We will use Sass again to correct these issues. Again, open the scss/includes/_navbar.scss file. Remember that we set the vertical padding of the navbar to 0 before. Now wrap this declaration into a CSS media query as follows to only apply it for the larger viewports:

```
@include media-breakpoint-up(md) {
    padding-top: 0;
    padding-bottom: 0;
}
```

As already explained, the media-breakpoint-up mixin is part of Bootstrap's Sass mixin and can be used to hide or show elements according to Bootstrap's media query ranges. The SCSS preceding code compiles into CSS as follows:

```
@media (min-width: 768px) {
  .navbar {
    padding-top: 0;
    padding-bottom: 0;
  }
}
```

To get the logo in line with the toggle button, you will have to change the display property of the logo image from block to inline-block. You can establish that by editing the following SCSS code in the scss/includes/_navbar.scss file:

```
.navbar {
  @include media-breakpoint-down(sm) {
    .navbar-brand,
    .nav-item {
      float: none;
      > img {
        display: inline-block;
      }
    }
  }
}
```

Finally, inspect the latest version of your `scss/includes/_navbar.scss` file. In your browser, the results should look like the following screenshot:

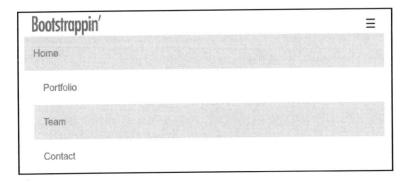

Now, let's add icon powers.

Adding icons

It's time to add icons to our navigation. **Glyphicons** that come with Bootstrap 3 are dropped in Bootstrap 4. Here, we'll use the large library of icons offered by **Font Awesome**. Other icon font sets can be found around the Web.

Font Awesome is a font icon set that offers 628 icons at the time of writing this book. Font Awesome icons are free, open source, and built to play nice with Bootstrap. You can see the Font Awesome home page at `http://fortawesome.github.io/Font-Awesome/`.

Let's fold Font Awesome into our workflow.

In *Chapter 2*, *Creating Your Own Build Process with Gulp*, you saw to use Font Awesome by loading it from CDN. Here, we compile the CSS code of Font Awesome into our main `app.css` file:

1. First, install Font Awesome in your project folder by running the following command in your console:

```
bower install font-awesome --save
```

2. After that, you can import Font Awesome's main SCSS file into your `scss/app.scss` file:

```
@import "includes/variables";
@import "font-awesome/scss/font-awesome.scss";
@import "includes/bootstrap";
@import "includes/navbar";
```

3. Last but not least, copy the font files to your assets folder:

```
cp bower_components/font-awesome/fonts/*
  assets/fonts/
```

4. The Font Awesome `scss` files include a variable specifying the path to the Font Awesome web fonts. We need to check to make sure that this variable matches our folder structure. Ensure that the `$fa-font-path` variable is set to `../fonts` as follows in our `scss/includes/_variables.scss` file:

```
$fa-font-path:      "../fonts";
```

This path is relative to the compiled CSS file, which is in our `css` directory

Now, in the `html/includes/header.html` file, let's update the icon for the Team navbar item to use the Font Awesome icon named `fa-group`. We also need the standalone `fa` class: `<i class="fa fa-group"></i>` Team

5. Save this change to the `html/includes/header.html` file, and refresh your browser.

If all works as it should, you should see the following result:

If you see a strange symbol or nothing, that's a sign that the web fonts are not coming through. Double-check that your icon classes are correct (including the `fa` class), your Font Awesome web font files are in your fonts directory, and the path is set correctly in the `scss/includes/_variables.scss` file.

Now update your icon markup in the `html/includes/header.html` file to make use of the desired Font Awesome icons.

The Font Awesome icon page `http://fortawesome.github.io/Font-Awesome/icons/` allows you to scan your options. Our mock-up calls for these icons in the navbar:

```
<i class="fa fa-home"></i> Home
<i class="fa fa-desktop"></i> Portfolio
<i class="fa fa-group"></i> Team
<i class="fa fa-envelope"></i> Contact
```

This has the following result:

This completes our nav, or almost completes it. We've inadvertently created a small problem that we need to fix before moving on.

It's time to move on to the carousel.

Styling the carousel

We're going to take Bootstrap's default carousel styles and apply some significant customization. Let's create a new `_scss/includes/carousel.scss` file and import it into our `scss/app.scss` file.

Now to begin customizing and making aesthetic enhancements.

Adding top and bottom padding

Let's add some top and bottom padding to the `.carousel` element itself and add our `@gray-lighter` color for a background color:

```
.carousel {
  padding-top: 4px; // added
  padding-bottom: 28px; // added
  background-color: @gray-lighter; // added
}
```

After saving and reloading (run the `bootstrap watch` or `gulp` command), you'll see the light gray background appears in our newly created space above and below the carousel images. This provides a bit of framing to set them off from the other elements above and below. In a bit, we'll take advantage of the extra bottom padding to position our carousel indicators in a way that allows them to stand out much more clearly.

Now to style the carousel indicators.

Repositioning the carousel indicators

The carousel indicators serve to inform the user how many slides are in our carousel, and highlight the current spot in the rotation. At present, these indicators are barely visible, languishing near the bottom center edge of our portfolio images:

Note that I have temporarily set the border color to white to make the preceding picture as follows:

```
.carousel-indicators li {
  border: 1px solid white;
}
```

Let's move these indicators into their own space, just below the image:

1. We want to move the indicators down even closer to the bottom edge, into our light gray area created by the padding we added previously. So, let's adjust the bottom positioning. In addition, we need to remove the default bottom margin by zeroing it out. Write down the following SCSS in the `_scss/includes/carousel.scss` file:

   ```
   .carousel-indicators {
    position: absolute;
     bottom: 0;
     margin-bottom: 0;
   }
   ```

2. Save the file; if you have run the `bootstrap watch` command already, your browser automatically reloads.

This brings our desired result. The indicators now stay positioned in the desired space across all screen dimensions:

Now let's update their appearance to make them larger and easier to see.

Styling the indicators

We'll make our carousel indicators more visible by using our gray variables. We'll also increase their size a bit. We can get a start in our `scss/includes/_variables.scss` file:

1. In `scss/includes/_variables.scss`, just after the `$carousel-control` variables, you'll find two variables beginning with `$carousel-indicator`:

   ```
   $carousel-indicator-active-bg:          #fff;
   $carousel-indicator-border-color:       #fff;
   ```

   These are used to provide a white border around the default indicators, and then fill the active indicator with the background color.

2. Let's add a default background color variable here, so that we may fill the default indicators with our `$gray-light` value:

   ```
   $carousel-indicator-bg:          $gray-light;
   ```

3. Then, we'll update the active background color:

   ```
   $carousel-indicator-active-bg:     $gray-lightest;
   ```

4. Finally, we'll make the border color transparent:

   ```
   @carousel-indicator-border-color: transparent;
   ```

5. Save, compile, and refresh.

At present, this has the effect of making all but the active item invisible:

Now for some work in the _scss/includes/_carousel.scss file:

1. In the _scss/includes/_carousel.scss file, move to the first set of rules for .carousel-indicator where we were previously working:

   ```
   .carousel-indicators {
     position: absolute;
   ```

2. Look for the li selector nested under it. Here, let's edit several values. Specifically, we'll perform the following actions:
   - Increase the width and height to 16px
   - Remove the margin
   - Add background color using our newly created variable $carousel-indicator-bg
   - Remove the border line altogether (the transparent value we set for the border variable is now merely a failsafe)
   - I've implemented these changes in the following code snippet:

   ```
   .carousel-indicators {
   position: absolute;
   bottom: 0;
   margin-bottom: 0;
   li {
   background-color: $carousel-indicator-bg;
   &,
   &.active {
   border: 0;
   height: 16px;
   width: 16px;
   margin: 0;
   }
   }
   }
   ```

3. In Bootstrap's default CSS, the active indicators are a little larger (12 px) than normal indicators (10 px); because of that, you have to set the new size (16 px) for both the normal and active indicators. You can accomplish that by using the Sass and parent reference as in the preceding code snippet. Consider the following snippet of SCSS code:

   ```
   .selector {
   &,
   &.active,
   &.otherstate {
   ```

```
    property: equal-for-all-states;
  }
}
```

4. This SCSS code compiles in CSS code like the one shown here:

```
.selector, .selector.active, .selector.otherstate {
  property: equal-for-all-states;
}
```

Save, and check out the result!

Carousel adjustments accomplished! We've learned a lot in the process—a lot about Bootstrap and perhaps a little about Sass as well.

Let's move on to the next section. What remains is considerably simpler.

Tweaking the columns and their content

Let's fine-tune the blocks of content under the three headings **Welcome!**, **Recent Updates**, and **Our Team**:

1. First, let's add the arrow-circle icon to the button in each of these three blocks. Recall that we're using Font Awesome for our icon selection.

2. Visit the Font Awesome documentation at
   `http://fortawesome.github.io/Font-Awesome/icons/`. You'll find the icon that
   we're after:

3. In the `html/pages/index.html` file, add an `i` tag with the appropriate classes
   inside each link. Here is the first one, which I've spaced out by adding an extra
   carriage return between elements:

```
<p>
  <a class="btn btn-primary pull-right" href="#">
    See our portfolio  <i class="fa fa-arrow-circle-
      right"></i>
  </a>
</p>
```

4. Repeat for each link.

You should now have the desired icon in each of the three buttons:

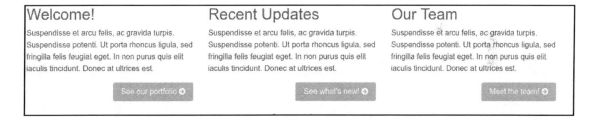

While we're at it, let's add a bit of vertical padding between the carousel and this section of
text. Right now, it's pretty tight.

The question that comes up at this point is where best to compose the styles that we'll need
for this; adding extra padding around page content sections will likely be a pretty normal
practice for us now and in the future. Let's create a Sass file to hold these and other tweaks
to the ordinary contents of pages (as it happens, we'll need this file for an additional and
more important responsive adjustment, so it seems well justified):

1. Create a file named `scss/includes/_page-contents.scss`.

2. Save it in your `scss` folder alongside your other custom Sass files:

```
<image of the directory scss>
```

3. Comment the file:

```
//
// Page Contents
// -------------------------
```

4. Now, let's create a sensible class for this purpose and add our desired padding, including some padding for the bottom:

```
.page-contents {
  padding-top: 20px;
  padding-bottom: 40px;
}
```

5. Save the file.

6. Add the `scss/includes/_page-contents.scss` file to the imports in the `scss/main.scss` file. I'll add mine in a new section near the bottom of the file and include a helpful comment for orientation purposes:

```
// Other custom files
@import "includes/page-contents";
```

7. Now let's add the necessary class to our markup. Open the `html/pages/index.html file` and add the class `page-contents` to the `div` with the class container, which follows just after the carousel including:

```
{{> carousel}}<!-- /#homepage-feature.carousel -->
<div class="page-contents container">
  <div class="row">
```

Save, and you should see the padding added.

Next, we need to tidy up the narrow-screen view of these blocks. Note that, when viewed in single-column layout, the headings do not clear the floated buttons:

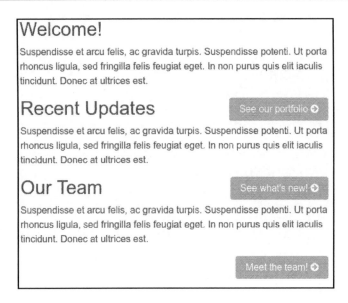

Fixing this is just a little tricky. We might want to add a clear fix to the `div` containing each of these three blocks. However, that won't work because we need these blocks to float side by side once the viewport width is 768 px or higher.

This calls for a media query. Knowing that our three-column view begins at the medium breakpoint, or 768 px, let's set a rule to clear floats when the window is 1 pixel below this breakpoint. As seen before, we can use Bootstrap's Sass media query mixin to do this.

While we're at it, let's also add some bottom padding to our columns so that they have a bit of extra vertical breathing room when stacked.

Inside the media query mixin, we'll add a CSS2 attribute selector to select all elements with a class that contains `col-`, so that the same rules will apply to a column of any size:

```
.page-contents {
  padding-top: 20px;
  padding-bottom: 40px;
  @include media-breakpoint-down(sm) {
    [class*="col-"] {
      clear: both;
      padding-bottom: 40px;
    }
  }
}
```

Save. The result is much improved!

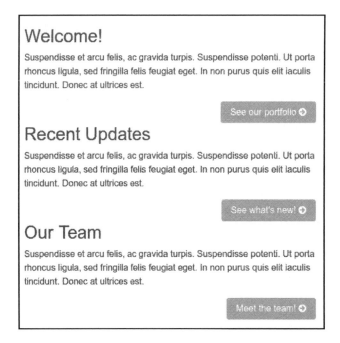

Much better! Now let's move on to the footer!

Styling the footer

The biggest feature of the footer is our social icons. Font Awesome to the rescue!

Consulting the Font Awesome documentation, we find a slew of available icons under the category of **Brand Icons**. Here is the direct link:

`http://fortawesome.github.io/Font-Awesome/icons/#brand`

Now we only need to replace the text for each social link in our footer, in the `html/includes/footer.html` file, with i elements, using the appropriate classes:

```
<ul class="social">
  <li><a href="#" ><i class="fa    fa-twitter"></i></a></li>
  <li><a href="#" ><i class="fa    fa-facebook"></i></a></li>
  <li><a href="#" ><i class="fa    fa-linkedin"></i></a></li>
  <li><a href="#" ><i class="fa fa-    google-plus"></i></a></li>
  <li><a href="#" ><i class="fa fa-    github-alt"></i></a></li>
</ul>
```

This updated markup puts our icons in place:

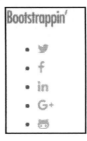

Now, perform the following steps to lay them out horizontally and align them to the center:

1. Create a new file, `scss/includes/_footer.scss`, to manage these styles.

2. Save the file to the `scss` directory.

3. Add an import variable for this file in `__main.less`:

```
// Other custom files
@import "includes/navbar";
@import "includes/carousel";
@import "includes/page-contents";
@import "includes/footer";
```

Now we'll write the styles we need. Let me simply lay them out, and then list what they do:

```
//
// Footer
// ------------------------

ul.social {
  margin: 0;
  padding: 0;
  width: 100%;
  text-align: center;
  > li {
    display: inline-block;
    > a {
      display: inline-block;
      font-size: 18px;
      line-height: 30px;
      @include square(30px); // see includes/mixins/_size.scss
      border-radius: 36px;
      background-color: $gray-light;
      color: #fff;
      margin: 0 3px 3px 0;
      &:hover,
```

```scss
        &:focus    {
            text-decoration: none;
            background-color: $link-hover-color;
          }
        }
      }
    }
```

Because Bootstrap tries to avoid both element and child selectors in Sass, you can consider rewriting the preceding SCSS code as follows:

```scss
.social {
  margin: 0;
  padding: 0;
  width: 100%;
  text-align: center;
}

.social-item {
 display: inline-block;
}

.social-link {
  display: inline-block;
  font-size: 18px;
  line-height: 30px;
  @include square(30px);
  // see includes/mixins/_size.scss
  border-radius: 36px;
  background-color: $gray-light;
  color: #fff;
  margin: 0 3px 3px 0;
  @include hover-focus {
    // bootstrap/scss/mixins/_hover.scss
    text-decoration: none;
    background-color: $link-hover-color;
    color: #fff;
  }
}
```

When you're using the latest SCSS code to compile your CSS code, you also have to modify your HTML code according to it. Modify the HTML of the footer links in the `html/includes/footer.html` file so that it looks like the snippet shown here:

```html
        <ul class="social">
            <li class="social-item"><a href="#" class="social-link" ><i
    class="fa fa-twitter"></i></a></li>
            <li class="social-item"><a href="#" class="social-link" ><i
```

```
class="fa fa-facebook"></i></a></li>
            <li class="social-item"><a href="#" class="social-link" ><i
class="fa fa-linkedin"></i></a></li>
            <li class="social-item"><a href="#" class="social-link" ><i
class="fa fa-google-plus"></i></a></li>
            <li class="social-item"><a href="#" class="social-link" ><i
class="fa fa-github-alt"></i></a></li>
        </ul>
```

Here's what's happening:

- The normal margin and padding is stripped away from the `ul`
- It is stretched to 100 percent width
- Its content is center aligned
- The list items are displayed inline to the block, thereby centering them
- The links are displayed inline to block, so that they fill up their available space
- The font size and line height are increased
- The width and height are set to 30px square, using a custom mixin (note that this mixin is copied from Bootstrap 3)
- To see this mixin, open `includes/mixins/_size.scss`, and you'll find the following relevant lines:

```
// Sizing shortcuts

@mixin size($width, $height) {
  width: $width;
  height: $height;
}

@mixin square($size) {
  @include size($size, $size);
}
```

- The `border-radius` property is set large enough to make the icons and their backgrounds appear circular
- The `background-color`, `color`, and `margin` properties are set
- The underline is removed from the hover and focus states, and the background color is altered to a lighter gray

With these steps done, let's polish off the footer by adding a healthy bit of top and bottom padding, and then center aligning the content in order to move our logo to the center, above the social icons:

```
footer[role="contentinfo"] {
  padding-top: 24px;
  padding-bottom: 36px;
  text-align: center;
}
```

The result is as follows:

Recommended next steps

Let me strongly recommend at least one additional step you'll need to take before taking a project like this to production. It's imperative that you take time to optimize your images, CSS, and JavaScript. These steps are not difficult:

- Compressing images takes just a bit of time, and it addresses the single largest cause for large page footprints. I've already used the *save to web* process option of Photoshop, but chances are you can squeeze a few more bytes out. In *Chapter 2, Creating Your Own Build Process with Gulp*, you can see how to add an image compress task to your gulp build process.
- In addition, we badly need to remove unneeded Bootstrap Sass files from the import sequence in the `scss/includes/_bootstrap.scss file`, and then compress the resulting `main.css` file.

- Finally, we need to slim down our `plugins.js` file by replacing Bootstrap's all-inclusive `bootstrap.min.js` file with compressed versions of only the three plugins that we're actually using: `carousel.js`, `collapse.js`, and `transitions.js`. We then compress the final `plugins.js` file.

Combined, these steps can cut the footprint of this website by roughly half. In an age where speed matters—both for user retention and for SEO ranking—that's a big deal. Also, read `Chapter 2`, *Creating Your Own Build Process with Gulp,* to learn how to get your code ready for production.

In addition, there is one other very sensible step you may want to take: We know that users of touch-enabled devices appreciate the ability to swipe their way forward and back through a carousel.

But, for the present moment, let's stop and celebrate.

Summary

Let's take stock of what we've accomplished in this chapter. We started a new Bootstrap project, powered by Panini, Sass, and Gulp, by using Bootstrap CLI. After that, we leveraged Bootstrap's responsive navbar, carousel, and grid system, and customized several of Bootstrap's Sass codes and mixins. You also learned how to create your own Sass files and folded them seamlessly into the project. Last but not least, you folded the Font Awesome icons into our workflow. At the end, you improved future maintenance of the site by implementing a thoughtful file organization scheme—all without creating code bloat.

With this experience under your belt, you're equipped to bend Bootstrap to your will, using its power to speed website development, and then customizing the design to your heart's content. In future chapters, we'll expand your experience further. First, however, let's take this design to create a complex business home page.

6
Bootstrappin' Business

We've built our portfolio site. Now, it's time to flesh out our portfolio with some projects that demonstrate the range of our powers. Let's now turn to designing a complex business home page.

Take a moment to survey the home pages of successful businesses, such as these:

- Zappos (http://www.zappos.com)
- Amazon (http://www.amazon.com)
- Adobe (http://www.adobe.com/)
- HP (http://www.hp.com)

While each has its own approach, what these sites have in common is that they manage considerable complexity.

We can get a grasp of some common features by breaking the website down into three categories, as follows, based on regions of the page:

- **Banner/masthead**: This part contains the logo, main navigation with drop-down menus, a secondary or utility navigation, and a login or register option
- **Main content area**: This features a complex layout with at least three columns, if not more
- **Footer**: This is filled with multiple columns of links and information

Let's demonstrate our ability to manage this degree of complexity. To do so, we will take full advantage of Bootstrap's responsive 12-column grid system.

Here is the design we'll create, when viewed in medium and wide viewports:

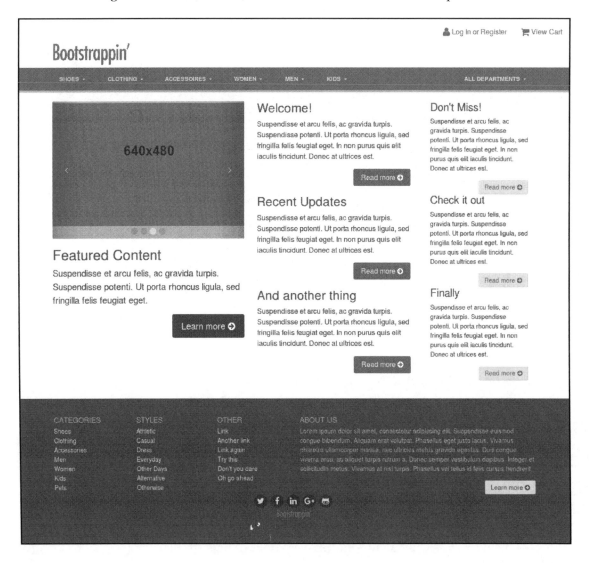

In narrow viewports, it will adapt considerably, as shown in the following screenshot:

After that, we will perform the following steps:

1. Begin with a set of starter files based on the Portfolio project from `Chapter 5`, *Bootstrappin' Your Portfolio*.
2. Create a complex banner with the logo above the navbar and a utility navigation in the top-right corner, in desktop viewports.
3. For smaller viewports, we'll enable our utility options to appear only as icons atop the collapsed responsive navbar.
4. Implement a business-style color scheme.
5. Make adjustments to both the responsive and desktop versions of the navbar.
6. Set up complex multicolumn grids for the main content and footer areas.

First things first: let's size up our project starter files.

Sizing up our beginning files

As with all the projects in this book, the beginning files for this project can be downloaded from the Packt Publishing website at `http://www.packtpub.com/support`. You'll find the files for this project in the `chapter6/start` folder.

These files are a copy of our results from Chapter 5, *Bootstrappin' Your Portfolio*. Thus, we have the benefit of the following key components:

- A complete build process, including the Sass compiler and the Panini template engine
- Bootstrap SCSS and JavaScript files
- The Panini HTML templates

In addition to these key assets, we have some of the custom Sass touches we created during the project in Chapter 5, *Bootstrappin' Your Portfolio*. They can be found in the following files, which are present in the `scss` and `scss/includes` directories:

- `_main.scss`: This is customized to import Bootstrap's Sass files from the `bower_components/bootstrap/scss` directory, as well as Font Awesome font icons and our custom Sass files
- `_carousel.scss`: This file has custom touches on the carousel padding, background, and indicators
- `_footer.scss`: This file contains styles for the layout and design of the logo and social icons
- `_navbar.scss`: This has adjusted padding in the `.navbar-brand` class to enable the navbar logo to fit
- `_page-contents.scss`: This contains styles to ensure that columns with floated buttons clear one another in narrow single-column layouts
- `_variables.scss`: This has custom versions of gray and some adjustments to variables for the navbar and carousel

Font Awesome font icons include the following:

- Icon fonts in the `fonts` directory
- Sass files in the `bower_components/font-awesome` directory

- In order to start using these files, you should run the following commands in your console:

```
bower installing
npm install
```

After that, you can run the `npm start` or `bootstrap watch` command to compile your project and start watching your changes in the browser.

Setting up the basics of your design

We start modifying the result of `Chapter 5`, *Bootstrappin' Your Portfolio*, and should end up with the basics, similar to that shown in the following screenshot:

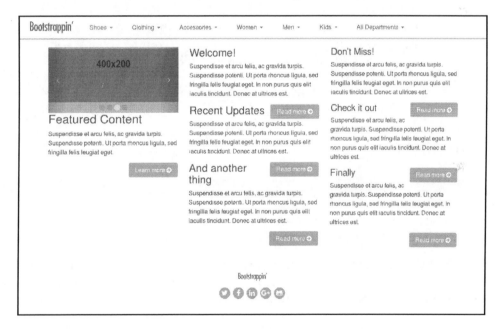

Note the following features:

- A complex navbar that has seven main `nav` items, each with a drop-down menu
- The first of the three columns is equipped with a carousel, followed by a heading, paragraph, and button

- The second and third columns, which have headings, paragraphs, and **Read more ->** buttons
- A footer that has the logo and social icons

You'll recognize elements we've already worked with in Chapter 5, *Bootstrappin' Your Portfolio*. The carousel is now smaller—constrained by its containing column. Otherwise, the markup is the same.

Adding drop-down menus to our navbar

Bootstrap's JavaScript Dropdown Plugin enables you to create drop-down menus with ease. You can also add these drop-down menus to your navbar.

Open the `html/includes/header.html` file in your text editor. Notice that the Gulp build process uses the Panini HTML compiler to compile our HTML templates into HTML pages. Panini is powered by the Handlebars template language. In your templates, you can use helpers, iterations, and custom data. In this example, you'll use the power of Panini to build the navbar items with drop-down menus.

First, create an `html/data/productgroups.yml` file that contains the titles of the navbar items:

```
- Shoes
- Clothing
- Accessories
- Women
- Men
- Kids
- All Departments
```

The preceding code is written in the YAML format. YAML is a human-readable data serialization language that takes concepts from programming languages and ideas from XML; you can read more about it at the following URL: http://yaml.org/.

Using the preceding data, you can use the following HTML and template code to build the navbar items:

```
<ul class="nav navbar-nav navbar-toggleable-sm collapse"
id="collapsiblecontent">
{{#each productgroups}}
  <li class="nav-item dropdown {{#ifCond this
'Shoes'}}active{{/ifCond}}">
    <a class="nav-link dropdown-toggle" data-toggle="dropdown" href="#"
    role="button" aria-haspopup="true" aria-expanded="false">
```

```
      {{ this }}
    </a>
      <div class="dropdown-menu">
        <a class="dropdown-item" href="#">Action</a>
        <a class="dropdown-item" href="#">Another action</a>
        <a class="dropdown-item" href="#">Something else here</a>
        <div class="dropdown-divider"></div>
        <a class="dropdown-item" href="#">Separated link</a>
      </div>
  </li>
{{/each}}
</ul>
```

The preceding code uses a (for) each loop to build the seven navbar items, and each item gets the same drop-down menu. The Shoes menu gets the active class. Handlebars, and therefore Panini, does not support conditional comparisons by default. The if statement can only handle a single value, but you can add a custom helper to enable conditional comparisons. The custom helper, which enables us to use the ifCond statement, can be found in the html/helpers/ifCond.js file. Read my *How to set up Panini for different environments* blog post, at http://bassjobsen.weblogs.fm/set-panini-different-environments/, to learn more about Panini and custom helpers.

The HTML code for the drop-down menu is in accordance with the code for drop-down menus described for the Dropdown plugin at http://getbootstrap.com/components/dropdowns/.

The navbar collapses for smaller screen sizes. By default, the drop-down menus look the same on all grids:

Setting the bottom border for the page header

Create a new Sass partial file and add the following SCSS code to it to give our page header a clear boundary:

```
header[role="banner"] {
  border-bottom: 4px solid $gray-lighter;
}
```

Adding images with holder.js

One other wrinkle is that I've used the excellent `holder.js` JavaScript plugin to dynamically generate placeholder images for our carousel.

You can install the holder.js plugin with Bower by running the following command in your console:

```
bower install holderjs --save-dev
```

After installing the plugin, you can use the `compile-js` Gulp task in `Gulpfile.js` to link it together with your other JavaScript code into the `app.js` file as follows:

```
gulp.task('compile-js', function() {
  return gulp.src([
        bowerpath+ 'jquery/dist/jquery.min.js',
        bowerpath+ 'tether/dist/js/tether.min.js',
        bowerpath+ 'bootstrap/dist/js/bootstrap.min.js',
        bowerpath+ 'holderjs/holder.min.js', // Holder.js for project
        development only
        'js/main.js'])
    .pipe(concat('app.js'))
    .pipe(gulp.dest('./_site/js/'));
});
```

If you examine the markup, you'll see near the bottom of the page that I've included the `holder.js` script right before `plugins.js`, as follows:

```
<!-- Holder.js for project development only -->
<script src="js/vendor/holder.js"></script>
```

We won't be using placeholder images in our final production site, so it makes sense to link it separately with a prominent comment.

With `holder.js` in place, we can conveniently build image tags that reference `holder.js` as their source. The remainder of the pseudo-URL specifies dimensions, color, and filler text, as follows:

```
<img src="holder.js/600x480/auto/vine/textmode:literal"    alt="Holder
Image">
```

For more information about `holder.js`, consult the documentation at `htt ps://github.com/imsky/holder`.

With these elements in place—and thanks in particular to Bootstrap's ready repertoire of styles and behaviors—we're starting out in good shape. Let's get to the details.

First, we'll reposition our navbar within a more complex banner design.

Creating a complex banner area

Let's start from the top and create our complex banner area with the following features:

- A site logo positioned above the navbar for desktops and larger viewports
- A navbar with many menu items, including drop-down menus
- A utility navigation area
- A login form with username and password
- An option to register

Here is the mockup of our desired end goal on a desktop-width viewport:

On a narrow viewport, it will adjust to this:

We'll start by working on a new arrangement for our top logo.

Placing a logo above the navbar

In this new design, we need a logo in two spots, for two contexts:

- For desktop and widescreen viewports, we want the logo to display above the navbar
- For tablet and phone viewports, we want the logo to display within the responsive navbar

Thanks to Bootstrap's responsive utility classes, we can do both! Here's how:

1. Open the `html/includes/header.html` file in your editor.
2. Move the logo and toggle button outside the `nav` element and wrap them with `<div class="container">...</div>` to constrain it within Bootstrap's centered grid space.
3. Remove the width attribute from the img element of the logo.
4. Then wrap the `<ul class="nav navbar-nav"></ul>` with `<div class="container">...</div>` too.
5. Move `navbar-toggleable-sm` and collapse the classes to the second container's div.
6. At the end, your HTML code in the `html/includes/header.html` file should look as follows:

```
<header role="banner">
<div class="container">
<button class="navbar-toggler hidden-md-up" type="button"
data-toggle="collapse" data-target="#collapsiblecontent">
≡
</button>
<a class="navbar-brand" href="/"><img
src="{{root}}/images/logo.png"
alt="Bootstrappin'"></a>
</div>
<nav class="navbar navbar-full" role="navigation">
<div class=  "container navbar-toggleable-sm collapse"
id="collapsiblecontent">
<ul class="nav navbar-nav">
...
</ul>
</div>
```

```
</nav>
</header>
```

7. After your HTML changes, you can use the power of Sass again to style the logo depending on the width of the viewport. Edit the following SCSS code in the scss/includes/_header.scss file:

```
header[role="banner"] {
  .navbar-brand {
  > img {
      width: 120px;
      padding-left: $spacer-x;
      @include media-breakpoint-up(md) {
        padding-left: 0;
        width: 180px;
      }
    }
  }
}
```

In the preceding steps, a couple of predefined Bootstrap classes are used. The hidden-md-up helper class hides content for the medium viewport and up and so ensures that the toggle button is only visible on the small viewports. On the other hand, the `navbar-toggleable-sm` class only affects small and extra-small viewports.

On narrow viewports, the logo gets a width of 120 pixels. For medium grids and larger, the left padding of the logo is removed and the width is set to 180 pixels.

Recall that our original logo image is large, about 900 pixels wide. We've resized it to 120 pixels wide via the width attribute (we could alternatively use CSS rules) in order to pack its pixels tighter for retina screens.

Save the changes and refresh the page, and you should see these results! In medium and large viewports, the larger logo will appear:

Bootstrappin'

Shoes ▾   Clothing ▾   Accessories ▾   Women ▾   Men ▾   Kids ▾   All Departments ▾

In small and extra-small viewports, a `small version of the logo` will appear:

Ah, the beauty of Bootstrap!

Now, let's make some adjustments to our navbar.

Reviewing and checking navbar drop-down items

The navbar, with its seven items and submenus, reflects the needs of a large complex website.

The markup for the drop-down menus is taken directly from the Bootstrap drop-down documentation at `http://getbootstrap.com/components/dropdowns/`.

If you look at our resulting markup, you'll notice these special classes and attributes:

- `class="dropdown"` on the parent `li`
- `class="dropdown-toggle"` on the link
- `attribute="data-toggle"` also on the link
- `class="dropdown-menu"` on the submenu div element
- `class="dropdown-item"` on each drop-down menu item

Here is the resulting markup:

```
<li class="nav-item dropdown">
  <a class="nav-link dropdown-toggle" data-toggle="dropdown" href="#"
  role="button" aria-haspopup="true" aria-expanded="false">
    Shoes
  </a>
  <div class="dropdown-menu">
    <a class="dropdown-item" href="#">Action</a>
    <a class="dropdown-item" href="#">Another action</a>
    <a class="dropdown-item" href="#">Something else here</a>
    <div class="dropdown-divider"></div>
    <a class="dropdown-item" href="#">Separated link</a>
  </div>
</li>
```

Also note that the small drop-down indicator is a CSS triangle, as already described in Chapter 3, *Customizing Your Blog with Bootstrap and Sass*. Bootstrap uses the following SCSS code in the `bower_components/bootstrap/scss/_` to create these triangles:

```scss
.dropdown-toggle {
  // Generate the caret automatically
  &::after {
    display: inline-block;
    width: 0;
    height: 0;
    margin-right: .25rem;
    margin-left: .25rem;
    vertical-align: middle;
    content: "";
    border-top: $caret-width solid;
    border-right: $caret-width solid transparent;
    border-left: $caret-width solid transparent;
  }

  // Prevent the focus on the dropdown toggle when closing dropdowns
  &:focus {
    outline: 0;
  }
}
```

When working with plugins and components, make sure that the required SCSS and JavaScript code is included in your project. Sass partials are imported into `main.scss` file. The import `scss/includes/_bootstrap.scss` in its turn imports the SCSS code for Bootstrap's components. The JavaScript plugins are included in the file in the Gulp task.

With the Sass, JavaScript, and HTML markup in place, our navbar and its dropdowns should presently look and work as shown in the following screenshot (*note that Bootstrap dropdowns responds on click*):

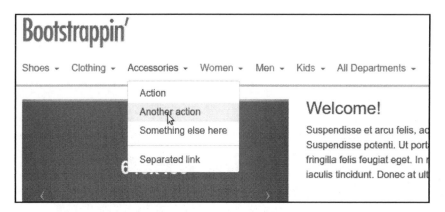

Now that we're familiar with the HTML markup structure and have ensured everything's working as it should, let's move the **All Departments** menu to the right-hand end of the navbar, setting it apart from the others.

To do this, we need to nest this list item within its own unordered list, as follows:

1. Before the **All Departments** list item, close the ul tag for ul class="nav", which surrounds all previous menu items.
2. Start a new ul tag with the nav and navbar-nav classes before the **All Departments** menu item. Once this opening tag is added, it will nest this list item in the standard structure for navigation menus.
3. In addition to the nav and navbar-nav classes, add a third class, pull-right, which is a convenient Bootstrap utility class, to float an element to the right.

The newly added lines are highlighted in the following snippet—after which I'll include the original list item and link in context:

```
<ul class="nav navbar-nav">
{{#each productgroups}}
  {{#ifCond this 'All Departments'}}</ul><ul class="nav navbar-nav
  pull-md-right">{{/ifCond}}
  <li class="nav-item dropdown {{#ifCond this
'Shoes'}}active{{/ifCond}}">
    <a class="nav-link dropdown-toggle" data-toggle="dropdown" href="#"
    role="button" aria-haspopup="true" aria-expanded="false">
    {{ this }}
    </a>
```

```
        <div class="dropdown-menu">
          <a class="dropdown-item" href="#">Action</a>
          <a class="dropdown-item" href="#">Another action</a>
          <a class="dropdown-item" href="#">Something else here</a>
          <div class="dropdown-divider"></div>
          <a class="dropdown-item" href="#">Separated link</a>
        </div>
    </li>
  {{/each}}
  </ul>
```

Notice that we've used the `IfCond` helper again to make sure that the `</ul><ul class="nav navbar-nav pull-md-right">` snippet is only inserted before the beginning of the All Departments category.

Save the changes and inspect the results in your browser. If you have not run the `bootstrap watch` or `gulp` command already, you should run it now. You should see the **All Departments** drop-down menu item float to the right-hand end of the navbar, as follows:

Instead of modifying your HTML code, you can also use the following SCSS code to accomplish the same thing:

```
.nav-item:last-child {
  float:right;
}
```

So far so good! Now, let's add our utility navigation.

Adding utility navigation

This project requires utility navigation to allow users to log in or register and to view their carts.

On medium, large, and extra-large viewports, we'll place this utility navigation in the very top-right corner of our banner area, as follows:

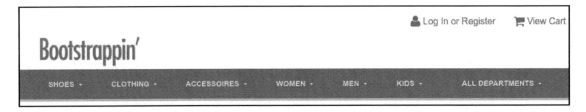

On smaller screens, we'll display icons at the far right of the collapsed navbar:

Notice that the collapsed navbar has a different color scheme; we'll discuss how to do this later on.

Now let's set the navbar changes up.

First, to give the logo a little more space in the the `scss/includes/_header.scss` file, set top-padding for only the larger viewports, as follows:

```
header[role="banner"] {
  .navbar-brand {
    > img {
      width: 120px;
      padding-left: $spacer-x;
      @include media-breakpoint-up(md) {
        padding-top: $spacer-y * 3;
        padding-left: 0;
        width: 180px;
      }
    }
  }
}
```

Then, still working in the `html/includes/header.html file,` we need to add the markup for our utility navigation within the banner, just after the `navbar-brand` attribute. Here is the full markup, beginning with the opening `header` tag for our banner area. I've highlighted the new `utility-nav` markup in the following code snippet:

```
<header role="banner">
  <div class="container">
    <button class="navbar-toggler hidden-md-up" type="button"
    data-toggle="collapse" data-target="#collapsiblecontent">
      ≡
    </button>
    <a class="navbar-brand" href="/"><img src="{{root}}/images/logo.png"
    alt="Bootstrappin'"></a>
    <div class="utility-nav">
      <ul>
        <li><a href="#" ><i class="icon fa
        fa-user fa-lg"></i> Log In or Register</a></li>
        <li><a href="#" ><i class="icon fa fa-shopping-cart
        fa-lg"></i> View Cart</a></li>
      </ul>
    </div>
  </div>
...
</header>
```

Note a few things about this markup:

- The `utility-nav` class is simply created for our use. It is not a Bootstrap-specific class and has no specific styles attached.
- I've included Font Awesome's user and shopping cart icons and added the class of `fa-lg` to increase their size by 33 percent. See Font Awesome's documentation on this at `http://fontawesome.io/examples/#larger`.

Save the changes and inspect the results in your browser, and you should see our new `utility-nav` class appear on the right-hand side of the logo, as follows:

Now, to complete the layout and related adjustments, we need to apply some custom styles. We need a new file to manage styles for our banner area.

We need to set the position of .utility-nav to absolute, at the top right. We'll specify header[role="banner"] as the context for these styles. Add the following SCSS code to the scss/includes/_header.scss file:

```scss
header[role="banner"] {
  // Banner Area Styles
  .utility-nav {
    position: absolute;
    top: $spacer-y;
    right: 0;
  }
}
```

Now, let's refine the details as follows:

1. Remove bullets from the unordered list.
2. Float the list items on the left.
3. Add padding to the link.
4. Remove underlines from the hover effect.

The following lines will accomplish these goals:

```scss
.utility-nav {
  ul {
    list-style: none;
    li {
      float: left;
      a {
        padding: 0 $spacer-x;
        @include hover {
          text-decoration: none;
        }
      }
    }
  }
}
```

Save the changes and ensure that it compiles. In the preceding code, we've set the padding for the anchors to padding: 0 $spacer-x;. We could accomplish this by adding Bootstrap's utility classes for spacing into the HTML code.

The following HTML code also sets a padding of `$spacer-x` on the left- and right-hand sides of the `<a>` element:

```
<a href="#" class="p-1-x">
```

Then make sure your browser window is at desktop width. You should see your `utility-nav` class take its place at the top right of the banner:

That takes care of medium viewports and larger. Now, let's address the needs of the collapsed responsive navbar.

Making responsive adjustments

On small screens, the elements of our page header may overlap:

We need to move the toggle to the left-hand side of our navbar. This can be done as follows:

1. Open the `scss/includes/_header.scss` file in your editor and add the following SCSS code to it:

```scss
header[role="banner"] {
  .navbar-toggler {
  float: left;
  }
}
```

2. Save and compile these changes, and you'll see the navbar toggle shift to the left end of the collapsed navbar, as shown in the following screenshot:

So far so good.

Now to address the problem of crowding by hiding the text for all devices except for screen readers on the collapsed navbar. In an uncluttered collapsed navbar, the icons will be enough to communicate the point, especially if we make the icons larger. Let's do that:

1. In the `html/includes/_header.html` file, place `span` tags around the text within each link of our `utility-nav` class, as follows:

   ```
   <li><a href="#" ><i class="icon fa
   fa-user fa-lg"></i> <span>Log In or    Register</span></a></li>
   <li><a href="#" ><i class="icon fa
   fa-shopping-cart fa-lg"></i> <span>    View Cart</span></a></li>
   ```

2. This will give us a handle for our upcoming style adjustment.
3. Now, in `_headers.scss`, we'll add a media query to target these `span` tags. Thanks to the power of Sass, we can nest the media query precisely where we want it to do its work. We'll use Bootstrap's `@media-breakpoint-down(sm)` mixin, setting a `max-width` query to the small breakpoint value minus one, since at this point our navbar makes the transition from collapsed to expanded. Within this media query, we'll use the `sr-only` utility class as a mixin to hide text from all devices except screen readers. (See the documentation on this class at `http://getbootstrap.com/components/utilities/#screen-readers-and-keyboard-users`.)
4. Instead of the sr-only mixin, you can also add the `sr-only` class to your HTML. The `sr-only-focusable` mixin and `sr-only-focusable` CSS class are available to make content hidden by the the `sr-only` class visible on focus, which is useful for keyboard-only users.
5. Here is the code snippet:

   ```
   header[role="banner"] {
     @include media-breakpoint-down(sm) {
       top: 0;
       span {
         @include sr-only;
       }
     }
   }
   ```

6. This will hide the text between our `span` tags, leaving us only with the icons!
7. Now, we will increase the size of the icons and add some line height to position them vertically. We'll do this within the same media query:

   ```
   header[role="banner"] {
     @include media-breakpoint-down(sm) {
   ```

```
      top: 0;
      span {
        @include sr-only;
      }
      .icon {
        font-size: 2em;
        line-height: 1.2;
      }
    }
  }
}
```

Save your changes, run the `bootstrap watch` command if you haven't already done so, and you should see the following result:

Take a minute to resize your browser window back and forth across the breakpoint. You should see the entire banner and navbar adjust seamlessly across the breakpoint.

If you're like me, it's hard not to be pleased with a framework that enables us to be this efficient at building such an adept and responsive interface.

Next up, we need to begin implementing the color scheme.

Implementing the color scheme

We've been provided with a business-friendly palette of blue, red, and gray. Let's work these colors into our color variables:

1. Open `scss/includes_variables.scss` in your editor. We'll be working at the beginning of the file, in the color variables.

2. Let's review the range of grays we have available. If you've begun with the chapter5/finish files, you'll see we've carried these variables over from Chapter 5, *Bootstrappin' Your Portfolio*. They served us well there, and we'll make use of them again here:

```
x`
// -----------------------

@gray-darker:           #222; // edited
@gray-dark:             #454545; // edited
@gray:                  #777; // edited
```

```
@gray-light:            #aeaeae; // edited
@gray-lighter:          #ccc; // edited
@gray-lightest:         #ededed; // edited
@off-white:             #fafafa; // edited
```

3. Now, below the grays, let's fold in our new brand colors. We'll modify the value for @brand-primary and create a @brand-feature variable for red:

```
@brand-primary:         #3e7dbd; // edited blue
@brand-feature:         #c60004; // added new red
```

4. Now, let's adjust our link-hover color so that it will lighten (rather than darken) the @brand-primary color, which is already dark:

```
// Links
// ------------------------
@link-color:            @brand-primary;
@link-color-hover:      lighten(@link-color, 15%);
```

5. Finally, let's define the colors for our navbar. We'll create two sets of variables the −xs− variables for the small screens and the −md− variables for the larger screens:

```
// Navbar
$navbar-xs-color:              $body-color;
$navbar-xs-bg:                 #fff;
$navbar-md-color:              $gray-lightest;
$navbar-md-bg:                 $brand-primary;

// Navbar links
$navbar-xs-color:              $navbar-xs-color;
$navbar-xs-hover-color:        $navbar-xs-color;
$navbar-xs-hover-bg:           darken($navbar-xs-bg, 5%);
$navbar-xs-active-color:       $navbar-xs-color;
$navbar-xs-disabled-color:     $navbar-xs-hover-bg;

$navbar-md-color:              $navbar-md-color;
$navbar-md-hover-color:        $navbar-md-color;
$navbar-md-hover-bg:           darken($navbar-md-bg, 5%);
$navbar-md-active-color:       $navbar-md-color;
$navbar-md-disabled-color:     $navbar-md-hover-bg;
```

Having set up these fundamental color variables, we're ready to work on our navbar.

Styling the collapsed navbar

While still in _navbar.less, search for // Navbar, which will take you to the navbar variables. Note that most of the standard values specified here will affect both the collapsed responsive navbar for small viewports and the expanded navbar for wider viewports.

We want the background, text, and link colors for the collapsed responsive navbar to remain largely consistent with the default values but then change to our blue background and a light text color for medium and larger viewports.

We'll develop a responsive color scheme to accomplish the preceding color changes based on the viewport.

Open the scss/includes/_navbar.scss file and edit the default values for the small viewport as follows:

```
// responsive color scheme
.navbar {
  background-color: $navbar-xs-bg;
  color: $navbar-xs-color;
  .nav-link
  {
    @include hover-focus-active {
      background-color: $navbar-xs-hover-bg;
    }
  }
}
```

As you can see, we'll use the -xs- variables now. For medium and large viewports—where our navbar stretches out horizontally below the logo—we want our navbar to take on the blue color. Using Bootstrap's media query mixins again, we can change the colors for the larger viewports, as follows:

```
// responsive color scheme
.navbar {
  background-color: $navbar-xs-bg;
  color: $navbar-xs-color;
  .nav-link
  {
    @include hover-focus-active {
      background-color: $navbar-xs-hover-bg;
    }
  }
  @include media-breakpoint-up(md) {
    background-color: $navbar-md-bg;
    color: $navbar-md-color;
```

```
    .nav-link
    {
      color: $navbar-md-color;
      @include hover-focus-active {
        background-color: $navbar-md-hover-bg;
      }
    }
  }
}
```

Customizing the drop-down menus

We will use the power of Sass again to customize the drop-down menus for smaller screens. Edit the following code in the scss/includes/_navbar.scss file:

```
@include media-breakpoint-down(sm) {
  .navbar {
    .nav-item + .nav-item {
      margin-left: 0;
    }
    .dropdown {
      position: initial;
    }
    .dropdown-menu {
      position: initial;
      z-index: initial;
      float: initial;
      border: initial;
      border-radius: initial;
    }
  }
}
```

In the preceding code, we've used Bootstrap's media query mixins to reset the styles for screens smaller than 768 pixels. The initial value the initial value of a property to an element. So the preceding code sets the position to again and removes the float, border, and border-radius, and the drop-down menu will look like a "normal" list now:

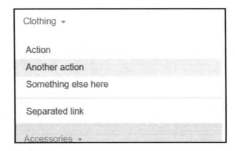

Fantastic! Now we can address the horizontal navbar.

Styling the horizontal navbar

When you move your mouse over the navbar links, you'll find that the hover background color of the link is smaller than the height of the navbar:

You can solve this issue by applying padding on the links instead of the navbar. Use the following SCSS code in the file to change the padding:

```scss
.navbar {
  @include media-breakpoint-up(md) {
    padding-top: 0;
    padding-bottom: 0;
  }
  .nav-link
  {
    padding: $spacer;
    @include media-breakpoint-only(md) {
      padding: $spacer-y ($spacer-x / 2);
    }
  }
}
```

Now your navbar links should look like the following screenshot:

And finally, let's transform the text to upper case, reduce its size a bit, and make it bold. In `_navbar.scss`, add these highlighted lines:

```scss
.nav-link
{
  padding: $spacer;
  @include media-breakpoint-up(md) {
   text-transform: uppercase;
   font-size: 82%;
   font-weight: bold;
  }
}
```

This will yield the following result:

Our banner and navbar are complete!

Enabling Flexbox support

As already explained in Chapter 1, *Getting Started with Bootstrap*, Bootstrap 4 comes with optional flexbox support. You can simply enable flexbox support by declaring `$enable-flex: true;` in the `scss/includes/_variables` file. If you do so, you'll have clear the floats of the container of the navbar because of we've implement flexbox support for it. You can clear the floats by adding the following SCSS code to the file:

```
header[role="banner"] {
  // header container do not use the flexbox layout, so floats have to be
cleared
  @if $enable-flex {
    .container {
      @include clearfix();
    }
  }
}
```

Now it's time to move on to the main content of our page.

Designing a complex responsive layout

Let's imagine we've emerged from client meetings with a plan to organize the home page content in three tiers, ranked by importance.

In medium and wide viewports, this content will be laid out in three columns, as shown in the following screenshot:

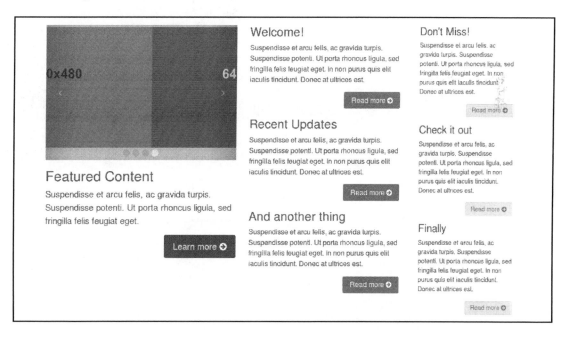

In a narrow viewport, these will be laid out one after another, in a single vertical column:

And in a small and medium `tablet-width` viewport, we'll arrange the content in two side-by-side columns, with the third tier of content laid out beneath it as a horizontal row, as shown in the following screenshot:

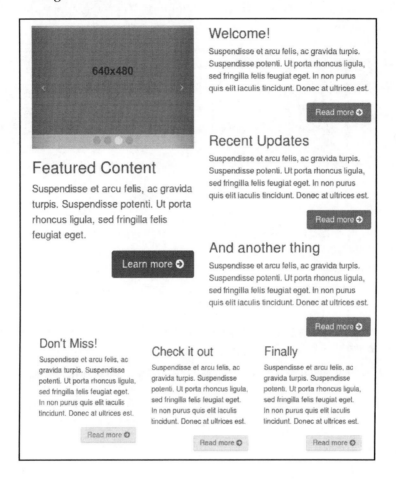

To get us started, I've provided the basic markup for three equal columns. Let's review what we have and then adapt it to the needs of this design. We'll begin with the three-column layout for medium and wide viewports.

Adjusting the large and extra-large layout

Currently, in large and extra-large viewports, our three columns are equal in width, font size, button size, and color. As a result, the presentation lacks visual hierarchy, as seen in the following screenshot:

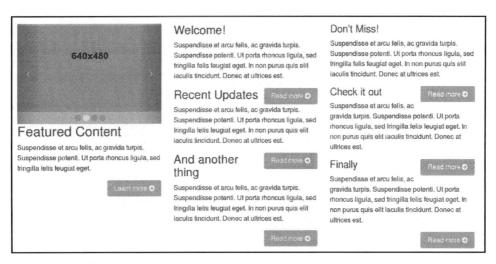

We can take significant strides by adjusting column width, font size, button size, and color to establish a clearer hierarchy between these tiers of content. Let's do that. We'll start by adjusting column widths:

1. In `html/pages/index.html`, search for the `section` tag for the primary content:

   ```
   <section class="content-primary col-md-4">
   ```

2. Note that the `col-md-4` class sets the width of this column to one-third of the width of the parent element, beginning at the small viewport width (768 pixels and up).

3. We want to save the three-column layout for the large and extra-large viewports (992 pixels and up), and we want this first column to be wider than the others.

4. Edit the `col-md-4` class to read `col-lg-5`, as follows:

   ```
   <section class="content-primary col-lg-5">
   ```

5. This will set this column to 5/12 width with the medium viewport and larger.

6. Now search and find the opening `section` tags for the next two columns and adjust the column classes to `col-lg-4` and `col-lg-3` respectively:

```
<section class="content-secondary col-lg-4">
...
<section class="content-tertiary col-lg-3">
```

Save, refresh, and you'll see the desired visual hierarchy in the width of our columns:

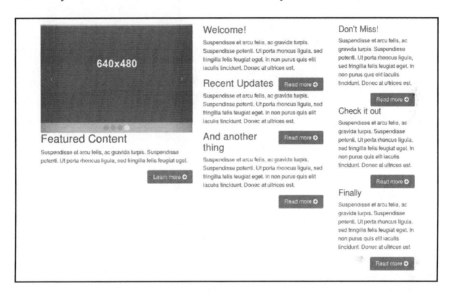

You might have noticed that the headings in the middle of the secondary and tertiary columns are not clearing the buttons above them. Let's adjust these, as well as our buttons and font sizes after adjusting the medium layout.

Adjusting the medium layout for tablet-width viewports

First notice that the navbar is too small for the number of items on the medium layout. The items render into two rows, as follows:

To get the items on a single row again, you may reduce the margin and padding of the navbar items or change the collapsing point of the navbar.

First, try the margin and padding solution; you can use the power of Sass again. Open the file in your editor and add the following SCSS code:

```scss
.navbar {
  @include media-breakpoint-only(md) {
    .nav-item + .nav-item {

      margin-left: 0;

    }
  }
  .nav-link
  {
    padding: $spacer;
    @include media-breakpoint-only(md) {
      padding: $spacer-y ($spacer-x / 2);
    }
  }
}
```

Notice that I've wrapped the code in the `media-breakpoint-only()` mixin. The `media-breakpoint-only()` mixin works just like the media-breakpoint-up and media-breakpoint-down mixins you've seen before, but only targets a single grid by setting both the min-width and max-width for the media query.

Consider the following SCSS code, for example:

```scss
@include media-breakpoint-only(md) {
  padding: $spacer-y ($spacer-x / 2);
}
```

The preceding SCSS code compiles into CSS code similar to the following:

```css
@media (min-width: 768px) and (max-width: 991px) {
  .navbar .nav-link {
  padding: 1rem 0.5rem;
  }
}
```

A `media-breakpoint-between()` mixin is available too. The `media-breakpoint-between()` mixin enables you to target a range of grids between two breakpoints. The `@include media-breakpoint-only(sm,md){}` call targets both small and medium grids.

You may have noticed that your file contains a lot of media queries now. Sass does not merge media queries, so the compiled CSS code contains a lot of media queries too. Merging the same CSS media query rules into one media query rule may be a performance improvement for your CSS code. The css-mqpacker node package can process your CSS code pack's same CSS media query rules into one media query rule.

You can run the package with the gulp-postcss package just like the autoprefixer plugin. More information about css-mqpacker and how to integrate it in your Gulp build process can be found at the following URL: https://www.npmjs.com/package/css-mqpacker

A `media-breakpoint-between()` mixin is available too. The `media-breakpoint-between()` mixin enables you to target a range of grids between two breakpoints. The `@include media-breakpoint-only(sm,md){}` call targets both the small and medium grids.

Alternatively, you may change the collapsing point of the navbar. First, open the html/includes/header.html file and change the appearance of the navbar toggler as follows:

```
<button class="navbar-toggler hidden-lg-up" type="button"
data-toggle="collapse" data-target="#collapsiblecontent">
```

The `hidden-lg-up` class in the preceding code now shows the toggle button on the medium screen too. Then, change the breakpoint for the toggleable navbar from `navbar-toggleable-sm` to `navbar-toggleable-md`, as shown in the following HTML snippet:

```
<div class="container navbar-toggleable-md collapse"
id="collapsiblecontent">
```

Now you'll find a collapsed navbar on the medium grid too. Notice that we've made some changes to the navbar items and the submenus for the collapsed navbar before. You should change the media queries for these changes too. You can change the media queries in the scss/includes/_navbar.sccs file:

```
.navbar {
  @include media-breakpoint-down(md) {
    .navbar-brand,
    .nav-item {
      float: none;
      > img {
        display: inline-block;
      }
    }
  }
```

```
      // dropdown menus
      .nav-item + .nav-item {
        margin-left: 0;
      }
      .dropdown {
        position: initial;
      }
      .dropdown-menu {
        position: initial;
        z-index: initial;
        float: initial;
        border: initial;
        border-radius: initial;
      }
    }
  }
```

Also change the breakpoint for the navbar class in the `scss/includes/_header.scss` file:

```
.navbar-brand {
  > img {
    width: 120px;
    padding-left: $spacer-x;
    @include media-breakpoint-up(lg) {
      padding-top: $spacer-y * 3;
      padding-left: 0;
      width: 180px;
    }
  }
}
```

And finally, in the file, replace the `pull-md-right` class with the `pull-lg-right` class for the last navbar item in the `html/includes/header.html` file, as shown in the following HTML template snippet:

```
{{#ifCond this 'All Departments'}}</ul><ul class="nav navbar-nav pull-lg-
right">{{/ifCond}}
```

The navbar is ready now for the medium grid. Let's prepare our content columns too. On the medium grid, we'll move the third column below the other columns and display each item in a column. See screenshot under section *Adjusting the medium layout for tablet-width viewports*.

The first row contains two columns whose combined width is 50% of the container, and the second row contains three columns stretching one-third of the width of the container.

We can accomplish the layout described previously by using Bootstrap's predefined grid classes again. First, open the `html/pages/index.html` file again and add the grid classes for the medium grid, as follows:

```
<section class="content-primary col-md-6 col-lg-5">
  ...
</section>
<section class="content-secondary col-md-6 col-lg-4">
  ...
</section>
<section class="content-tertiary col-md-12 col-lg-3">
  ...
</section>
```

The `col-md-*` classes in the preceding code only affect the medium, because the `col-lg-*` classes overwrites them for the larger grids, according to mobile first coding.

A grid row contains 12 columns; on the medium grid you'll have 24 (2 *x md-6* + *md-12*) columns now. The columns will automatically split up into two rows. The first row contains the first two (*md-6*) columns, and the second row is filled with the *md-12* column.

Now you will have to lay out the items of the content-tertiary column on the medium grid. Bootstrap's grid rows can also be nested. We'll use nesting to split up the second row into three equal-width columns. To nest your content with the default grid, add a new row class and set of `col-*-*` columns within an existing `col-*-*` column. In your layout, wrap each column into the following HTML structure:

```
<article class="col-md-4 col-lg-12">
  ...
</article>
```

You'll not only have to add a `col-md-4` class, but also a `col-lg-12` class to ensure the nesting does not influence the columns on the large and extra-large grids. Wrap the columns in a new row and the HTML code of the tertiary column should now look like the following:

```
<section class="content-tertiary col-md-12 col-lg-3">
<div class="row">
<article class="col-md-4 col-lg-12">
<h4>Don't Miss!</h4>
<p>Suspendisse et arcu felis, ac gravida turpis. Suspendisse potenti.
Ut porta rhoncus ligula, sed fringilla felis feugiat eget. In non purus
quis elit iaculis tincidunt. Donec at ultrices est.</p>
```

```
<p><a class="btn btn-primary pull-right" href="#">Read more
<span class="icon fa fa-arrow-circle-right"></span></a></p>
</article>
<article class="col-md-4 col-lg-12">
<h4>Check it out</h4>
<p>Suspendisse et arcu felis, ac gravida turpis. Suspendisse potenti.
Ut porta rhoncus ligula, sed fringilla felis feugiat eget. In non purus
quis elit iaculis tincidunt. Donec at ultrices est.</p>
<p><a class="btn btn-primary pull-right" href="#">Read more
<span class="icon fa fa-arrow-circle-right"></span></a></p>
</article>
<article class="col-md-4 col-lg-12">
<h4>Finally</h4>
<p>Suspendisse et arcu felis, ac gravida turpis. Suspendisse potenti.
Ut porta rhoncus ligula, sed fringilla felis feugiat eget. In non purus
quis elit iaculis tincidunt. Donec at ultrices est.</p>
<p><a class="btn btn-primary pull-right" href="#">Read more
<span class="icon fa fa-arrow-circle-right"></span></a></p>
</article>
</div>
</section>
```

In the browser, the last column should look like that shown in the following screenshot:

Adjusting headings, font sizes, and buttons

Let's begin by adjusting our headings so that they consistently clear the buttons above them, which have been floated to the right. For this purpose, we'll use the file we previously created to manage the details of the page contents, _page-contents.scss.

Here's how to do it:

1. In `_page-contents.scss`, let's write a selector to select headings h1 through h4 when they're nested inside a Bootstrap column class. We'll use the CSS2 attribute selector and cover our bases by targeting any element whose classes include the `col-` string.

 Later in this chapter, we will equip our footer with its own set of responsive columns. Thus, we need to make sure we nest these rules within the selector for the main element.

2. Within this context, we'll select all heading tags we might potentially use and set them to clear floated elements, with some added padding for separation:

```
[class*="col-"] {
  h1, h2, h3, h4 {
    clear: both;
    padding-top: $spacer-y;
  }
}
```

3. This gives the necessary separation between our headings and floated buttons. But it also creates unneeded padding at the top of the secondary and tertiary columns.

4. In the following screenshot, the lower arrows highlight the improvement accomplished now that our headings clear the floated buttons. Also, the ragged top edge of our columns, where padding causes a problem:

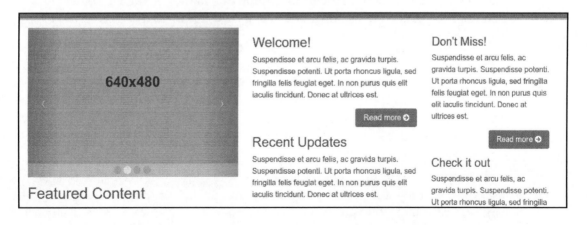

5. Let's remove the margin and padding from the uppermost heading in each column. We'll use the `:first-child` selector for these headings, nesting these lines within our heading selectors. We'll use the `&` combinator, which in this formulation allows us to select any first-child instance of these headings:

```
&:first-child {
  margin-top: 0;
  padding-top: 0;
}
```

6. This removes the extra margin and padding and evens up the top edge of the second:

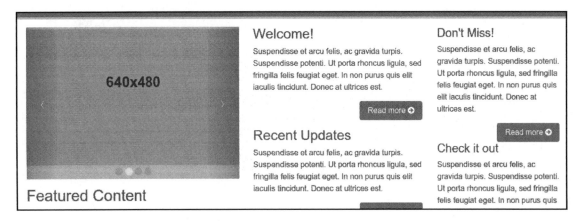

7. But now there is a problem with the third column. The `:first-child` selector matches each h4 element in the third column due to the nesting we added before. You can solve this issue by creating a new h4 selector in your Sass code, as follows:

```
h4 {
  clear: both;
  padding-top: $spacer-y;
}
> article:first-child h4 {
  margin-top: 0;
  padding-top: 0;
}
```

8. However, we only want to remove this top margin and padding in medium, large, or extra-large viewports, which accommodate multiple columns. Thus, we need to nest this rule within a media query corresponding with the breakpoint at

which our layout expands from a narrow single-column layout to a wider multi-column layout.

9. Thus, we need to nest what we've just done within a media query for medium viewports and larger:

```
[class*="col-"] {
  h1, h2, h3, h4 {
    clear: both;
    padding-top: $spacer-y;
    @include media-breakpoint-up(md) {
      &:first-child {
        margin-top: 0;
        padding-top: 0;
      }
    }
  }
  h4 {
    clear: both;
    padding-top: $spacer-y;
  }
  @include media-breakpoint-up(md) {
    > article:first-child h4 {
      margin-top: 0;
      padding-top: 0;
    }
  }
}
```

With the preceding media query, we've retained the padding we need between elements in the single-column layout for narrow viewports, as seen in the following screenshot:

With this accomplished, we can move on to adjust buttons and font sizes to reflect the informational hierarchy of our content. Let's begin by enlarging the font size, button size, and color in our primary content area.

Enhancing the primary column

First, let's increase the font size of our primary column content:

1. In Bootstrap's `_variables.scss` file, the `$font-size-large` variable is set to the following by default:

   ```
   $font-size-lg: 1.25rem !default;
   ```

2. Now, in the `scss/includes/_page-contents.scss` file, add these lines to use this font size for our primary content:

   ```
   .content-primary {
     font-size: $font-size-lg;
   }
   ```

Save these changes, compile the file, and refresh your browser. You should see the font size increase accordingly!

Now, let's adjust the color of our button to utilize the red `$brand-feature` color. We'll utilize the `$brand-feature` variable we set up in the local `scss/includes/_variables.scss` file.

```
$brand-feature:          #c60004;
```

We'll also utilize an excellent `button-variant()` mixin provided in the Bootstrap `mixins/_buttons.scss` file. You may want to take a moment to check it out. Open the `mixins/_buttons.scss` in the Bootstrap's source code in the `bower_components` directory and search for `// Button` variants. You'll find a mixin that begins as follows:

```
@mixin button-variant($color, $background, $border) {
```

The mixin does the following:

- Specifies the button font, background, and border colors (in other words, the three parameters that the mixin accepts)
- Generates hover, focus, active, and disabled states for the button, adjusting font color, background color, and border

If you'd like to, you can see how Bootstrap uses this mixin in `bootstrap/_buttons.scss` under the `// Alternate buttons` comment. Here are the lines generating styles for the default and primary buttons:

```
//
// Alternate buttons
//

.btn-primary {
  @include button-variant($btn-primary-color, $btn-primary-bg, $btn-primary-border);
}
.btn-secondary {
  @include button-variant($btn-secondary-color, $btn-secondary-bg, $btn-secondary-border);
}
.btn-info {
  @include button-variant($btn-info-color, $btn-info-bg, $btn-info-border);
}
```

 You will find the variables beginning with `$btn-primary-` and `$btn-secondary-` in the `bower_components/bootstrap/scss/_variables.scss` file.

Following this pattern, we can generate our custom feature button in four simple steps:

1. First, we'll set up a new set of button variables. In the `_scss/includes/_variables.scss` file, under `// Buttons`, make a copy of the three `$btn-primary-` variables, and customize them, replacing `-primary-` with `-feature-` and using `$brand-feature` as the background color:

   ```
   $btn-feature-color:             #fff;
   $btn-feature-bg:                $brand-feature;
   $btn-feature-border:            darken($btn-feature-bg, 5%);
   ```

2. Next, we can make a file to keep our custom buttons. Create `scss/includes/_buttons.scss` and write a mixin based on the `.btn-primary` mixin from `bootstrap/_buttons.scss`, as follows:

```
.btn-feature {
    @include button-variant($btn-feature-color, $btn-feature-bg,
    $btn-feature-border);
```

3. Save this file and add it to the import sequence in `scss/app.scss` as follows:

```
@import "includes/carousel"; @import "includes/buttons"; // added
```

4. Now, in the `html/pages/index.html` file, change the button class from `btn-primary` to `btn-feature`. While we're at it, we want to make the button large, so add the `btn-lg` class:

```
<a class="btn btn-feature btn-lg pull-right" href="#">   Learn more
```

Save your work. Run the `bootstrap watch` command, and you should see the following result. The primary column to the left now has a larger font size and a large button with our `brand-feature` color:

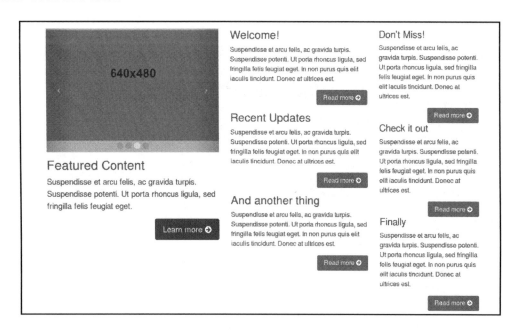

Meanwhile, the font size and button colors of the secondary (center) column are exactly what we want. What needs to happen next is this: we need to de-emphasize the tertiary column content so that it takes its appropriate place in the informational hierarchy.

Adjusting the tertiary column

Our task for the tertiary content is fairly straightforward. We have to reduce the font size and de-emphasize the buttons. This can be accomplished as follows:

1. First, we'll adjust the `font-size`. In Bootstrap's `_variables.scss file`, the `$font-size-sm` variable is set as follows:

    ```
    $font-size-sm:                    .875rem !default;
    ```

2. Now we need only add these lines to the `_scss/includes/_page-contents.scss` file:

    ```
    .content-tertiary {
      font-size: $font-size-sm;
    }
    ```

3. If you have run the `bootstrap watch` command already, you should see the font size reduce, after saving your changes.

4. Next, in the `html/pages/index.html` file, we need to edit our button classes. We'll change them from `btn-primary` to `btn-secondary`, and we'll reduce their size using the `btn-sm` class:

    ```
    <a class="btn btn-secondary btn-sm pull-right" href="#">Read more
    ```

    . . .

5. This will reduce the button size and turn the button's background white.

6. Let's adjust the background to a light gray and adjust the font color and border as well. In the `_variables.scss` file, adjust the values for the three `$btn-secondary-` variables as follows:

```
$btn-secondary-color:          $gray;
$btn-secondary-bg:             $gray-lightest;
$btn-secondary-border:         darken($btn-secondary-bg, 5%);
```

Save the changes, compile the file, and refresh your browser.

We now have a clear visual hierarchy, from the primary content (on the left), to the secondary (center), and tertiary (right):

Now, take a moment to notice that our adjustments work reasonably well in the narrow single-column layout as well:

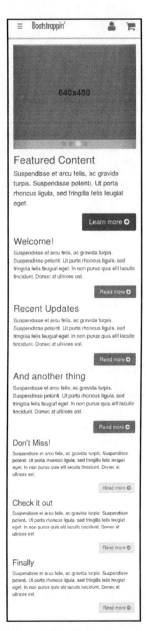

In narrow viewports, our three columns stretch out vertically, one after the other, with primary content first, followed by secondary and tertiary.

All that remains is some fine-tuning to make our content even more user friendly across devices and viewports.

Fine touches for multiple viewports

It's always good to give our content—and our viewers' eyes—some room to breathe. Visual indicators of section boundaries are good as well. Let's fold these in:

1. First, we'll add padding above and below our content. Add a bit of top padding to the `main` element itself. This padding will serve us well in all viewports, so we won't need a media query:

```
main {
  padding-top: $spacer-y;
  padding-bottom: $spacer-y * 2;
}
```

That's it. Our main content layout is ready. Now for the complex footer area.

Laying out a complex footer

In the following steps, we'll create a complex footer built to manage multiple goals, including three lists of links to key sections of our website, a bit of **About Us** text, social icons, and our logo.

Setting up the markup

We will start by creating the footer markup. We want this footer to be as functional and useful for the user as possible. We'll build the markup as follows:

1. Start with the footer of the Portfolio project from `Chapter 5`, *Bootstrappin' Your Portfolio*. You'll find the HTML Markup code of the footer in the html/includes/footer.html file.

2. Move HTML code for the logo and add it directly under the social links and create a new include for the additional footer content as follows:

```
<footer role="contentinfo">
{{> footercolumns}}

<div class="container social-logo">
<ul class="social">
  <li class="social-item"><a href="#" class="social-link"
  ><i class="fa fa-twitter"></i></a></li>
  <li class="social-item"><a href="#" class="social-link"
  ><i class="fa fa-facebook"></i></a></li>
  <li class="social-item"><a href="#" class="social-link"
  ><i class="fa fa-linkedin"></i></a></li>
  <li class="social-item"><a href="#" class="social-link"
  ><i class="fa fa-google-plus"></i></a></li>
  <li class="social-item"><a href="#" class="social-link"
  ><i class="fa fa-github-alt"></i></a></li>
</ul>

<p><a href="{{root}}index.html"><img src="{{root}}images/logo.png"
 width="80" alt="Bootstrappin'"></a></p>
</div>
</footer>
```

3. Now create a new HTML partial called `html/includes/footercolumns.html`. You can pass the additional footer content into this file.

4. Before pasting the content, let's prepare to utilize the Bootstrap grid system. To do this, we'll wrap the area within `div class="row"`, as follows:

```
<div class="container">
  <div class="row">
    . . .
  </div><!-- /.row -->
</div><!-- /.container -->
```

5. Now, paste the new content in place.

6. Next, we'll wrap each of the three lists of links, along with their headings, in a `col-lg-2` class `div`. This way, each list will take one-sixth of the available width in medium and larger viewports. Together, these three lists will take half the available viewport width.

7. Now, to complete our row, wrap the **About Us** heading and its paragraph in `col-lg-6` class `div` so that it takes up the remaining half of the available width:

```
<div class="about col-lg-6">
  <h3>About Us</h3>
```

 Be sure to add the necessary closing tags for each new `div` element.

8. Save, run the `bootstrap watch` or `gulp` command, and check your results.

After performing the preceding steps, you should end up with the following HTML code:

```
<div class="container">
  <div class="row">
    <div class=col-lg-2">
      <h3>Categories</h3>
      <ul>
        <li><a href="#">Shoes</a></li>
        <li><a href="#">Clothing</a></li>
        <li><a href="#">Accessories</a></li>
        <li><a href="#">Men</a></li>
        <li><a href="#">Women</a></li>
        <li><a href="#">Kids</a></li>
        <li><a href="#">Pets</a></li>
      </ul>
    </div>
    <div class="col-lg-2">
      <h3>Styles</h3>
      <ul>
        <li><a href="#">Athletic</a>  </li>
        <li><a href="#">Casual</a></li>
        <li><a href="#">Dress</a></li>
        <li><a href="#">Everyday</a></li>
        <li><a href="#">Other Days</a></li>
        <li><a href="#">Alternative</a></li>
        <li><a href="#">Otherwise</a></li>
      </ul>
    </div>
    <div class="col-lg-2">
      <h3>Other</h3>
      <ul>
        <li><a href="#">Link</a></li>
        <li><a href="#">Another link</a></li>
        <li><a href="#">Link again</a></li>
```

```
      <li><a href="#">Try this</a></li>
      <li><a href="#">Don't you dare</a></li>
      <li><a href="#">Oh go ahead</a></li>
    </ul>
  </div>

  <!-- Add the extra clearfix for only the required viewport -->
  <div class="clearfix hidden-sm-down hidden-lg-up"></div>

  <div class="about col-lg-6">
    <h3>About Us</h3>
    <p>Lorem ipsum dolor sit amet, consectetur adipiscing elit.
    Suspendisse euismod congue bibendum. Aliquam erat volutpat.
    Phasellus eget justo lacus. Vivamus pharetra ullamcorper massa, nec
    ultricies metus gravida egestas. Duis congue viverra arcu, ac aliquet
    turpis rutrum a. Donec semper vestibulum dapibus.
    Integer et sollicitudin
    metus. Vivamus at nisi turpis. Phasellus vel tellus id felis cursus
    hendrerit.</p>
    <p><a class="btn btn-secondary btn-sm pull-right" href="#">Learn more
    <span class="fa fa-arrow-circle-right"></span></a></p>
  </div>
  </div><!-- /.row -->
</div><!-- /.container -->
```

Due to the Bootstrap grid classes we've added in our HTML in a viewport of 980 pixels and larger, our columns should organize themselves as follows:

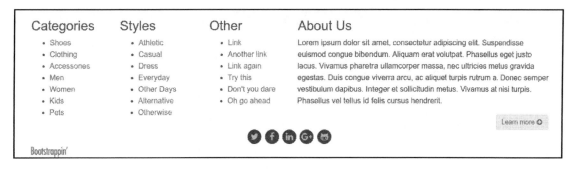

This is the layout we want in large and extra-large viewports. Extra-small screen sizes are served just fine by the single-column layout. However, for tablet-width screen sizes that fall within the range of 768 to 980 pixels, our layout can benefit from some adjustments. Let's address that.

Adjusting for tablet-width viewports

Test the layout in a viewport that falls between 768 and 980 pixels. Bootstrap refers to this as the medium breakpoint and `col-md-` grid classes. At this width, the single-column layout leaves unnecessary white space. Here is what you'll see:

Categories

- Shoes
- Clothing
- Accessories
- Men
- Women
- Kids
- Pets

Styles

- Athletic
- Casual
- Dress
- Everyday
- Other Days
- Alternative
- Otherwise

Other

- Link
- Another link
- Link again
- Try this
- Don't you dare
- Oh go ahead

About Us

Lorem ipsum dolor sit amet, consectetur adipiscing elit. Suspendisse euismod congue bibendum. Aliquam erat volutpat. Phasellus eget justo lacus. Vivamus pharetra ullamcorper massa, nec ultricies metus gravida egestas. Duis congue viverra arcu, ac aliquet turpis rutrum a. Donec semper vestibulum dapibus. Integer et sollicitudin metus. Vivamus at nisi turpis. Phasellus vel tellus id felis cursus hendrerit.

Learn more ⊙

Bootstrappin'

We can improve this layout by allowing our three lists of links to float next to each other. Using the Bootstrap `col-md-*` column classes for Bootstrap's grid, let's set the three lists of links to be one-third width, or `col-sm-4`, and the **About Us** column to be full width, or `col-sm-12`:

```
<div class="col-md-4 col-lg-2">
...
<div class="col-md-4 col-lg-2">
...
<div class="col-md-4 col-lg-2">
...
<div class="about col-xs-12 col-lg-6">
```

Save this and try it out in the medium viewport range. You will see the following result:

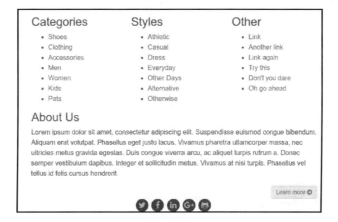

Much improved! But we're not quite finished. Try clicking on the links in the upper three columns. Chances are that you won't be able to. Inspect the element and you'll find that the fourth `div` element contains the code for the **About Us** column. This code does not clear the floated columns above it. Though the **About Us** heading and its paragraph will appear below the three floating columns, the `div` element itself will overlap them.

Adding a targeted responsive clearfix

In a standard Bootstrap layout situation, we would use a `div` element with the `row` class to clear the floating columns. Here, we need a different solution, as we want this block of content to clear floats only within this specific breakpoint.

To accomplish this, we could write custom styles in our Sass files. But we can also use a Bootstrap responsive utility class to provide a targeted `clearfix` directly in the markup. Since we've already specified grid classes in our markup, let's use the second option in this context.

You can find the approach we'll use mentioned in Bootstrap's documentation at `http://get bootstrap.com/layout/grid/#example-responsive-column-resets`. Following that method, we'll create a `div` element with the `clearfix` class, and add a Bootstrap responsive utility class to make it visible only on small screens. We'll place this new div element immediately prior to the **About Us** column:

```
<!-- Add the extra clearfix for only the required viewport -->
<div class="clearfix hidden-sm-down hidden-lg-up"></div>

<div class="about col-xs-12 col-lg-6">
```

The `clearfix` class will force this element to clear the floats above it. The `hidden-sm-down` and hidden-lg-up classes will allow this `div` to display only within our targeted breakpoint. At other breakpoints, it will be as if this `div` does not exist.

Save this, and you should find that the **About Us** column now clears the floats above it and that the links are clickable.

Task complete. Now for a few finishing touches.

Refining the details

We have a few final touches we want to implement as we finish our footer. These include the following:

- Refining the presentation of our three lists of links
- Adjusting margins and padding
- Reversing the color scheme to match our navbar colors

To accomplish these refinements, we'll write some custom styles. Let's tackle this in cascading fashion, starting with general rules for the footer and moving to the specific rules:

1. Open `_footer.scss`, the file for custom footer styles, in your editor.
2. Here, you'll find some initial rules that are carried over from Chapter 5, *Bootstrappin' Your Portfolio*. These include some initial padding for the footer, as well as styles for the social icons and the footer version of the logo.

3. Now to add the refinements we need for our new complex footer. Let's start by reducing the footer font size and inverting the color scheme to correspond with the inverted navbar—a blue background with light text. I'll begin with those colors and then darken them slightly. To do this, I'll make use of appropriate variables from Bootstrap's `_variables.scss` and the local `scss/includes/_variables.scss` files, including `$font-size-sm`, `$navbar-md-bg`, and `$navbar-md-color`:

```
footer[role="contentinfo"] {
  padding-top: 24px;
  padding-bottom: 36px;
  font-size: $font-size-sm;
  background-color: darken($navbar-md-bg, 18%);
  color: darken($navbar-md-color, 18%);
}
```

In this and all that follows, we need to nest our new rules within `footer[role="contentinfo"]`.

4. Next, we need to adjust our links and buttons to fit the new color scheme. Still nesting rules within `footer[role="contentinfo"]`, I've done this as follows:

```
footer[role="contentinfo"] {
  a {
    color: $navbar-md-color;
    @include hover-focus-active {
      color: $navbar-md-hover-color;
    }
  }
  .btn-secondary {
    color: darken($navbar-md-bg, 18%) !important;
  }
}
```

5. Now to address the four h3 headings. I'll adjust font size, trim the bottom margin, and convert the text to uppercase:

```
footer[role="contentinfo"] {
  h3 {
    font-size: 120%;
    margin-top: $spacer-y;
    margin-bottom: 4px;
    text-transform: uppercase;
  }
```

```
    }
```

6. Having done this, we can next remove bullets from our list of links, and adjust their padding and margin:

```
ul {
   list-style: none;
   padding: 0;
   margin: 0;
}
```

7. And we can center the logo and social icons:

```
footer[role="contentinfo"] {
  .social-logo {
    text-align: center;
  }
}
```

8. Finally, let's adjust our social icons. We'll add a bit of top padding and then adjust their colors to work better with the new color scheme. Since these are Font Awesome icons, we can do this simply by adjusting the `color` and `background-color` values, as follows:

```
.social-link {
   display: inline-block;
   font-size: 18px;
   line-height: 30px;
   @include square(30px); // see includes/mixins/_size.scss
   border-radius: 36px;
   background-color: darken($navbar-md-bg, 27%);
   color: darken($navbar-md-color, 18%);
   margin: 0 3px 3px 0;
   @include hover-focus { // bootstrap/scss/mixins/_hover.scss
   text-decoration: none;
     background-color: darken($navbar-md-bg, 32%);
     color: $navbar-md-hover-color;
   }
}
```

That's it. Save, run the `bootstrap watch` command, and enjoy! Here is our result in the large and extra-large viewports:

Here is the result for the medium viewport:

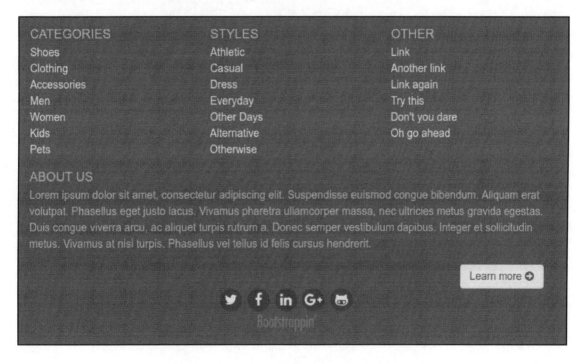

And this is for extra-small and small viewports:

Not bad! We have built a footer capable of managing a complex array of content across the full spectrum of extra-small, small, medium, large, and extra-large viewports.

Summary

This project has enabled us to beef up our Bootstrappin' skills in a number of ways. We've designed a responsive layout for the main content of our page, providing an appropriate visual hierarchy for three tiers of information. At the top of our page we've built a complex responsive navbar, so that it appears below the logo and banner area in medium, large, and extra-large viewports and yet collapses into a mobile-friendly navbar on smaller screens. The footer part of the project effectively manages multiple blocks of links and text across viewports.

Congratulations! In the next chapter, we'll build on these skills by designing a products page suitable for an e-commerce section for this website.

7
Bootstrappin' E-Commerce

Having built our business home page, it's time to design our online store.

We'll build on the design from the previous chapter, adding a new page with the following elements:

- A grid of product thumbnails, titles, and descriptions
- A left-hand sidebar with options to filter our products by category, brand, and so on
- Breadcrumbs and pagination to ease navigation through our inventory

Take a few moments to visit websites such as Zappos (http://www.zappos.com) and Amazon (http://www.amazon.com). Search or browse for products and you will see product grids with features similar to what we will be creating in this chapter.

When complete, we want our products page to look like the following screenshot on medium, large and extra-large screens:

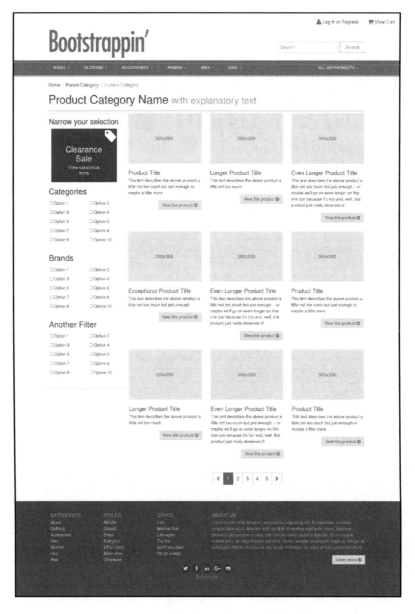

Layout for medium large and extra-large screens

On extra-small screens, we want our products page to adjust to the following single column layout:

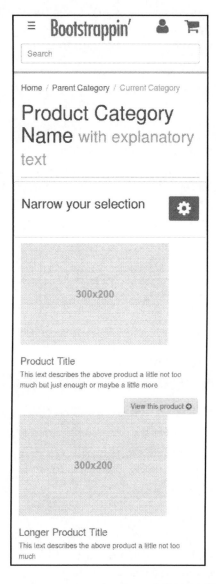

Bootstrap gives us a big head start in accomplishing this design-after which we can use the power of Sass to refine things to completion.

Surveying the markup for our products page

You'll find this chapter's files prepared and ready in the folder `chapter7/start`. This project builds directly on the completed design from `Chapter 6`, *Bootstrappin' Business*. If anything in these files seems strange, you may want to review `Chapter 6`, *Bootstrappin' Business*, before proceeding.

 If you've not already downloaded the exercise files, you can find them at `h ttp://packtpub.com/support`.

Run the `bower install` and `npm install` commands in your console before going on with the next steps! For this chapter, there is one new file in the `html/pages` directory, `products.html`.

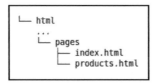

Open `products.html` in your editor to view the markup. Let's survey its contents.

Inside the `main role="main"` element is where we'll find what's new. Here, you'll find the following elements in the same order as they appear:

- Breadcrumb links marked up as an ordered list
- A page title within a `h1` heading
- A series of options for filtering products
- Nine products with thumbnails, titles, descriptions, and a button
- An unordered list of pagination links just below the products and before

You can run the `bootstrap watch` command and point your browser to `http://localhost:8080/products.html` to view the file in your browser. You'll see that much remains to be done. Breadcrumbs do not yet look like breadcrumbs, the filtering options look like a long series of bulleted lists, the layout of our product items is uneven (and in places broken), and so on.

Don't let these current imperfections worry you. These are the things that we'll be addressing in the following steps. Here is what's coming:

- We will apply Bootstrap's built-in styles to the breadcrumbs, page title, and pagination, and then customize them further
- We will improve the layout of the nine product items, innovating the Bootstrap grid system to maintain a visually well-organized grid across breakpoints
- We will style the filtering options by enhancing the layout and then using the Font Awesome icons to provide checkboxes

Run the `bootstrap watch` or `gulp` command in your console and point your browser to `http://localhost:8080/products.html`. Your browser will automatically reload now after saving the Sass or HTML templates.

Now that we have a plan, let's get started!

Styling the breadcrumbs, page title, and pagination

In the following steps, we'll apply Bootstrap styles to our breadcrumbs, page title, and pagination, and then customize them to fit our design:

1. Open `products.html` in your editor.
2. Find the ordered list just above the h1 page title, add the `"breadcrumb"` class to the `ol` tag, and then add the `"active"` class to the last list item, as follows:

```
<ol class="breadcrumb">
  <li class="breadcrumb-item"><a href="/">Home</a></li>
  <li class="breadcrumb-item"><a href="#">Parent Category</a></li>
  <li class="breadcrumb-item active">Current Category</li>
</ol>
```

> These classes correspond with Bootstrap breadcrumb styles, which you will find documented at `http://v4-alpha.getbootstrap.com/components/breadcrumb/`.
>
> Save and refresh your browser. You should see the result shown in the following screenshot:

3. To customize the breadcrumbs for this design, let's remove the light gray background and the extra padding.

- Let's set the `padding` to 0 and remove the `background-color` entirely

- Create a new Sass partial in the `scss/_includes` directory called `_breadcrumb.scss` and add the following SCSS to it:

```scss
.breadcrumb {
padding: 0;
background-color: initial;
}
```

4. Do not forget to import the new `_breadcrumb.scss` partial file into your `app.scss` file as follows:

```scss
// Components
@import "includes/breadcrumb";
```

5. Now for the page title. The page title works by nesting the top-level page heading within a `div` tag of the `page-header` class. The SCSS code for the `page-header` class can be edited in a new `scss/includes/_page-header.scss` partial and may look as shown here:

```scss
// Page header
// -----------------------
.page-header {
  padding-bottom: ($spacer / 2);
  margin: $spacer 0 ($spacer / 2);
  border-bottom: 1px solid $page-header-border-color;
}
```

Notice that you'll have to declare the `$page-header-border-color;` variable in the `scss/includes/_varaibels.scss` file and of course also have to import the `scss/includes/_page-header.scss` partial in the main `app.scss` file.

6. Let's adjust our markup accordingly. For the title, a `h1` tag with Bootstrap's `display-*` classes will be used. Let's also add some text within a `small` tag having Bootstrap's `text-muted` class to take advantage of the Bootstrap style for adding the explanatory notes to our headings:

```html
<div class="page-header">
  <h1 class="display-5">Product Category Name <small class="text-
```

```
muted">with explanatory text</small></h1>
    </div>
```

That will produce the following result:

Product Category Name with explanatory text

7. You can read more about Bootstrap's typography and heading classes at the following URL: v4-alpha.getbootstrap.com/content/typography/#headings.

8. Finally, the pagination. Our markup for this is found just a few lines above the closing main tag (</main>). Above that closing tag, you'll see commented closing div tags for the .container, .row, and .products-grid:

```
        </div><!-- /.products-grid -->
      </div><!-- /.row -->
    </div><!-- /.container -->
  </main>
```

Bootstrap's documentation for pagination styles is found at v4-alpha.getbootstrap.com/components/pagination.

To apply these styles here, we only need to add class="pagination" to the ul tag that you will find a few lines above the closing .products-grid tag:

```
<ul class="pagination">
  <li class="page-item">
    <a class="page-link" href="#" aria-label="Previous">
      <span aria-hidden="true" class="fa fa-chevron-left"></span>
      <span class="sr-only">Previous</span>
    </a>
  </li>
  <li class="page-item active">
    <a class="page-link" href="#">1 <span class="sr-only">(current)</span></a>
  </li>
  <li class="page-item"><a class="page-link" href="#">2</a></li>
  <li class="page-item"><a class="page-link" href="#">3</a></li>
  <li class="page-item"><a class="page-link" href="#">4</a></li>
  <li class="page-item"><a class="page-link" href="#">5</a></li>
  <li class="page-item">
    <a class="page-link" href="#" aria-label="Next">
      <span aria-hidden="true" class="fa fa-chevron-right"></span>
      <span class="sr-only">Next</span>
    </a>
```

```
    </li>
  </ul>
```

The markup for the navigation links may contain different classes to set the state of a link. The active CSS class makes clear that the link has an active state, whilst the disabled CSS class enables you to give some links a disabled state.

The HTML code for a disabled item may look like the following:

```
<li class="page-item disabled">
  <a class="page-link" href="#" tabindex="-1" aria-label="Previous">
    <span aria-hidden="true">&laquo;</span>
    <span class="sr-only">Previous</span>
  </a>
</li>
```

Neither disabled nor active items are clickable. You can add the add pagination-lg or pagination-sm CSS classes for larger or smaller pagination as follows:

```
<ul class="pagination pagination-lg">
  ...
</ul>
```

Also notice that Bootstrap takes accessibility into account. The navigation contains various `aria-*` attributes. **Accessible Rich Internet Applications (ARIA)** is a set of special accessibility attributes that can be added to any markup, but is especially suited to HTML. You can read more about ARIA in HTML at the website of the **World Wide Web Consortium (W3C)**, see `https://www.w3.org/TR/html-aria/`. Elements with Bootstrap's sr-only class provided additional information for only screen readers.

For the `Next` and `Prev` items, I've already provided the `span` tags for the Font Awesome icons, `fa-chevron-left` and `-right`. This gives us the result shown in the following screenshot:

9. Let's center align the pagination below our grid. First, wrap it in a parent `div` tag. We'll place the `row` class on this to ensure it clears the content above it, and then we'll add an appropriately named Bootstrap class `text-xs-center`. The `xs` in the naming means for the extra small grid and up:

```
<nav class="text-xs-center">
<ul class="pagination">
<li> ...
</ul>
</nav>
```

Adjusting the products grid

Before you start you should notice that the product images, provided by the holder.js image placeholders as described in Chapter 6, *Bootstrappin' Business*, are not responsive. Let's make all images responsive by default by adding the following lines of SCSS code to our app.scss file:

```
// make images responsive by default
img {
  @extend .img-fluid;
}
```

The process of making images responsive by default was described in Chapter 1, *Getting Started with Bootstrap* before. It influence all images. The logo in the also becomes responsive now and ignores the width we've set in the scss/includes/_header.scss file before. You can solve that by putting the SCSS code for the responsive image before the import of the _header.scss file in the app.scss file.

You should also inspect the footer logo after making the images responsive by default. You'll find that the logo does not center anymore. The img-fluid class changes your images into block level element. Block level elements cannot be centered by the text-align: center; declaration. You can use the following CSS code in the file to center the logo again:

```
.social-logo {
  img {
    margin 0 auto;
  }
}
```

Now let's make our products grid look as it should. Before we start, we move the product grid to its own HTML template file. Create a new HTML partial called html/includes/products-grid.html.

In the `html/includes/products.html` file, use the following code to include the product grid:

```
<div class="products-grid col-md-9">
  {{> products-grid }}
</div>
```

If you inspect the markup for our product items, you'll see that each item has been given a class of `col-sm-4`:

```
<div class="product-item col-sm-4">
```

While this constrains the width of each of our product items and the grid automatically wraps the columns into the row, it has failed to produce an effective grid.

The primary problem here is that our items have varying heights. Thus, when trying to float left, as Bootstrap grid components do, these items bump into one another. This results in a broken, uneven layout, as shown in the following screenshot:

Currently, in a medium, large, or extra-large viewport, product items 4 to 7 refuse to float neatly due to their uneven heights. The problem of your columns don't clear quite right as one is taller than the other can be solved by using an additional div element with a combination of the `clearfix` class and the responsive utility classes. You can read more about the `clearfix` and the responsive utility classes in the `Chapter 1`, *Getting Started with Bootstrap* chapter.

Now, let's fix our layout problem. We should clearfix the layout after each third item. You can do this by adding the following HTML snippet after each third item in the `html/pages/products.html` file:

```
<!-- Add the extra clearfix for only the required viewport -->

<div class="clearfix hidden-sm-down"></div>
```

Then we want our grid to reduce to two products per row for the medium screens, while large and extra-large viewports will have three items per row. To accomplish this, we need to find and replace the classes in each of our product items so that they are as follows:

```
<div class="product-item col-md-6 col-lg-4">
```

These classes will set each product item to half width within extra-small and small viewports, and then transition to one-third width for medium and large viewports.

The preceding change also means that we have to replace and extend our responsive column resets as follows:

1. After each third item the HTML code should look as follows:

```
<!-- Add the extra clearfix for only the required viewport -->
<div class="clearfix hidden-md-down"></div>
```

2. The `hidden-sm-down` class in the preceding code has been replaced with the class `hidden-sm-down`. And then add the following lines of HTML after each second item:

```
<!-- Add the extra clearfix for only the required viewport -->
<div class="clearfix hidden-sm-down hidden-lg-up"></div>
```

3. After the sixth item you will get the following HTML code now:

```
<!-- Add the extra clearfix for only the required viewport -->
<div class="clearfix hidden-md-down"></div>
<!-- Add the extra clearfix for only the required viewport -->
<div class="clearfix hidden-sm-down hidden-lg-up"></div>
```

4. The HTML code after the sixth item above should be replaced with this:

```
<!-- Add the extra clearfix for only the required viewport -->
<div class="clearfix hidden-sm-down">
```

5. Product items will now be laid out in two columns on a medium viewport:

6. Then, our grid will transform to a three-column layout in large and extra-large viewports:

7. Let's adjust the styles of our grid items to enhance their visual presentation. Having done that, we can fix this layout problem.

8. As we'll be writing custom styles, create and have the `sccs/includes/_products-grid.scss` file open in your editor and import it into the main `app.scss` file.

9. Let's write styles to adjust image width, font size, padding, and margins, as shown in the following lines of code:

```
.product-item {
  padding-bottom: ($spacer-y * 2);

  h2 {
    font-size: $font-size-lg;
    line-height: $line-height-lg;
    padding: 0;
    margin-top: ($spacer-y / 7);
    margin-bottom: ($spacer-y / 8);
  }
  p {
    font-size: $font-size-sm;
    line-height: $line-height-sm;
    color: $gray;
  }
}
```

10. These styles will accomplish the following:
    1. Add bottom padding to each product item.
    2. Reduce the `h2` heading font size to the size of our `$font-size-lg`.
    3. Reduce the `p` font size to our `$font-size-sm` value.
    4. Reduce `h2` padding by adding `!important` to override any conflicting rules .that we've written to apply in the standard pages.
    5. Set the `p` font color to `$gray`.

Save these new styles, and run the `bootstrap watch` or `gulp` command. Though the layout will still be broken in places, you should see significant improvement in the styling of the product items, as shown in the following screenshot:

It's a beautiful thing to behold.

Don't forget the Card module

In the preceding section you used Bootstrap Grid to build to the product grid. You can also use Bootstrap's new card module to build the product grid. Cards include header, footers, top and bottom image caps. You've already meet the Card module in *Chapter 4*, *Bootstrappin' a WordPress Theme*, when you created the Masonry grid layout for the WordPress theme.

First, create a new HTML partial called `html/includes/product-grid-cards.html` to rebuild the product grid using the Cards module. The HTML code for each card should look as follows:

```
<div class="card">
  <a href="#"><img data-src="holder.js/300x200?auto=yes"
  alt="sample product" /></a>
  <div class="card-block">
    <h4 class="card-title"><a href="#">Product Title</a></h4>
    <p class="card-text">This text describes the above product a
    little not too much but just enough or maybe a little more</p>
    <a class="btn btn-secondary btn-sm pull-sm-right" href="#">View
    this product <i class="fa fa-arrow-circle-right"></i></a>
  </div>
</div>
```

Bootstrap enables you to organize your cards in Groups or Decks. In this example, you will use decks. Decks contain a set of equal width and height cards that aren't attached to one another. The HTML structure of a Deck of Cards will look as follows:

```
<div class="card-deck-wrapper">
  <div class="card-deck">
    <div class="card product-item">
    ---
    </div>
    <div class="card product-item">
    ---
```

You'll have to wrap each block of three cards into its own card-deck wrapper.

The Card and Deck groups got a single breakpoint at between the extra small and small grid at 576 pixels. Below the breakpoint, the cards will stack. For the small grid between 576 and 768 pixels there are three cards in a row too. This cards are very small, so you'll have to reduce the size of the button for the small grid by using the following SCSS code:

```
.product-item {
  .btn-sm {
    @include media-breakpoint-only(sm) {
        font-size: $font-size-sm * 0.8;
    }
  }
}
```

In the preceding code, we've reduced the size of the button in the small viewport. Now let's add some space between the card for the larger viewports.

In `scss/includes/_product-grid.scss` you can add the following SCSS code to create some space between the cards:

```
@include media-breakpoint-up(sm) {
    .card-deck {
        padding-bottom: ($spacer-y * 2);
    }
}
```

With the Card Deck, your product grid may look like the following screenshot:

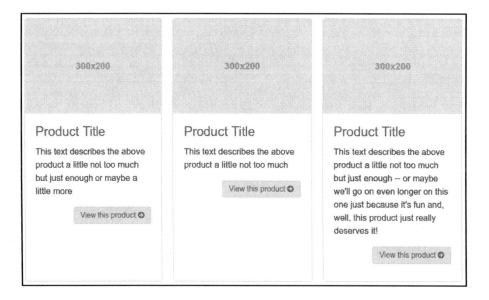

Cards with the CSS3 Flexbox layout module

As already explained in Chapter 1, *Getting Started with Bootstrap*, has Bootstrap option flexbox support built in. You can enable flexbox support by setting the $enable-flex Sass variable to true.

Create a new HTML partial called html/includes/product-grid-cards-flexbox.html to test the flexbox layout. Don't forget to replace the include statement in the html/product.html file as follows:

```
{{> products-grid-cards-flexbox}}
```

In the scss/includes/_variables.scss file, add the following line of SCSS code:

```
// Options
//
// Quickly modify global styling by enabling or disabling optional
features.
$enable-flex:          true;
```

The html/includes/product-grid-cards-flexbox.html file may contain HTML code similar to the HTML code used in the html/includes/product-grid-cards-flexbox.html file. The card-deck-wrapper wrapper is not required when the flexbox support is enabled. You can wrap all Cards into a single card-deck wrapper. The breakpoint is still set at 576 pixels. For viewports wider than the breakpoint the flexbox is responsive by default. The more space there is, the more Cards there are on each row. On large and extra-large viewports there are four cards on each row by default. Use the flex-basis property to get three cards on each row. The flex-basis property specifies the initial length of a flexible item. You can use the following SCSS code to set the flex-basis property:

```
.card-deck .card {
  flex-basis: 30%;
}
```

On a medium grid you will got two cards in each row. The last row has only one card, because of we have an odd number of cards. The last card takes 100% of the available space and will look like that shown in the following screenshot:

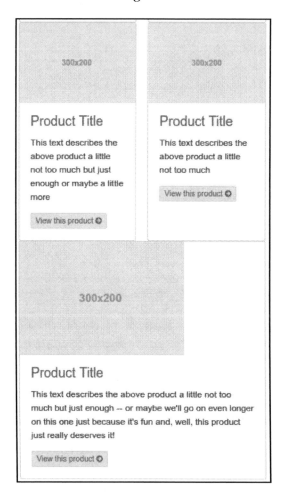

You can try to fix this with Sass by setting the max-width for each card as follows:

```
@include media-breakpoint-up(sm) {
  .card-deck .card {
    max-width: 46%;
  }
}
```

Or alternatively, add an empty card that's only visible on the medium grid by using Bootstrap's responsive utilities classes:

```
<div class="card hidden-xs-down hidden-lg-up">
    <!-- empty card -->
</div>
```

If you've not removed the borders and rounded corners of the cards, you should remove them for the empty card. You can remove the borders and/or rounded corners with Sass. Use the following SCSS code to remove the borders from the empty card:

```
@include media-breakpoint-up(sm) {
  .card-deck .card {
    &:last-child {
      border: initial; // 0
    }
  }
}
```

In the preceding code, :last-child is a CSS pseudo-class. CSS pseudo-classes can be added to selectors that specifies a special state of the element to be selected. The last-child pseudo-class selects any element that is the last child element of its parent. You can read more about the last-child pseudo-class at the following URL:
https://developer.mozilla.org/nl/docs/Web/CSS/:last-child.

Notice that the SCSS code with the & parent reference in front of the last-child pseudo-class compiles into CSS code as follows:

```
.card-deck .card:last-child
border: initial; }
```

You can read more about the & parent reference in Sass in Chapter 3, *Customizing Your Blog with Bootstrap and Sass*.

Now the last cards on the medium grid should look as follows:

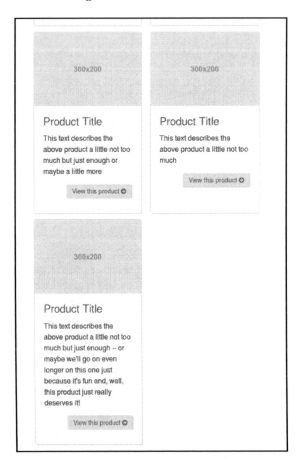

Of course, you can you can also remove just the rounded corners by using the following SCSS code:

```
.card-deck .card {
    border-radius: initial;
}
```

You can read more about the CSS3 flexbox layout module at the following URL: `https://developer.mozilla.org/en-US/docs/Web/CSS/CSS_Flex ible_Box_Layout/Using_CSS_flexible_boxes`. Internet Explorer 9 and earlier do not support flexbox.

Next, we'll style the filtering options sidebar.

Styling the options sidebar

Now, let's style our filtering options. These appear just before the markup for our product items. In small, medium, and large viewports, they appear as a left-hand sidebar.

At the moment, they appear like the following screenshot:

Narrow your selection

Clearance Sale

View clearance items

Categories

- Option 1
- Option 2
- Option 3
- Option 4
- Option 5
- Option 6
- Option 7
- Option 8
- Option 9
- Option 10

For our final design, we want to transform the **Clearance Sale** link into an attractive extra-large button and arrange the filtering options into two columns with checkboxes rather than bullets, as shown in the following screenshot:

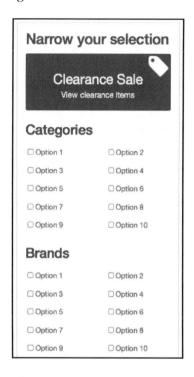

Let's begin by setting up some basic styles to lay a basic groundwork.

Setting up basic styles

We'll start by adjusting fonts, colors, margins, and padding.

Let's add these rules to a new Sass partial called _grid-options.scss:

```
.grid-options {
  @extend .card;
  padding-top: 12px;
  padding-bottom: 24px;
  > h2 {
    margin-top: 0;
    font-size: 1.3 * ($font-size-lg);
    line-height: 1.2;
    color: $gray-dark;
```

```
    }
}
```

The preceding code does the following:

- Adds Bootstrap Card styles to our sidebar (see the relevant Bootstrap documentation at `v4-alpha.getbootstrap.com/components/card/`)
- Adds top and bottom padding to the sidebar so that our new background extends past the sidebar content
- Adjusts font size, line-height, and color for the `h2` heading

Notice that you should not forget to import the `_grid-options.scss` file into your `app.scss` file.

Next, we will style the **Clearance Sale** link.

Styling the Clearance Sale link

We want to transform our **Clearance Sale** link into an extra-large attractive button.

Let's adjust the markup to do the following:

- Turn the linked heading and paragraph into a button.
- Add the custom button `btn-feature` class, which we created in Chapter 6, *Bootstrappin' Business*, to give the button our special featured color—red.
- Add a Font Awesome icon for a sale tag. We'll make it three times the normal size by using Font Awesome's built-in `icon-3x` class.

 For more information about Font Awesome's special sizing classes, see the documentation at `http://fontawesome.io/examples/#larger`.

The resulting HTML markup is as follows:

```html
<a class="btn btn-feature choose-clearance" href="#">
  <span class="icon fa fa-tag fa-3x"></span>
  <h3>Clearance Sale</h3>
  <p>View clearance items</p>
</a>
```

This immediately gives us a good start towards our desired result as shown in the following screenshot:

Now to polish it up, perform the following steps:

1. Display the **Clearance Sale** button as a block-level element by setting the display property to block and center it by extending Bootstrap's `m-x-auto` class. The `m-x-auto` class is part of Bootstrap's Utility classes and centers fixed-width block level content by setting the horizontal margins to auto.
2. Force its width to fill 92.5 percent of its containing column.
3. Add top and bottom padding.
4. Override Bootstrap's `white-space:nowrap` rule for buttons, so that our text can wrap as it should (See Bootstrap's `white-space` rule in `/bootstrap/scss/_buttons.scss`. You can learn more about the `white-space` property at `http://css-tricks.com/almanac/properties/w/whitespace/`.)
5. Position it relatively so that we can apply absolute positioning to the tag icon.
6. Adjust font, color, font-size, and margins on our heading and paragraph.
7. Position the tag icon at the top right.

We can accomplish these goals by adding the following style rules:

```
.choose-clearance {
  @extend .m-x-auto;
  display: block;
  width: 92.5%;
  padding-top: $spacer-y * 2;
  padding-bottom: $spacer-y;
  font-size: 90%;
  white-space: normal;
  position: relative;
  h3 {
    font-weight: normal;
    color: #fff;
```

```
    padding-top: $spacer-y / 2;
    margin: $spacer / 3;
  }
  p {
    margin: $spacer / 3 $spacer * 2;
    line-height: 1.2;
  }
  .icon {
    position: absolute;
    top: 0;
    right: 2px;
  }
}
```

Notice that the background-color of the **Clearance Sale** button is set by the class in the HTML code in the `html/pages/products.html` file. The `btn-feature` class is generated via the `scss/includes/_buttons.scss` partial file with the following SCSS code:

```
.btn-feature {
  @include button-variant($btn-feature-color, $btn-feature-bg,
  $btn-feature-border);
}
```

At the end, this gives us a pleasing result, as is evident from the following screenshot:

As a bonus, these styles work well across viewport sizes. Take a few moments to test it. Then of course, as always, feel free to take what we've begun and beautify it further.

Meanwhile, let's move down to the options for filtering our products.

Styling the options list

In this section, we will transform our lists of product filtering options.

If you take a moment to examine the markup of product filtering options in a store such as Amazon (http://www.amazon.com) or Zappos (http://www.zappos.com), you'll find that they are composed lists of links that have been specially styled to appear like checkboxes. We will style our links to look like checkboxes, which will appear as checked once selected, and we'll adjust them to work nicely across devices, such as tablet and phone devices.

 On e-commerce websites such as Amazon and Zappos, the filter options are connected to a content management system, which dynamically updates the grid of shown products in response to the options selected. Bootstrap is a frontend design framework, and not a content management system. Thus, we will not be dynamically filtering our products as a part of this project. Instead, we will prepare a design that is ready to be used in the context of a complete content management system.

In the coming section, we'll use the HTML code from the `html/pages/products.html` file. The HTML code of an option list may look as follows:

```
<h3>Brands</h3>
  <ul class="options-list options-brands">
    <li><a href="#">Option 1</a></li>
    <li><a href="#">Option 2</a></li>
    <li><a href="#">Option 3</a></li>
    <li><a href="#">Option 4</a></li>
    <li><a href="#">Option 5</a></li>
    <li><a href="#">Option 6</a></li>
    <li><a href="#">Option 7</a></li>
    <li><a href="#">Option 8</a></li>
    <li><a href="#">Option 9</a></li>
    <li><a href="#">Option 10</a></li>
  </ul>
```

Edit your SCSS code in the `scss/includes/_grid-options.scss` partial file. We'll start with the `h3` headings for the lists, adjusting their size, line-height, margin, and color:

```
.grid-options {
  > h3 {
    font-size: $font-size-lg;
    line-height: 1.2;
    margin-top: $spacer-y / 2;
    color: $gray-dark;
  }
}
```

We need to use the >h3 child selector since we don't want these rules to apply to other h3 tags, especially the one within our **Clearance Sale** button.

Now, let's turn our attention to the unordered lists. These have a special class of options-list, which we'll use as our selector to ensure we're targeting only these special lists.

First, let's remove bullets and padding:

```
.options-list {
  list-style-type: none;
  padding-left: 0;
}
```

Now we'll style the links. Shortly, we'll also style the list items, so we'll include them in the sequence of nested selectors.

```
.options-list {
  list-style-type: none;
  padding-left: 0;
  li {
    a {
      @extend .btn;
      @extend .btn-sm;
      padding-left: 0;
      padding-right: 0;
      color: $gray;
      @include hover-focus-active {
        color: $link-color;
      }
    }
  }
}
```

The rules we just set accomplish the following:

- We'll use the power of Sass' extend feature to pull in the fundamental button styles associated with the btn class that includes displaying the inline-block link and the addition of padding.
- Since we added no other button class, there is no background color
- What we gain from these basic button styles is a convenient way to make our links user-friendly click targets-including fingers on touch devices

- We then extend the styles associated with the `btn-sm` class to reduce padding and for the font-size to be a bit smaller than the standard button (for a refresher on Bootstrap button classes, go to `v4-alpha.getbootstrap.com/components/buttons/`)
- We then remove unneeded left and right padding
- We change the color of our link text to `$gray`
- Finally, we set the color of hovered, focused, and active links to our `$link-color` value

You may want to save, compile, and test the results. The following screenshot depicts the result we get:

Categories
Option 1
Option 2
Option 3
Option 4

Our option links have gained improved padding and font size and taken our desired colors.

 You may be wondering why I've chosen to extend the button styles by using the `.btn` and `.btn-sm` classes in our Sass files rather than adding the classes directly to the markup. We could do the latter, but given the number of option links, I think you will agree that it is far more efficient to apply the styles via CSS as we've done. In the section that follows, I will continue this pattern and extend it by bringing in Font Awesome icons via Sass rather than by adding markup.

Now we'll add checkboxes to our option links.

Adding Font Awesome checkboxes to our option links

In this section, we'll use Font Awesome icons to add an empty checkbox to the left of each option link. Rather than adding icons in the markup, we will do it here via Sass as it will be far more efficient. Then we'll push a step further, adding styles to pull in an alternate Font Awesome icon-for a checked checkbox – to the hovered, focused, and active option links.

Adding icons via Sass requires extending Font Awesome styles. First, we will take these fundamental styles from the fa base class, which can be found in the `_core.scss` file in the `bower_components/font-awesome` folder. In this file, you'll find the following key styles:

```
.#{$fa-css-prefix} {
  display: inline-block;
  font: normal normal normal #{$fa-font-size-base}/#{$fa-line-height-base}
  FontAwesome; // shortening font declaration
  font-size: inherit; // can't have font-size inherit on line above,
  so need to override
  text-rendering: auto; // optimizelegibility throws things off #1094
  -webkit-font-smoothing: antialiased;
  -moz-osx-font-smoothing: grayscale;
}
```

In the preceding code we've used the `.#{$fa-css-prefix}` selector, which is based on Sass' variable interpolation. The Sass compiler uses the #{} interpolation syntax to compile variables into selectors and property names. Read more about variable interpolation in Sass at the following URL: `http://sass-lang.com/documentation/file.SASS_REFERENCE.html#interpolation_`

These styles establish the fundamental rules for all Font Awesome icons, including the Font Awesome icon for the font family and then refine the details of its presentation.

For our present purposes, we do not need the selector or the braces but only the rules. We will take these and apply them to our links. Primarily, we'll use the `:before` pseudo-element as it ensures the best results.

For more information about the CSS2.1 `:before` pseudo-element, go to `http://coding.smashingmagazine.com/2011/07/13/learning-to-use-the-before-and-after-pseudo-elements-in-css/`.

So edit the following rules in the `_grid-options.scss` file, nested as follows:

```
.options-list {
  li {
    a {
      &:before {
        @extend .#{$fa-css-prefix};
      }
    }
  }
}
```

These rules establish the fundamentals. Next, we need to specify which Font Awesome icon to use. Browsing the options at `http://fontawesome.io/icons/`, we find the following open checkbox icon:

☐ fa-square-o

The Sass rules for this icon are found in the `_icons.scss` file inside the `font-awesome` folder. By opening that file and searching for the `}-square-o` string (including the closing curly brace before `-square-o` to narrow the results), we can find the following relevant line:

```
.#{$fa-css-prefix}-square-o:before { content: $fa-var-square-o; }
```

From the previous line, we only need `content: $fa-var-square-o`, which we can copy and paste in the `_grid-options.scss` file directly after the preceding rules, which are applied to our `a:before` selector or alternatively extend the `.fa-square-o:before` selector:

```
.options-list {
  li {
    a {
      &:before {
        @extend .#{$fa-css-prefix};
          @extend .#{$fa-css-prefix}-square-o:before;
      }
    }
  }
}
```

Finally, we want to grab Font Awesome styles to give our icons a fixed width and to avoid any shifting when the icon changes to the checked version. These styles are found in the `_fixed-width.scss` file inside the `font-awesome` folder. Extend the `.fa-fw` class as follows:

```
.options-list {
  li {
    a {
      &:before {
        @extend .#{$fa-css-prefix};
        @extend .#{$fa-css-prefix}-square-o:before;
        @extend .#{$fa-css-prefix}-fw;
      }
    }
  }
}
```

After adding these rules, run the bootstrap watch command and inspect the results in your browser. You should see the checkboxes appear as shown in the following screenshot:

Now, following the same approach, we'll add the following selectors and rules to apply the checked version of the Font Awesome icon to the hovered, focused, and active states of our links:

```
.options-list {
  li {
    a {
      &:before {
        @extend .#{$fa-css-prefix};
        @extend .#{$fa-css-prefix}-square-o:before;
        @extend .#{$fa-css-prefix}-fw;
      }
      @include hover-focus-active {
        color: $link-color;
        &:before {
          content: $fa-var-check-square-o;
        }
      }
    }
  }
}
```

Bootstrap's `hover-focus-active` mixin can be found in the `bower_components/bootstrap/scss/mixins/_hover.sccs` partial. You can use this mixin to set the active, hover, and focus states once.

Save the file, and inspect the results in your browser. You'll find that the checked version of the square icon appears when you hover on one of the links, as shown in the following screenshot:

As a reminder, it is not currently possible to force one of these links to stay in the active state as we have no content management system in place. What we do have is a set of styles ready and waiting to go to work in the context of such a content management system.

That's it! We've successfully given our links the appearance of checkboxes to provide desired user feedback.

Next, let's make more efficient use of our space by floating our options side by side.

Using Sass mixins to arrange option links in columns

In the previous section, we used custom Sass rules to accomplish things that might have been accomplished by adding markup. Given the number of option links we need to manage, this has proven significantly more efficient. The same dynamic applies when we want to arrange our option links into columns.

We might accomplish our desired result by using Bootstrap row and column classes, adjusting our markup with the following pattern:

```
<ul class="options-list options-categories row">
    <li class="col-xs-6"><a href="#">Option 1</a></li>
    <li class="col-xs-6"><a href="#">Option 2</a></li>
    ...
```

In Chapter 6, *Bootstrappin' Business*, you saw that the Panini template engine does support loops and iterations. Using loops in your template is also an alternative for DRY coding and preventing duplicate code.

An example can be found in the `html/pages/products.html` file. The code of the first list looks as follows:

```
{{#each numbers-10}}
<li><a href="#">Option {{this}}</a></li>
{{/each}}
```

The numbers-10 variable is read from the file, which contains the number 1 through 10 in YAML format. Using the index of the iteration seem to make more sense, but unfortunately, Panini does not support this feature of Handlebars. See also `https://github.com/zurb/panini/issues/67`.

Thanks to the power of Bootstrap's mixins, we can accomplish the same result with a few lines of Sass, as shown in the following steps:

1. First, we'll apply the `make-row()` mixin to the `options-list` selector, as follows:

```
.options-list {
  @include make-row();
}
```

2. This mixin applies the same styles to our options list that we would have gained by applying the `row` class in the markup. In this case, it's simply more efficient to do it here.

3. Next, we can use a `make-col(6)` mixin and set the number of column to six to apply column rules to our list items as follows:

```
.grid-options {
  @include make-row();
  li {
    @include make-col-ready();
    @include make-col(6);
  }
}
```

4. This will apply the same styles to our list items as would be applied if we had added the `col-xs-6` class to each of the relevant `li` tags. Later on, you will read how to make the columns responsive.

After adding the preceding lines, save the file, compile to CSS, and refresh your browser. You should see the option links line up in two columns:

Not bad!

We will now make some adjustments for smaller viewports.

Adjusting the options list layout for tablets and phones

We need to constrain the width of our options panel so that it does not range too widely in tablet-width devices.

On the medium grid for tablets, between 768 and 992 pixels, neither the **Clearance Sale** button nor the options fit the column, as shown in the following screenshot:

We can fix this issues with the options by using Sass and force the options into a single column again for the medium grid as follows:

```
.grid-options {
  @include make-row();
  li {
    @include make-col-ready();
    @include make-col(6);
    @include media-breakpoint-only(md) {
      @include make-col(12);
    }
  }
}
```

The preceding SCSS code does not fix the **Clearance Sale** button for the medium grid. You may try the reduce the font size to fix it.

Alternatively, you can adopt the main grid the solve the issues on the medium grid. In the `html/pages/products.html` file change the grid classes as shown here:

```
<div class="grid-options col-md-4 col-lg-3">
  ...
</div>
<div class="products-grid col-md-8 col-lg-9">
  ...
</div>
```

The grid-options area will span four columns on the medium grid now. The problems for the medium grid are fixed. Let's take on the small grid.

Right now, our **Clearance Sale** button stretches too wide, and our options list items spread too far apart on viewports between 480 pixels and 768 pixels wide. Thus, they can end up appearing like the following screenshot:

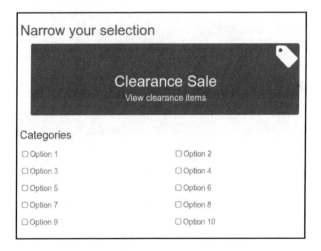

This can be easily fixed by setting a `max-width` property with a value of 480 pixels for the entire options panel:

```
.grid-options {
  max-width: 480px;
}
```

Now let's adjust our option list items so that they organize themselves in three columns in small viewports. Using Sass, we can nest a media query within the appropriate selector and add an adjusted `make-col(4)` mixin, as shown in the following code snippet:

```
.grid-options {
  @include make-row();
  li {
    @include make-col();
    @include make-col(6);
    @include media-breakpoint-down(sm) {
      @include make-col(4);
    }
  }
}
```

After making these adjustments, save the file and test in a narrow viewport. You should see the result shown in the following screenshot:

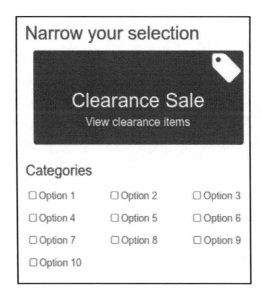

Now let's address the next problem facing our single-column layout: we need to hide our options away until they're needed.

Collapsing the options panel for phone users

At present, our options take up a considerable amount of vertical space. This creates a problem in narrow viewports. The single-column layout winds up pushing our grid of products far down the page.

This is a great deal of vertical space for options that are not needed. The products themselves are priority items. We need to allow users of phones to find the products more quickly while still allowing them to access the filtering options when desired.

We'll use Bootstrap's collapse plugin for this. In the following steps, we'll apply the collapse plugin to the options panel, add a button to expand the panel when desired, and restrict the behavior to narrow viewports only:

1. Open your editor with `products.html`.

2. Add a new `div` tag to wrap our **Clearance Sale** button and three options lists. We need to give this new `div` a special class of collapse as well as a distinctive ID so that we can target it with our JavaScript plugin. For good measure, we'll give it a matching special class as well:

   ```
   <h2>Narrow your selection</h2>
   <div id="options-panel" class="options-panel collapse">
   . . .
   </div>
   ```

3. Notice that the `collapse` class in the previous step hides the content for all viewports. You can add the `navbar-toggleable-sm` class to ensure the content is always visible on larger viewports:

   ```
   <h2>Narrow your selection</h2>
   <div id="options-panel" class="options-panel collapse
   navbar-toggleable-sm">
   . . .
   </div>
   ```

Bootstrap's collapse JavaScript plugin is what powers the collapsible responsive navbar. It may also be put to other uses, such as the one shown in the Bootstrap documentation at `v4-alpha.getbootstrap.com/components/collapse/`.

4. Save the file and refresh it in your browser. You should see that the **Clearance Sale** button and options lists will now be hidden from view. All that remains of the options panel content will be the h2 heading **Narrow your selection**, as shown in the following screenshot:

5. Now we need a toggle button to expand our filter options when clicked.
6. Within the still visible h2 heading that reads **Narrow your selection**, add a button element with the following attribute structure:

```
<h2 class="clearfix">Narrow your selection
  <button type="button"
    class="options-panel-toggle btn btn-primary pull-right hidden-md-up"
    data-toggle="collapse" data-target="#options-panel">
    <span class="icon fa fa-cog fa-2x"></span>
  </button>
</h2>
```

7. The following points explain what the preceding markup will do:
   1. The clearfix class will ensure that the h2 heading will contain the toggle button, which will float to the right due to the pull-right class.
   2. The btn and btn-primary classes will style our new button element with the Bootstrap's btn styles, which includes our background color of $brand-primary
   3. The hidden-md-up class hides the button on larger viewports.
   4. Within the button element, we've placed a Font Awesome icon using the fa-2x class to double its size.
   5. Save this and find the following result in your browser:

8. In narrow viewports, the options list is collapsed and the toggle button is visible:

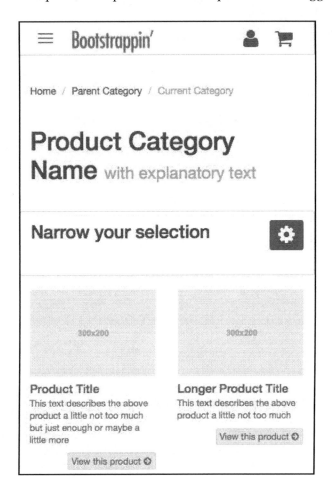

9. In small, medium, and large viewports, the toggle button is hidden, and the options list is visible:

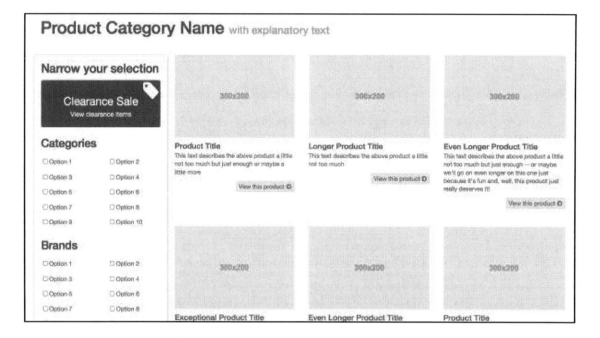

Adding a search form to your designing

In the preceding sections we've build a navigation structure. About fifty percent of your visitors will use this navigation, the other half will prefer to search your content. So a good ability to search the content and your products must always be represented on your pages.

We can add a search form in the header of our page, which should look as follows:

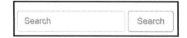

Edit the following HTML code in the `html/includes/header.html` file:

```
<div class="utility-nav">
   <ul>
     <li><a href="#" ><i class="icon fa fa-user
     fa-lg"></i><span> Log In or Register</span></a></li>
     <li><a href="#" ><i class="icon fa fa-shopping-cart
```

```
       fa-lg"></i><span> View Cart</span></a></li>
     </ul>
  </div>
  <form class="search-form form-inline pull-md-right">
    <input class="form-control" type="text" placeholder="Search">
    <button class="btn btn-outline-success hidden-sm-down"
    type="submit">Search</button>
  </form>
  </div>
```

The following points explain what the preceding markup will do:

- The form-inline and form-control classes are Bootstrap classes for inline forms. You can read more about Bootstrap's inline forms at the following URL: v4-alpha.getbootstrap.com/components/forms/#inline-forms.
- The pull-md-right class will ensure that the form float on the right side of the header for
- The hidden-sm-down class hides the search button on the small viewports; only the search input is visible in these viewports.

The preceding code overlaps the icons; you can fix this by setting a padding-top using the following SCSS code in the scss/includes/_header.scss Sass partial:

```
header[role="banner"] {
  .search-form {
    @include media-breakpoint-up(md) {
      padding-top: $spacer-y * 6;
    }
  }
}
```

The media-breakpoint-up(md) mixin call ensures that the padding is only added for medium and larger viewports.

Using the Typeahead plugin

Adding an autocomplete function to your search form may improve the usability of search function. The typeahead plugin from Bootstrap 2 can be used to build an autocomplete function. More information about this plugin can be found at the following URL: https://github.com/bassjobsen/Bootstrap-3-Typeahead. The plugin is ready to use with Bootstrap 4.

The following steps describe how to integrate the Typeahead plugin in your project:

- First, add the plugin to your bower project dependencies to the bower.json file of your project, as follows:

```
"dependencies": {
 "bootstrap": "4",
 "tether": "^1.1.2",
 "font-awesome": "^4.6.1",
 "bootstrap3-typeahead": "git://github.com/bassjobsen/Bootstrap-3-
 Typeahead.git#master"
}
```

- Then run the `bootstrap update` or `bower update` command in your console.
- Then edit the `compile-js` task in Gruntfile.js to ensure that the plugin is included in your project:

```
gulp.task('compile-js', function() {
  return gulp.src([
        bowerpath+ 'jquery/dist/jquery.min.js',
        bowerpath+ 'tether/dist/js/tether.min.js',
        bowerpath+ 'bootstrap/dist/js/bootstrap.min.js',
        bowerpath+ 'holderjs/holder.min.js', // Holder.js for project
        development only
        bowerpath+ 'bootstrap3-typeahead/bootstrap3-typeahead.min.js',
        'js/main.js'])
    .pipe(concat('app.js'))
    .pipe(gulp.dest('./_site/js/'));
});
```

- Then initiate the plugin and attached it to the search form. Open the `js/main.js` and edit the following JavaScript code into it:

```
$('.search-form .form-control').typeahead( { items: 4, source:
["Alabama","Alaska","Arizona","Arkansas","California","Colorado","Connectic
ut","Delaware","Florida","Georgia","Hawaii","Idaho","Illinois","Indiana","I
owa","Kansas","Kentucky","Louisiana","Maine","Maryland","Massachusetts","Mi
chigan","Minnesota","Mississippi","Missouri","Montana","Nebraska","Nevada",
"New Hampshire","New Jersey","New Mexico","New York","North Dakota","North
Carolina","Ohio","Oklahoma","Oregon","Pennsylvania","Rhode Island","South
Carolina","South
Dakota","Tennessee","Texas","Utah","Vermont","Virginia","Washington","West
Virginia","Wisconsin","Wyoming"] });
```

- And lastly, set the CSS z-index value of the suggestions menu to prevent the navbar overlapping it. You can set the `scss/includes/_header.scss` partial by using the following SCSS code:

```
header[role="banner"] {
  .search-form {
    @include media-breakpoint-up(md) {
      padding-top: $spacer-y * 6;
    }
    .typeahead.dropdown-menu {
      z-index: 2000;
    }
  }
}
```

Now your search form with autocomplete is ready. Run the Bootstrap watch command and expect the result in your browser. Type the capital A in the search form and you will find that a drop-down list with suggestions appears:

The Bootstrap team dropped the typeahead plugin in version 3 in favor of using `typeahead.js`; see `https://github.com/twitter/typeahead.js`. To use `typeahead.js` with Bootstrap 4, some additional CSS code is required. The required CSS code, include the generation SCSS code, can be found at the following URL: `https://github.com/bassjobsen/typeahead.js-bootstrap4-css/`.

Congratulations! With the search form, we have accomplished our design.

Summary

In this chapter, we have employed Bootstrap styles to quickly set up breadcrumbs, a page title, and pagination customized according to our needs. Then we created a visually pleasing grid of product items, all of the same height so as to ensure a regular grid by using Bootstrap's mobile first and responsive grid styles.

We finished our design by adding a complex **Clearance Sale** button with a `$brand-feature` red background color and a list of filter options that are easily clickable. We also used Bootstrap column classes with responsive adjustments to arrange our options list items optimally for multiple viewport widths.

At the end, we also added a search form with an autocomplete function.

Congratulations! We now have an attractive business website with a well-crafted e-commerce section.

Next, let's take our skills another step forward by rebuilding our project with Angular 2.

8

Bootstrappin' a One-Page Marketing Website

We've developed some significant skills with Bootstrap. Now it's time to bring an extra touch of beauty and creativity to helping our clients achieve their full online marketing potential. So, let's create a beautiful, one-page, upscale marketing site.

We'll cover the following topics in this chapter:

- A large introductory carousel with a customized responsive welcome message
- A section for customer reviews with images and captions laid out in the masonry format
- A features list with large Font Awesome icons
- A signup section with custom-designed pricing tables
- A ScrollSpy navbar with animated scrolling behavior

Overview

We've been approached by a new prospective client. She is stricken by the beauty of one-pagers websites that scroll vertically, providing a visually stimulating presentation of a product or message with a clear call to action at the end. She wants one of these.

This client is knowledgeable and discerning. She frequents `http://onepagelove.com` and has a list of her current favorites to hand. Her desired features include:

- A clean, modern, aesthetic website.
- An introductory welcome message with a visually intriguing background image.

- An efficient presentation of the main features of her product, accentuated with visually appealing icons.
- Customer testimony presented in a visually stimulating way.
- An easy-to-understand overview of three basic packages that a customer can choose from. These need to be presented clearly in a way that makes it easy to choose the right fit and then sign up!
- Conversions! Everything should draw the user down the page, making it nearly impossible to avoid clicking on the Signup button at the end.

To protect the secrecy of her upcoming product launch, our client has chosen not to reveal the exact nature of her product or service to us. Rather, she has provided mock-ups of the design she would like us to create by using a dummy copy for placeholders.

The first section will open with an interesting full-width image, a large welcome message, and an invitation to scroll down the page to learn more, as shown in the following screenshot:

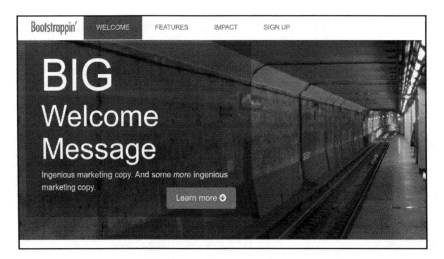

The second section will list six key features of the product, which are laid out in a three-column grid, and illustrated by appropriate icons as shown in the following screenshot:

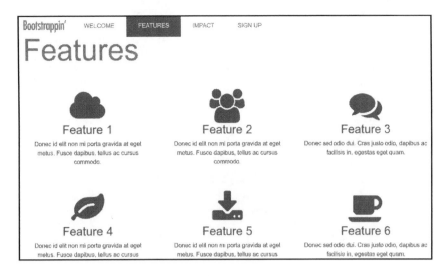

The third section will feature client testimonies with photos and quotations laid out in the masonry style:

The fourth and final section will feature three available plans, each with a pricing table, and will have a visual emphasis on the center of the three tables, as shown in the following screenshot:

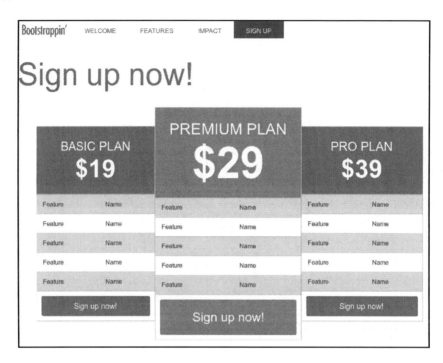

Savvy client that she is, she further demands that the design adapt beautifully to tablets and phones.

A great plan. No problem. Let's get to work.

Surveying the starter files

Let's survey the initial files for this exercise. Create a new project by using Bootstrap CLI, as already described in Chapter 1, *Getting Started with Bootstrap*.

You can install Bootstrap CLI by running the following command in your console:

```
npm install -g bootstrap-cli
```

Then you can set up your project by running the following command:

```
bootstrap new
```

Again, choose the **An empty new Bootstrap project. Powered by Panini, Sass and Gulp** option when prompted.

You'll see files similar to the template we set up in Chapter 1, *Getting Started with Bootstrap*:

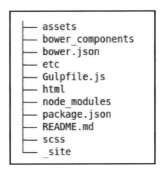

There are a few additions you will have to make now:

1. Create a new assets/images folder.
2. Copy the files in the images folder to the new assets/images folder. It contains five images:
   1. One logo image, named logo.png.
   2. Two background images for the intro section.
   3. Seven images of happy people for the **Impact** section.
3. The images are automatically copied to the _site folder by the copy task in the Gulpfile.js file:

```
// Copy assets
gulp.task('copy', function() {
  gulp.src(['assets/**/*']).pipe(gulp.dest('_site'));
});
```

The html folder, which contains your Panini HTML templates, should have the file and folder structure shown as follows:

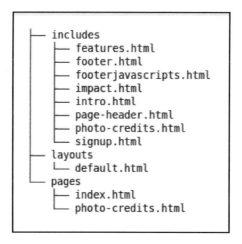

```
├── includes
│       ├── features.html
│       ├── footer.html
│       ├── footerjavascripts.html
│       ├── impact.html
│       ├── intro.html
│       ├── page-header.html
│       ├── photo-credits.html
│       └── signup.html
├── layouts
│       └── default.html
└── pages
        ├── index.html
        └── photo-credits.html
```

You can read more about Panini at https://github.com/zurb/panini.

Instead of the modifications described above, you can also start with the files found in the chapter8/start folder. In this folder, run the npm install and bower install commands first. After running the npm and bower commands, you can run the bootstrap watch or gulp command to view the results in your browser.

Viewing the page content

Run the bootstrap watch command and watch the page in your browser at http://localhost:8080/. You'll see the following major components in place. Each component got its own HTML partial. Of course, at present, they will be displayed with default Bootstrap styles, awaiting the customization that needs to be done:

- A fixed top navbar
- A jumbotron with a big welcome message
- A features section with icons, headings, and text organized in three columns
- The **Impact** section with photos of six happy customers and placeholder content for their positive testimony
- A **Sign up now!** section with three tables laying out the **Basic Plan**, **Premium Plan**, and **Pro Plan** packages, with a **Sign up now!** button under each
- A footer logo

- Photo credits (images are attribution-licensed)

To view the markup, open the corresponding Panini HTML partial in your editor. We will get very familiar with the markup in the steps that follow!

Adding Font Awesome to our project

Font Awesome gives you scalable vector **icons** that can instantly be customized: size, color, drop shadow, and anything that can be done with the power of CSS. In Chapter 5, *Bootstrappin' Your Portfolio,* you can read how to compile Font Awesome's CSS code into your local CSS by using Sass.

Here, we simply load Font Awesome's CSS code from CDN by linking it in the html/layouts/default.html HTML template as follows:

```
<link rel="stylesheet"
href="https://maxcdn.bootstrapcdn.com/font-awesome/4.6.1/css/font-awesome.m
in.css">
```

Adjusting the navbar

This design calls for a fixed top navbar with a significant color shift for hovered and active links. I've already applied some of these styles by setting appropriate variables. Let me point those out, and then we'll move on to make some necessary adjustments to the markup.

The scss/_variables.scss file is based on Bootstrap's variables.scss file. I've customized the shades of gray in line with previous projects. You'll see these in the topmost section of the file.

I've further adjusted the following navbar variables, adjusting its height, margin, colors, and hover colors specifically for this design:

```
// Navbar
$navbar-bg:                      #fff;

// Navbar links
$navbar-link-color:              $gray;
$navbar-link-bg:                 #fff;
$navbar-link-hover-color:        #fff;
$navbar-link-hover-bg:           $gray;
$navbar-link-active-color:       #fff;
```

```
$navbar-link-active-bg:           $gray-dark;
```

We'll use the responsive navbar variant as already described in `Chapter 1`, *Getting Started with Bootstrap*. The HTML code for the navbar can be found in the `html/includes/page-header.html` file and looks like the following:

```html
<nav class="navbar navbar-fixed-top">
  <div class="container">
  <button class="navbar-toggler hidden-sm-up" type="button" data-
toggle="collapse" data-target="#exCollapsingNavbar2" aria-
controls="exCollapsingNavbar2" aria-expanded="false" aria-label="Toggle
navigation">
      ≡
  </button>
  <div class="collapse navbar-toggleable-xs" id="exCollapsingNavbar2">
    <a class="navbar-brand" href="index.html"><img
src="{{root}}images/logo.png" alt="Bootstrappin'"></a>
    <ul class="nav navbar-nav">
      <li class="nav-item active">
        <a class="nav-link" href="#">Welcome <span class="sr-
only">(current)</span></a>
      </li>
      <li class="nav-item">
        <a class="nav-link" href="#">Features</a>
      </li>
      <li class="nav-item">
        <a class="nav-link" href="#">Impact</a>
      </li>
      <li class="nav-item">
        <a class="nav-link" href="#">Sign up</a>
      </li>
    </ul>
  </div>
  </div>
</nav>
```

As you can see in the preceding code, the navbar also gets the `navbar-fixed-top` class, which fixes the navbar to the top of our page. The `navbar-fixed-top` class also sets the `border-radius property` to 0. The `navbar-fixed-top` class is one of Bootstrap's navbar classes determining the placement of the navbar; classes are available for static or fixed navbars.

Along with the custom variables, I've made a few adjustments to the `_navbar.scss` file.

I've customized the list items in the expanded navbar, adding padding, removing the spacing between the links, and transforming the text to uppercase:

```
.navbar {
  background-color: $navbar-bg;
  color: $navbar-link-color;
  padding: 0 1rem;

  .nav-item + .nav-item {
    margin-left: 0;
  }
  .nav-link, .navbar-brand {
    padding: $spacer-y * .75 $spacer-x * 2;
  }
}
.navbar-brand img {
  width: $brand-image-width;
}
.nav-link {
  color: $navbar-link-color;
  line-height: $brand-image-height;
  text-transform: uppercase;
  .active & {
    background-color: $navbar-link-active-bg;
    color: $navbar-link-active-color;
  }
  @include hover {
    background-color: $navbar-link-hover-bg;
    color: $navbar-link-hover-color;
  }
}
```

 Bootstrap's predefined CSS classes also contain some classes for text transformations. More information about these text capitalization classes can be found at the following URL: http://getbootstrap.com/componen ts/utilities/#text-transform.

The original logo image file had these settings: width 900 pixels and height 259 pixels. We can use these values to calculate the height in Sass when we resize its width to 120 pixels as follows:

```
$brand-image-width: 120px;
$brand-image-height: (259 * $brand-image-width / 900);
```

I use the $brand-image-height variable to set the line-height of the navbar links to ensure that the brand image and links are in line.

Now the total height of the navbar becomes `$brand-image-height + 2 * ($spacer-y * 0.75)`. We'll use this value to set the `padding-top` of the HTML body element, because the fixed navbar will overlap the body.

The `$brand-image-height` variable got pixel units, whilst the `$spacer-y` got rem units. Sass can't add up these values with different dimensions. You can remove the rem units by dividing with 1rem. Now the unitless value times `$font-size-root` will give you the value in pixels.

First, create a new `_page-contents.scss` in the main `scss/includes` folder.

Import it into `main.scss` just as shown in the following line:

```
@import "_page-contents";
```

Then calculating the padding-top value for the HTML body element in scss/app.scss will look like this:

```
body {
  padding-top: (2 * ($spacer-y * .75) / 1rem * $font-size-root) + $brand-image-height;
}
```

When combined, the adjusted variables and navbar customizations yield these visual results:

Let's move on to the jumbotron with its big welcome message.

Customizing the jumbotron

The jumbotron is a Bootstrap component highlighting the key message of your website. More information about the jumbotron and its HTML markup can be found at the following URL: `http://v4-alpha.getbootstrap.com/components/jumbotron/`.

In this section, we'll customize the jumbotron to display our client's big welcome message with stylistic touches in line with her mockup. This will include adding a large background image, enlarging the welcome message text, and then adjusting its presentation for multiple viewports.

In `index.html`, find the following markup:

```
<!-- INTRO SECTION -->
<section class="jumbotron" id="welcome">
  <div class="container">
  <h1 class="display-3"><strong>Big</strong> Welcome Message</h1>
  <p class="lead">
    Ingenious marketing copy. And some <em>more</em> ingenious
marketing copy.<a href="#features" class="btn btn-lg btn-primary pull-xs-
right">Learn more <span class="icon fa fa-arrow-circle-down"></span></a>
  </p>
  </div>
</section>
```

Let's start by expanding the height of our jumbotron and putting our desired background image in place:

1. Open a new custom `Sass partial` file, `scss/includes/_jumbotron.scss`, in your editor. Don't forget to import it in the `scss/app.scss` file too.

2. Now, let's set the height, background color, and font color for the `#welcome` section. While we're at it, we'll add some top margin to the button:

```
.jumbotron {
  height: 300px;
  background-color: $jumbotron-bg;
  color: $jumbotron-color;
  .btn {
    margin-top: $spacer-y;
  }
}
```

3. The background and font color of the jumbotron are set in the `scss/includes/_variable.scss` file as follows:

```
// Jumbotron
$jumbotron-bg: #191919;
$jumbotron-color: contrast($jumbotron-bg);
```

4. The `contrast()` Sass function can be found in the `scss/functions_contrast.scss` file. The `contrast()` function uses the built-in lightness function of Sass to return a light (white) or dark (black) color depending on the lightness of the input color.

Using color contrasts in your design may improve the accessibility of your projects. When your font colors depend on the background color and change automatically when you change the base colors of your design, the changes do not influence readability and accessibility. In this chapter, we'll use a simple contrast() function. Sass libraries such as Compass have their own contrast function.

Also read *Design Accessibly, See Differently: Color Contrast Tips And Tools by Cathy O' Connor* at the following URL: https://www.smashingmagazine.com/2014/10/color-contrast-tips-and-tools-for-accessibility/.

5. Next, let's use a media query to place our background image for large screens and up (991px, according to the current default Bootstrap media query breakpoint values).

6. If you like, take a few minutes to open and read the documentation about Bootstrap's responsive breakpoints again. The information can be found at the following URL: getbootstrap.com/layout/overview/#responsive-breakpoints. All media queries are available via Sass mixins.

7. We can use the power of Sass to nest a media query within the context of the jumbotron selector. Within this media query, we'll specify the subway-906x600.jpg image for the background. This image is scaled to be large enough for this breakpoint while still loading relatively quickly:

```
.jumbotron {
  @include media-breakpoint-down(md) {
    background: url('#{$images-path}subway-906x600.jpg') center center no-repeat;
  }
}
```

Remember that the preceding SCSS code compiles into CSS code as follows:

```
@media (max-width: 991px) {
.jumbotron {
background: url("../images/subway-906x600.jpg") center center no-repeat;
}
}
```

8. Save the file, run the `bootstrap watch` command, and inspect the results in your browser. You should see the new background image appear – but only within a window width of `991px` or less.

9. Next, let's expand the height of the jumbotron for tablet-sized viewports. We'll write a media query only the medium grid, which increases the `jumbotron` element's height to `480px` within this breakpoint:

```
@include media-breakpoint-only(md) {
  height: 480px;
}
```

10. Save the file, run the `bootstrap watch` command, and watch the results in your browser. You should see the jumbotron grow to `480px` in height for viewports between 768 px and `991px` in width.

11. Now, for medium and larger (greater than 992px in width) viewports, we'll increase the height of the jumbotron to 540px. At this width, we'll use the larger version of the `subway-1600x1060.jpg` background image. While we're at it, we'll set the background size to `cover`:

```
@include media-breakpoint-up(lg) {
   height: 540px;
   background: #191919 url('#{$images-path}subway-1600x1060.jpg') center
center no-repeat;
   background-size: cover;
}
```

12. With these style rules in place, large viewports will have a 1600px-wide background image.

13. Save the file, and test it in your browser. You should find that we have our major breakpoints nicely covered.

After these steps, the Jumbotron should look as shown in the following screenshot:

Notice that we've set a max-width for the small background image by using the `@include media-breakpoint-down(md)` mixin call. The preceding may break the mobile-first approach of Bootstrap. Media queries can be used to conditional-load background images based on screen size and so reduce load time and bandwidth on mobile phones and tablets. Read Media Query & Asset Downloading Results by Tim Kadlec for more information about testing a browser's file requests and media queries. You can find the test result at the following URL: `https://timkadlec.com/2012/04/media-query-asset-downloading-results/`.

Next, we can style our big marketing message for maximum impact.

Refining the jumbotron message design

Our client wants the welcome message in the jumbotron to be extra big. Bootstrap's display-3 styles in the jumbotron increase the font size by 350 % globally. We want to enhance the results further. We also want to constrain the width of the message on wide screens and put a dark translucent box behind it.

In our current results, we should reduce the font size for small and extra-small screens. We can, however, improve the contrast of our text by placing a translucent dark overlay behind the text. Let's do that here by performing the following steps:

1. In `index.html`, add a new `div` tag inside the jumbotron `container` class and above the `h1` heading and paragraph. Give this new `div` tag a class of `welcome-message`:

```
<section class="jumbotron">
  <div class="container">
    <div class="welcome-message">
      <h1 class="display-3"><strong>Big</strong> Welcome Message</h1>
      <p class="lead">
        Ingenious marketing copy. And some <em>more</em> ingenious
marketing copy.<a href="#features" class="btn btn-lg btn-primary pull-
right">Learn more <span class="icon fa fa-arrow-circle-down"></span></a>
      </p>
    </div>
  </div>
</section>
```

2. Now, to create some styles for this new div, in the `scss/includes/_jumbotron.sccs` file we will perform the following steps:

- Give it a translucent dark background using HSLA
- Stretch it to fill the full width and height of our jumbotron by positioning it as `absolute` and setting its top, bottom, left, and right values to `0`
- Position the jumbotron itself as `relative` using the `container` selector inside the jumbotron so that it will anchor our absolute-positioned welcome message
- Add internal padding to the welcome message
- Use the provided `strong` tag to transform the word **Big** to uppercase and increase its font size:

```
.jumbotron {    .container {      position: relative;      height: 100%;
.welcome-message {        background-color: hsla(0,0,1%,0.4); // translucent
overlay        position: absolute;        top: 0;        left: 0;        right:
0;        @include media-breakpoint-up(lg) {        right: 50%;        }
bottom: auto;        padding: 20px 40px;        strong {        font-size:
1.5em;        text-transform: uppercase;        }        @include media-
breakpoint-down(sm) {        .display-3 {        font-size: 1.5em;
}        }        }   }}
```

3. Save the file, run the bootstrap watch command, and inspect the results in your browser. You should see the background darken and the text stand out more clearly against it, as shown in the following screenshot:

4. Finally, let's address the medium and large viewports. We'll constrain the width a bit more. This can all be done under with Sass media query mixins again:

```
.jumbotron {
  .container {
    .welcome-message {
     right: 0;
      @include media-breakpoint-up(lg) {
        right: 50%;
      }
    }
  }
}
```

5. Again, save the file, and take a look in your browser. You should see the following result in a large viewport:

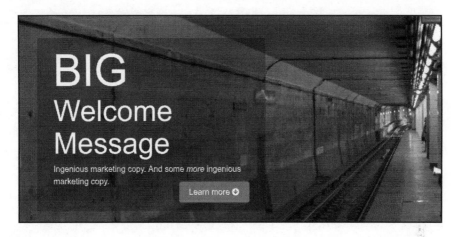

Mission accomplished!

Our customized jumbotron is finished, providing the large welcome message our client has asked for, including the ability to adapt to tablet- and phone-sized viewports, which we've accomplished efficiently with a mobile-first approach.

Now we're ready to move on to the features list.

Beautifying the features list

We need to enlarge the icons, align the text at the center, and iron out the grid layout. Let's review the markup structure for the features list:

```
<section id="features">
  <div class="container">
    <h1>Features</h1>
    <div class="row">
      <div class="features-item col-md-4">
        <span class="icon fa fa-cloud"></span>
        <h2>Feature 1</h2>
        <p>Donec id elit non mi porta gravida at eget metus. Fusce
dapibus, tellus ac cursus commodo. </p>
      </div>
  ...
```

Each feature with its icon, heading, and paragraph is wrapped in a `div` tag with two classes: `features-item` and `col-md-4`.

With this in mind, let's write the styles we need:

1. Create `scss/includes/_features.scss`, a new Sass partial, and do not forget to import it in the scss/app.scss file:

   ```
   @import "includes/navbar";
   @import "includes/jumbotron";
   @import "includes/features";
   ```

2. With `scss/includes/_features.scss` opened in your editor, add a new section with a comment for our `#features` section:

   ```
   // Features Section
   #features {

   }
   ```

3. Now let's focus on the `.features-item` section by aligning the text at the center, adding padding, providing a set height to keep the floating items from interfering with each other, and increasing the `.icon` font size to 90px:

   ```
   #features {
     .features-item {
       text-align: center;
       padding: 20px;
       height: 270px;
       .icon {
         font-size: 90px;
       }
     }
   }
   ```

4. Save the file, and test the results in your browser. Run the `bootstrap watch` command first, if you haven't already done so. You should see the following result in a medium viewport:

Feature 1

Donec id elit non mi porta gravida at eget metus. Fusce dapibus, tellus ac cursus commodo.

Feature 2

Donec id elit non mi porta gravida at eget metus. Fusce dapibus, tellus ac cursus commodo.

Feature 3

Donec sed odio dui. Cras justo odio, dapibus ac facilisis in, egestas eget quam.

Feature 4

Donec id elit non mi porta gravida at eget metus. Fusce dapibus, tellus ac cursus commodo.

Feature 5

Donec id elit non mi porta gravida at eget metus. Fusce dapibus, tellus ac cursus commodo.

Feature 6

Donec sed odio dui. Cras justo odio, dapibus ac facilisis in, egestas eget quam.

5. That's a great start! Now let's adapt our features section for small screens. Currently, our `.features-item` section includes a class of `col-md-4`. We can shift our small-screen layout to two columns, as shown in the following screenshot, by adding a class of `col-sm-6`:

Feature 1

Donec id elit non mi porta gravida at eget metus. Fusce dapibus, tellus ac cursus commodo.

Feature 2

Donec id elit non mi porta gravida at eget metus. Fusce dapibus, tellus ac cursus commodo.

Feature 3

Donec sed odio dui. Cras justo odio, dapibus ac facilisis in, egestas eget quam.

Feature 4

Donec id elit non mi porta gravida at eget metus. Fusce dapibus, tellus ac cursus commodo.

6. And then, of course, they'll arrange themselves in a single column for extra-small screens.

7. Unfortunately, at the upper range of extra-small screens, 500px to 767px, the full-width layout allows the descriptive text to range too wide.

8. We can fix this by adding a media query within which we set a maximum width on the .features-item section and center the content by setting the horizontal margins to auto:

```
// Features Section
#features {
   @include media-breakpoint-only(xs) {
    margin: 0 auto;
    max-width: 320px;
    }
  }
}
```

9. Bootstrap also includes a m-x-auto class for horizontally centering fixed-width block level content. The m-x-auto class replaces the center-block class and mixin from Bootstrap 3.

10. With these lines in place, our .features-item elements retain their desired dimensions across all viewports! On small viewports, our features will look like this:

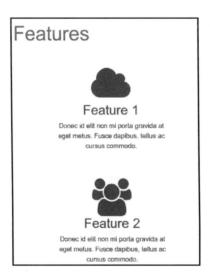

11. At this point, we have satisfied our client's demands for this section of her website! We're ready to move on to the customer reviews.

Tackling customer reviews

Our next section, named **Impact**, presents reviews from happy customers. In this section, we see smiling faces of happy customers with excerpts from their commentary about our client's product.

We'll use the Card module for this section again. As already described in Chapter 4, *Bootstrappin' a WordPress Theme*, the Card module is a flexible and extensible content container which replaces the panels, thumbnails, and wells used in earlier versions of Bootstrap.

Another application of the Card module can be found in Chapter 7, *Bootstrappin' E-commerce*.

In Chapter 4, *Bootstrappin' a WordPress Theme*, you used the Card module to create the masonry grid layout. A masonry grid layout works by placing elements in optimal position based on available vertical space, sort of like a mason fitting stones in a wall. You'll create a Masonry grid layout for the Impact section again. The Bootstrap masonry solution uses CSS only. If you need a JavaScript solution which works in older browsers too, you can use a JavaScript masonry plugin available at http://masonry.desandro.com.

The Card columns use the CSS multi-column layout; you can read more about it at the following URL: https://developer.mozilla.org/en-US/docs/Web/CSS/CSS_Columns/Using_multi-column_layouts.

The masonry grid layout is not available in IE9 and below as they have no support for the column-* CSS properties.

So the initial markup starts as follows:

```
<!-- IMPACT SECTION -->
  <section id="impact">
  <div class="container">
      <h1>Impact</h1>
  <div class="reviews card-columns">
```

Each review is marked up as follows using the hreview microformat:

Microformats are an extension of HTML to mark up things such as people, organizations, products, and reviews. Sites using microformats publish a standard API, which can be consumed by search engines, browsers, and other tools. **h-review** is a simple, open format for publishing reviews on the Web. More information can be found at the following URL: http://microformats.org/.

```
            <div class="hreview review-item-1 card">
               <img class="card-img img-fluid" src="{{root}}images/smiling1-
by-RomainGuy-600x900.jpg" alt="Customer Photo1">
               <div class="caption card-img-overlay">
                  <blockquote class="description card-img-overlayquote">
                     <p>Lorem ipsum dolor sit amet, consectetur adipiscing
elit. Proin euismod, nulla pretium commodo ultricies</p>
                     <footer>Smiling Customer1</footer>
                  </blockquote>
               </div>
            </div>
```

Each card image gets the `img-fluid` class to make the image responsive and fit the cards.

The class turns an image into a card background and overlays the card's text by setting the position property of the image to absolute and the card's position property to relative.

Each card (having the card class) will be automatically arranged in the grid due to the card-columns class of the selector.

The card-columns class creates CSS columns for the small grid and up by default. On the extra-small grid, the grid item will stack. Use the following SCSS code in the scss/includes/_impact.scss file for two columns on the small grid:

```
.card-columns {
  column-gap: $card-columns-sm-up-column-gap;
  @include media-breakpoint-up(sm) {
    column-count: 2;
  }
  @include media-breakpoint-up(md) {
    column-count: 3;
  }
  > .card {
    // see:
https://github.com/twbs/bootstrap/pull/18255#issuecomment-237034763
    display: block;
  }
}
```

You may read about the `hreview` microformat at http://microformats.org/wiki/hrevie
w-examples.

Save your modifications and run the `bootstrap watch` command. You'll find that the Impact section should now look like the following screenshot:

Both in terms of semantics and presentational starting points, we're off to a good start.

Because we wanted to arrive at a masonry layout, our images are a mixture of portrait and landscape aspect ratios. We've made them all of equal width in order to provide enough room for bright faces and textual overlays with short laudatory statements.

Before addressing the layout for larger viewports, let's start by tackling captions.

Positioning and styling captions

Let's begin by positioning our captions as overlays on top of their respective customer photos:

1. While editing the `scss/includes/_impact.scss` file, add a new comment and selector for the `#impact` section:

   ```
   // Impact Section
   #impact {
   }
   ```

2. Now, we can work on the captions. We'll add a translucent background and position them as `absolute` at the bottom of each image:

   ```
   .hreview {
     .caption {
       position: absolute;
        top: auto;
        left: 10px;
        right: 10px;
       bottom: 0;
       line-height: 1.1;
       background: hsla(0,0,10%,0.55);
     }
   ```

3. Now we can focus on the review text and specify the margin, border, font family, font size, and color:

   ```
   blockquote {
     margin-top: 4px;
     border: none;
      font-family: @font-family-serif;
      font-size: @font-size-large;
        color: #fff;
   }
   ```

4. Next, specify styles for the reviewer's name, which appears below the review text:

   ```
   .reviewer {
      margin-top: 2px;
      margin-bottom: 4px;
      text-align: right;
     color: $gray-lighter;
   }
   ```

5. Save the file, run the `bootstrap watch` command, and check your progress.

6. You should end up with an **Impact** section like that shown in the following screenshot:

Not bad! However, we can do it one step better.

Refining the caption position

Looking carefully at the available open space in the preceding screenshots and examining the overlap variations at various viewport widths in your responsive grid, you may want to position each caption in a way that works best for each customer's photo.

This is where the `review-item-1`, `review-item-2`, and so on classes become relevant and helpful, as we may use these specific classes to position each caption in a way that fits best with its image.

To demonstrate the positions of the caption, I've added the following lines in the `scss/includes/_impact.scss` file:

```
.hreview:nth-child(2n) .caption {
    top: 0;
    left: 62%;
```

```
      right: 10px;
      bottom: auto;
      .reviewer {
        margin-top: 6px;
        text-align: left;
      }
  }
  .hreview:nth-child(3n) .caption {
      top: 0;
      left: 17%;
      right: 10px;
      bottom: auto;
  }
```

The preceding markup adjusts the absolute positioning of each second and third caption, which yields the results shown in the following screenshot:

Instead of using the :nth-child() selectors in the above, you can also write your own SCSS to position each specific caption.

Adjusting for tiny screens

On the extra-small grid, the reviews are stacked, and on the small grid we'll arrange them in two columns.

First, we'll reduce the font size of the captions for the small grid. To reduce the font size, insert the following SCSS code into the `scss/includes/_impact.scss` file:

```scss
#impact {
  .caption {
    blockquote {
      font-size: $font-size-sm;
      @include media-breakpoint-only(sm) {
        font-size: $font-size-lg;
      }
    }
  }
}
```

On the small and extra-small grid, we'll only show the first four reviews. Hide the last reviews by default by using the following SCSS code:

```scss
// Impact Section
#impact {
 .hreview:nth-child(5), .hreview:nth-child(6) {
   display: none;
   @include media-breakpoint-only(md) {
     display: block;
   }
 }
}
```

Save the file and then test the results in your browser.

Voilà! The customer reviews are now performing entirely in line with our client's desires.

Now to take care of the last major item in our client's desired home page design: the pricing tables.

Creating attention-grabbing pricing tables

Let's revisit the mockup of how our client would like the pricing tables to look on desktop-sized screens:

Let's see how close we can get to the desired result, and what we can work out for other viewport sizes.

Setting up the variables, files, and markup

As shown in the preceding screenshot, there are a few tables in this design. We can begin by adjusting a few fundamental variables for all tables. These are found in Bootstrap's `_variables.scss file`. Search for the tables section and adjust the variables for background, accented rows, and borders as desired. I've made these adjustments as shown in the following lines of code, and saved them in the local `scss/includes/_variables.scss` file:

```
// Tables
//
// Customizes the `.table` component with basic values, each used across
all table variations.
```

```
$table-cell-padding:            .75rem;
$table-sm-cell-padding:         .3rem;

$table-bg:                      transparent;
$table-bg-accent:               hsla(0,0,1%,.1); // for striping
$table-bg-hover:                hsla(0,0,1%,.2);
$table-bg-active:               $table-bg-hover;

$table-border-width:            1px;
$table-border-color:            $gray-lighter;
```

Save the file, and run the `bootstrap watch` command to see the result as shown in the following screenshot:

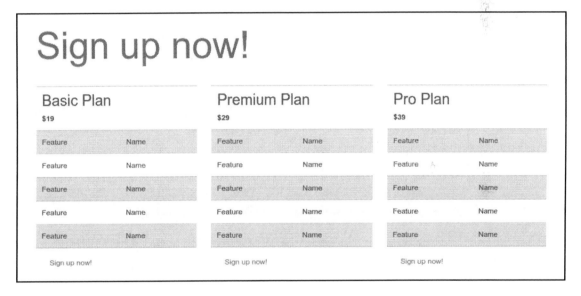

That's a start. Now we need to write more specific styles.

To carry the custom styles, let's create a new Sass file for these pricing tables:

1. Create `_pricing-tables.scss` in the main `scss/includes` folder.
2. Import it into `main.scss` just after the import of the `_impact.scss` file as shown in the following line:

   ```
   @import "_pricing-tables";
   ```

3. Open `_pricing-tables.less` in your editor and begin writing your new styles.

But before we begin writing styles, let's review the markup that we'll be working with.

We have the following special classes already provided in the markup on the parent element of each respective table:

- `package package-basic`
- `package package-premium`
- `package package-pro`

Thus, for the first table, you'll see the following markup on its parent `div`:

```
<div class="package package-basic col-lg-4">
  <table class="table table-striped">
...
```

Notice that the `table` and `table-striped` classes in the above HTML code are part of Bootstrap's styles to display content. You can use these styles by just adding the table base class to any `<table>` element, Extend the base class with custom styles or by including a modifier class such as the `table-striped` class. Read more about tables in Bootstrap at the following URL: `http://getbootstrap.com/content/tables/http://v4-alpha.getbootstrap.com/content/tables/`.

Similarly, we'll use `package package-premium` and `package package-pro` for the second and third tables, respectively.

These parent containers obviously also provide basic layout instructions using the `col-md-4` class to set up a three-column layout in medium viewports and up.

Next, we will observe the markup for each table. We see that the basic `table` and `table-striped` classes have been applied:

```
<table class="table table-striped">
```

The table uses the `<thead>` element for its topmost block. Within this, there is `<th>` spanning two columns, with an `<h2>` heading for the package name and `<div class="price">` to mark up the dollar amount:

```
<thead>
  <tr>
    <th colspan="2">
      <h2>Basic Plan</h2>
      <div class="price">$19</div>
    </th>
  </tr>
</thead>
```

Next is the `tfoot` tag with the **Sign up now!** button:

```
<tfoot>
  <tr><td colspan="2"><a href="#" class="btn">Sign up
now!</a></td></tr>
</tfoot>
```

Then there is the `tbody` tag with the list of features laid out in a straightforward manner in rows with two columns:

```
<tbody>
  <tr><td>Feature</td><td>Name</td></tr>
  <tr><td>Feature</td><td>Name</td></tr>
  <tr><td>Feature</td><td>Name</td></tr>
  <tr><td>Feature</td><td>Name</td></tr>
  <tr><td>Feature</td><td>Name</td></tr>
</tbody>
```

And finally, of course, the closing tags for the `table` and parent `div` tags:

```
  </table>
</div><!-- /.package .package-basic -->
```

Each table repeats this basic structure. This gives us what we need to start work!

Beautifying the table head

To beautify the `thead` element of all of our tables, we'll do the following:

- Align the text at the center
- Add a background color; for now, add a gray color that is approximately a midtone similar to the colors we'll apply to the final version
- Turn the font color white
- Convert the `h2` heading to uppercase
- Increase the size of the price table
- Add the necessary padding all around the tables

We can apply many of these touches with the following lines of SCSS code. We'll specify the `#signup` section as the context for these special table styles:

```
#signup {
  table {
    border: 1px solid $table-border-color;
    thead th {
```

```
        text-align: center;
        background-color: $gray-light;
        color: #fff;
        padding: 2 * $spacer-y 0;

        h2 {
          text-transform: uppercase;
          font-size: 2em;
        }
      }
    }
  }
}
```

In short, we've accomplished everything except increasing the size of the price tables. We can get started on this by adding the following lines of code, which are still nested within our #signup table selector:

```
.price {
    font-size: 4em;
    line-height: 1;
}
```

This yields the following result:

This is close to our desired result, but we need to decrease the size of the dollar sign. We can nest the first letter within our styles for .price:

```
.price {
  font-size: 4em;
  line-height: 1;
  &::first-letter {
    font-size: .5em;
    vertical-align: super;
  }
}
```

::first-letter is a pseudo element, which allows you to style the first letter in an element without needing to stick a <span> tag around that first letter in your HTML. You can read more about this pseudo element at the following URL: https://css-tricks.com/almanac/selectors/f/first-letter/.

These lines reduce the dollar sign to half its size and align it at the top. The following screenshot shows the result:

Styling the table body and foot

Continuing to focus on the styles that apply to all three pricing tables, let's make the following adjustments:

- Add left and right padding to the list of features
- Stretch the button to full width
- Increase the button size

We can accomplish this by adding the following rules:

```scss
#signup {
  table {
    tbody {
      td {
        padding-left: $spacer-x;
        padding-right: $spacer-x;
      }
    }
    a.btn {
      @extend .btn-lg;
      font-size: 1.25em;
      display: block;
      width: 100%;
      background-color: $gray-light;
      color: #fff;
    }
  }
}
```

In the preceding SCSS code, the @extend feature of Sass has been used to extend the button with Bootstrap's styles for large buttons. Bootstrap itself avoids the @extend feature, but you can use it.

Alternatively, you can use Bootssrap's `button-size()` mixin to set the large button styles.

You can read a little more about the `@extend` feature of Sass in `Chapter 1`, *Getting Started with Bootstrap*.

Notice that I have set font-size: 1.25em; afterward. The button mixin sets the font size in rem units and we want the font size to scale with its parent.

Save the file, run the `bootstrap watch` command, and you should see the following result:

We're now ready to add styles to differentiate our three packages.

Differentiating the packages

Let's begin by giving each package the desired color for the table head and the **Sign up now!** button. Our provided mockup uses blue for the **Basic**, green for the **Premium**, and red for the **Pro** packages. Let's prepare our color scheme by using the chosen color values in new variables for primary, secondary, and tertiary brand colors, as shown in the following lines of code:

```
$brand-primary:          #428bca;
$brand-secondary:        #5cb85c;
$brand-tertiary:         #d9534f;
```

Having set up these colors, we can efficiently apply them to the appropriate `thead` and `button` elements. We'll use the distinctive class that we applied earlier to each table's parent element, that is, `package-basic`, `package-premium`, and `package-pro`:

1. In the `scss/includes/_pricing-tables.scss` file, begin a new section with a comment:

   ```scss
   // Pricing Table Colors
   ```

2. We'll apply the primary brand color to the `.package-basic` table using the `$brand-primary` variable; we'll try it first on the `thead th` element:

   ```scss
   #signup .package-basic table {
   thead th {
       background-color: $brand-primary;
   }
   ```

3. Then, apply the primary brand color to the `thead th` element's button. Here, we'll use the `.button-variant()` mixin from the `bootstrap/mixins.less` file to efficiently apply styles to the `:hover` and `:active` states. The mixin takes three parameters: color, background color, and border color. We'll define them as follows:

   ```scss
       ...
       .btn {
           @include button-variant(#fff, $brand-primary, darken($brand-primary, 5%));
       }
   }
   ```

4. When compiled, this concise mixin will generate styles for the button and its hover and active states!

For a reminder of how the `button-variant()` mixin works, consult the `bootstrap/scss/mixins/_buttons.scss file`, where the mixin is defined, and then `bootstrap/scss/_buttons.scss`, where it is used to define the default Bootstrap button classes.

5. Now we need to repeat this for our `.package-premium` table; this time, however, use the `$brand-secondary` variable:

```
#signup .package-premium table {
  thead th {
    background-color: $brand-secondary;
  }
  .btn {
    @include button-variant(#fff, $brand-secondary, darken($brand-secondary,
      5%));
  }
}
```

6. Finally, we'll apply the tertiary brand color to the `.package-pro` table using the `$brand-tertiary` variable:

```
#signup .package-pro table {
  thead th {
    background-color: $brand-tertiary;
  }
  .btn {
    @include button-variant(#fff, $brand-tertiary, darken($brand-tertiary,
      5%));
  }
}
```

7. You might have noticed that the preceding steps and code are very repetitive. Sass can help you to code your CSS code DRY (**D**o not **R**epeat **Y**ourself). By wrapping the names in a Sass map and using an `@each` loop, you'll have to write the code only once.

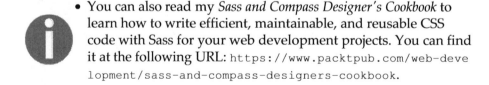

- You can also read my *Sass and Compass Designer's Cookbook* to learn how to write efficient, maintainable, and reusable CSS code with Sass for your web development projects. You can find it at the following URL: `https://www.packtpub.com/web-development/sass-and-compass-designers-cookbook`.

8. Save the file, and run the `bootstrap watch` command if you have not already run it. You should see the new colors we applied to our tables:

Nice!

Now let's check how our tables respond to various viewport widths.

Adjusting for small viewports

Thanks to the attention Bootstrap gives to responsive design, our tables perform quite well across viewport breakpoints. We've already seen how our tables fare in the medium breakpoint range. In large screens, the tables expand wider. In narrow viewports, the tables stack up vertically, quite nicely.

However, there is an awkward range of width approximately between 480px and 768px, where the tables expand to fill the full width of the screen. Clearly, they become too wide.

Because we have three tables, there is no benefit involved in having a two-column layout at this dimension. Instead, let's constrain the width of our tables and align them at the center with `auto` left and right margins. We'll use the media-breakpoint-down() media query mixin to set `400px` as our maximum width, and set the horizontal margins to auto to keep our tables at the center of the window:

```
//
// Constrain width for small screens and under
// ------------------------------------------

@include media-breakpoint-down(sm) {
  #signup .package {
      max-width: 400px;
      margin: 0 auto;
```

```
      }
   }
```

You cannot center the tables by using the @extend feature of Sass to extend the .m-x-auto class, because you may not @extend an outer selector from within @media.

On the medium grid, the tables are too wide for the grid columns, so we reduce the total font size for only the medium grid by using the following SCSS code:

```
#signup {
  font-size: 100%;
  @include media-breakpoint-only(md) {
    font-size: 70%;
  }
}
```

Save the file, and test the results in your browser. You should see nicely constrained tables aligned at the center within the window! The following screenshot shows our result:

At this point, our tables are differentiated by color and are responsive. However, one last step remains. In the medium and large viewport widths, we want the premium plan to stand out.

Providing a visual hierarchy to our tables

If we look back at the mockup, we see that the design – at least for desktop-sized viewports – calls for visual emphasis on the central Premium plan by increasing its size and bringing it visually into the foreground.

This can be accomplished with some adjustments to padding, margins, and font sizes. We'll do this within a media query for medium viewports and up:

```
//
// Visually enhance the premium plan
// ----------------------------------------
@include media-breakpoint-up(md) {

}
```

Our first aim is to bring the tables closer to one another. This can be done by removing the padding (the gutter of the grid) between the grid columns:

```scss
#signup {
  // Squeeze tables together
  .col-md-4 {
    padding: 0;
  }
}
```

Then we can enlarge the font size for the price information in the premium block as follows:

```scss
#signup {
  .package-premium .price {
    font-size: 7em;
  }
}
```

Nested within this media query, we can first reduce the widths of our basic and pro tables (the first and third) and add a little margin to the top to push them down a bit:

```scss
// Size down the basic and pro
#signup .package-basic {
  padding-left: 4 * $spacer-y;
}
#signup .package-pro {
  padding-right: 4 * $spacer-y;
}
#signup .package-basic table,
#signup .package-pro table {
  margin-top: 3 * $spacer-x;
}
```

Next, let's enhance the font size of our premium table and add padding to its button:

```scss
// Size up the premium
#signup .package-premium table {
  thead th {
    h2 {
      font-size: 2.5em;
    }
  }
  a.btn {
    font-size: 2em;
    padding-top: 1.5 * $spacer-x;
    padding-bottom: 1.5 * $spacer-x;
  }
}
```

Save the file, and inspect the results in the browser. You should see the following result in large viewports of 1,200px and above:

That's it! We've accomplished the last major challenge in our client's design. Now let's tidy things up by applying those little touches that hold it all together.

Adding the final touches

In this section, we will enhance the details that hold our design together. First, we'll enhance the h1 headings for each of our major sections and add some needed top and bottom padding to each section. Then, we'll enhance the navigation experience by adding ScrollSpy to the navbar and using jQuery to animate the scrolling action when triggered by a click on the navbar item.

Let's begin by enhancing the size and contrast of our major h1 headings for each section and increasing the top and bottom padding. If you pause to look at these h1 headings, you may note that they are rather lackluster.

Enlarging these headings, bringing the contrast down a little, and providing extra padding will make a big difference. We only want these rules to apply to the **Features**, **Impact**, and **Sign up** sections. We will select these by ID:

1. Open the `scss/includes/_page-contents.scss` file again in your editor.

2. At the top of the file, after the rule applying top padding to the body, add the following lines:

```
#features, #impact, #signup {
  padding-top: $spacer-y * 2.5;
  padding-bottom: $spacer-y * 3;
  h1 {
    font-size: 5em;
    color: $gray;
    line-height: 1.3;
    padding-bottom: $spacer-y * 1.5;
  }
}
```

3. Here, we've done the following:

- Added top and bottom padding to these sections
- Significantly increased the size of the `h1` heading
- Reduced the heavy contrast of that heading
- Ensured that the heading has room to breathe by setting the line height and bottom padding

4. Save your work and notice the difference in your browser:

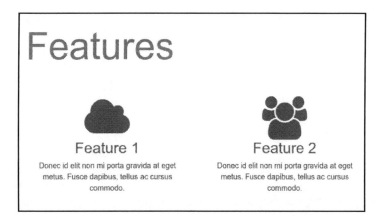

This yields a nice result across almost all viewport sizes. For small viewports, the `h1` font size is now a bit large. So, let's adjust this. As we do not want these styles to flow up to larger viewports, we'll wrap the styles we have already written in a query by limiting them to larger viewports. Finally, the refactored and mobile-first SCSS code should look like this:

```scss
#features, #impact, #signup {
  padding-top: $spacer-y * 1.5;
  padding-bottom: $spacer-y * 1;
  h1 {
    font-size: 3em;
    color: $gray;
    line-height: 1.3;
    padding-bottom: $spacer-y;
  }
  @include media-breakpoint-up(md) {
    padding-top: $spacer-y * 2.5;
    padding-bottom: $spacer-y * 3;
    h1 {
      font-size: 5em;
      padding-bottom: $spacer-y * 1.5;
    }
  }
}
```

The following screenshot shows our result:

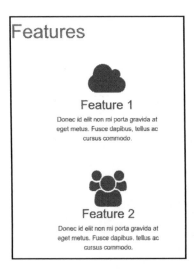

This is a much improved result! Now we'll enhance the navigation experience.

Adding ScrollSpy to the navbar

Let's configure our top navbar to indicate our location on the page. We'll add Bootstrap's ScrollSpy behavior to the navbar.

 Refer to Bootstrap's ScrollSpy plugin documentation at
`http://getbootstrap.com/javascript/#scrollspy`.

By default, the ScrollSpy plugin requires a Bootstrap nav component. Bootstrap's navbar contains a nav component already. The relative position is required too. You should set position:relative; in your CSS for the element you're spying on. In our situation, we'll have to set the relative position for the body element.

You can easily initiate the ScrollSpy plugin by adding data-attributes in the HTML code. First add data-spy="scroll" to the element you want to spy and then add the data-target attribute with the ID or class of the parent element of any Bootstrap .nav component.

 Data-attributes in HTML5 allow use to store extra information into standard semantic HTML elements. Read more about data-attributes in HTML5 at the following URL: `https://developer.mozilla.org/en-US/docs/Web/Guide/HTML/Using_data_attributes`.

ScrollSpy requires a resolvable ID target in our HTML code. We've already added the target in the preceding steps. For instance, the Intro section had `id="welcome"` in the section element as follows:

```
<section class="jumbotron" id="welcome">
```

The above HTML code can be found in the `html/includes/intro.html` file. The `id="welcome"` declaration corresponds with the resolvable id targets in the navbar links, as can be seen in the `html/includes/page-header.html file`. The HTML code of the `Welcome` should look as follows now:

```
<a class="nav-link active" href="#welcome">Welcome <span class="sr-only">(current)</span></a>
```

Now perform the following steps to initiate the ScrollSpy plugin in our project:

1. Edit the `scss/app.scss` file to set the relative position of the body element. Add the following SCSS code at the end of this file:

```
body {
  position: relative;
}
```

2. Then open `index.html` in your editor.

3. Add these ScrollSpy data-attributes to the `body` tag:

```
<body data-spy="scroll" data-target=".navbar">
```

4. Edit the file and set the resolvable ID targets in the navbar links. At the end, your HTML code should look like this:

```
<ul class="nav navbar-nav">
  <li class="nav-item">
    <a class="nav-link active" href="#welcome">Welcome <span
        class="sr-only">(current)</span></a>
  </li>
  <li class="nav-item">
    <a class="nav-link" href="#features">Features</a>
  </li>
  <li class="nav-item">
    <a class="nav-link" href="#impact">Impact</a>
  </li>
  <li class="nav-item">
    <a class="nav-link" href="#signup">Sign up</a>
  </li>
</ul>
```

With the resolvable id targets and the new data-attributes in place, save the file, refresh your browser, and scroll up and down the page. You should see your main navigation respond as it should, indicating your position on the page as shown in the following screenshot:

In the preceding step, we used data-attributes to initiate Bootstrap ScrollSpy behavior. You can also initiate the plugin via JavaScript by performing the following steps:

1. First add the `position: relative;` declaration for the body element in your CSS/SCSS:

```
body {
    position: relative;
}
```

2. Then call the ScrollSpy via JavaScript/jQuery as follows:

```
$('body').scrollspy({ target: '.navbar' })
```

Animating the scroll

Now let's animate the page scrolls that will be triggered by clicking on the navbar page anchors. We'll use jQuery to accomplish this.

jQuery is a JavaScript library and provides you with an API for HTML document traversal and manipulation, event handling, and animations. The `jQuery animate()` API call lets you create custom animations of CSS properties. You can read more about jQuery's animations at the following URL: `http://api.jquery.com/animate/`.

Animating the page scroll requires adding a few lines to our `main.js` file:

1. Open `js/main.js`.
2. Add the following lines within `$(document).ready(function() {`:

```
$('#nav-main [href^=#]').click(function (e) {
  e.preventDefault();
  var div = $(this).attr('href');
  $("html, body").animate({
  scrollTop: $(div).position().top
  }, "slow");
});
```

3. Save the file and refresh your browser.

What have we done here? We have done the following using the power of jQuery:

- Selected the links in our `.navbar` element that use page anchors as their targets and set a click event on them:

```
$('#nav-main [href^=#]').click(function (e) {}
```

- Prevented the default click behavior as follows:

```
e.preventDefault();
```

- Animated the scrolling behavior, setting its duration to slow as shown in the following snippet:

```
$("html, body").animate({
    scrollTop: $(div).position().top
}, "slow");
```

Click on one of the nav items and you should see it animate the scroll!

Summary

Take a moment to scroll back and forth through our page, appreciating its details and resizing it to see how it adjusts to viewport dimensions.

When we consider the variety of features packed into this page – and that they all work responsively across desktop-, tablet-, and phone-sized viewports – it's not a bad accomplishment!

To recap, we have given our client a beautiful, one-page marketing site with a large welcome section using Bootstrap's jumbotron styles, a bold background image, and responsive customizations, a features list making use of large-sized Font Awesome icons, a section of customer reviews with images and captions laid out in the masonry format, which adapts beautifully across viewports. We ended up with a signup section with custom-designed pricing tables built on Bootstrap styles and enhanced further to provide a visual hierarchy for medium and large viewports. As a finishing touch, we added a ScrollSpy-equipped navbar with animated scrolling behavior provided by a bit of extra jQuery. With this design, we have reached a point where there is nothing we can't do with Bootstrap.

Across this and previous projects, we have accomplished a great deal. We have learned the ins and outs of Bootstrap, and folded Bootstrap Sass and JavaScript into our own custom set of project files. We then used the robust Font Awesome icons. We also tweaked, customized, and otherwise innovated on Bootstrap styles to arrive the exact results we were seeking.

In the next and last chapter, you'll learn how to build an app with Angular 2 and Bootstrap.

Building an Angular 2 App with Bootstrap

9

In this chapter, you will use your Bootstrap skills to build an Angular 2 app. Angular 2 is the successor to AngularJS. You can read more about Angular 2 at the following URL: `https://angular.io/`. It is a toolset for building the framework most suited to your application development; it lets you extend the HTML vocabulary for your application. The resulting environment is extraordinarily expressive, readable, and quick to develop. Angular is maintained by Google and a community of individuals and corporations.

In this chapter, you will learn how to build with Angular 2 and Bootstrap:

- Set up a simple Angular 2 app
- Integrate Bootstrap HTML markup in your app
- Add Bootstrap's CSS code to your Angular 2 projects
- Use native Angular directives for Bootstrap
- Get introduced to some other build tools to deploy your Bootstrap 4 project

Overview

You can use Angular to build **single page applications (SPAs)** and rich web applications. Angular implements the **Model-View-Controller (MVC)** in JavaScript and HTML. The MVC is an architectural pattern that separates an application into three main logical components: the model, the view, and the controller. **Data**–*binding* in *Angular* apps is the automatic synchronization of data between the model and view components.

Angular's HTML compiler can attach a specified behavior to a **DOM element**. An Angular directive is a marker on a DOM element that tells the compiler what to attach or how to transform it.

Angular contains a built-in subset of jQuery, called **jQuery lite** or **jqLite**, which means that you should not use jQuery in your Angular apps. Bootstrap's JavaScript plugins require jQuery and so cannot, or should not, be used in your Angular apps.

Angular directives for Bootstrap can replace Bootstrap's plugins and enable you to use Bootstrap components in your Angular apps. You can use Bootstrap's CSS code, and even load it from CDN, together with these directives.

Setting up your first Angular app

Angular 2 is the successor of **AngularJS**. Those who are already familiar with Angular 2 may possibly skip this section. More information about Angular 2 can be found at the official website at the following URL: `https://angular.io/`. On this website, you'll find a *Getting Started* section, which includes a 5 MIN QuickStart guidance and a Tour of Heroes Tutorial!.

As this book is about Bootstrap, I won't discuss Angular 2 in detail, although I highly recommend you to try the QuickStart and tutorial before reading further.

We'll reuse the source code of the 5 MIN QuickStart guidance to build our own Angular 2 website with Bootstrap.

You can write Angular 2 apps in TypeScript, Dart, and JavaScript. In this book, I've used TypeScript.
TypeScript is a free and open source programming language developed and maintained by Microsoft. It is a strict superset of JavaScript, and adds optional static typing and class-based object-oriented programming to the language. TypeScript compiles to clean, simple JavaScript code which runs on any browser, in Node.js, or in any JavaScript engine that supports ECMAScript 3 (or newer).
You can read more about TypeScript at the following URL: `https://www.typescriptlang.org/`.

To start, run the following command in your console:

```
git clone  https://github.com/angular/quickstart start
```

Git is a `version-vcontrol` system that is used for software development and other version control tasks. The source code of the 5 MIN QuickStart guide is available for free at GitHub. GitHUB is a web-based Git repository hosting service.

The preceding command copies the source code of the 5 MIN QuickStart guide into a new folder called start. Navigate into the new folder and run the following command:

```
npm install && npm start
```

The preceding command creates a super-simple Angular 2 application in TypeScript. We'll use this application to create our own project. After running the `npm start` command, the TypeScript compiler and lite-server are watch for file changes. They should detect the change, recompile the TypeScript into JavaScript, and refresh the browser.

Without any modifications, the app should run in your browser at `http://localhost:3000`. Your browser screen should look like the following screenshot:

My First Angular 2 App

Now we can rebuild the app into a simple website with four pages.

Adding routing to our app

To learn more about routing in Angular 2, and for better understanding of the coming steps, you can visit the following URL: `https://angular.io/docs/ts/latest/tutorial/toh-pt5.html`.

Our simple website has the following pages: **Home**, **Features**, **Pricing,** and **About**. So we have to create four new components (views). For the home page, create a file call in `home.component.ts` in the `app` folder. The `home.component.ts` file should contain the following TypeScript code:

```
import { Component } from '@angular/core';
@Component({
  selector: 'home',
  template: '<h3>Home</h3>'
})
export class HomeComponent {
}
```

Repeat the preceding steps for each page, and create the `features, component.ts,` `pricing.component.ts,` and `about.component.ts` files too.

Then create a new `app/app.routes.ts` file, which should contain the following TypeScript code:

```
import { provideRouter, RouterConfig }  from '@angular/router';
import { HomeComponent } from './home.component';
import { FeaturesComponent } from './features.component';
import { PricingComponent } from './pricing.component';
import { AboutComponent } from './about.component';

const routes: RouterConfig = [
  {
    path: 'home',
    component: HomeComponent
  },
  {
    path: 'features',
    component: FeaturesComponent
  },
  {
    path: 'pricing',
    component: PricingComponent
  },
  {
    path: 'about',
    component: AboutComponent
  },
  {
  path: '',
  redirectTo: '/home',
  pathMatch: 'full'
  }
];
export const appRouterProviders = [
  provideRouter(routes)
];
```

After the preceding changes, you should also add base tags into the `index.html` in the root folder of your application. Open the `index.html` file in your editor and add the following HTML code:

```
<head>
  <base href="/">
```

Now you can start editing the `app/app.component.ts` file.

Setting up navigation

The original app component (app/app.component.ts) should only handle navigation now. So edit the app/app.component.ts file so that it contains the following TypeScript code:

```
import { Component } from '@angular/core';
import { ROUTER_DIRECTIVES }  from '@angular/router';
@Component({
    selector: 'my-app',
    template: `<ul>
    <li><a [routerLink]="['/home']" routerLinkActive="active">Home</a></li>
    <li><a [routerLink]="['/features']"
routerLinkActive="active">Features</a></li>
    <li><a [routerLink]="['/pricing']"
routerLinkActive="active">Pricing</a></li>
    <li><a [routerLink]="['/about']"
routerLinkActive="active">About</a></li>
    </ul>
    <router-outlet></router-outlet>`,
     directives: [ ROUTER_DIRECTIVES ]
    })
export class AppComponent { }
```

The router displays each component immediately below the `<router-outlet>` as we navigate through the application.

Inspect the result in your browser and you'll find that it look like that shown in the following screenshot:

You can click the links and will find that a new view is loaded when you do so. Now it's time to add Bootstrap to our project!

Adding Bootstrap's HTML markup code to your app

Open the `app/app.component.ts` file in your editor again. Replace the template metadata with a `templateUrl` property that points to a new `app/app.component.html` template file as follows:

```
@Component({
    selector: 'my-app',
    templateUrl: 'app/app.component.html',
    directives: [ ROUTER_DIRECTIVES ]
})
```

Now we can add Bootstrap HTML markup to the `app/app.component.html` template file. We replace the navigation list with a responsive navbar, and we add some containers and other grid classes. We should end up with HTML code like the following:

```
<div class="container">
 <div class="row">
   <h1>{{title}}</h1>
 </div>
</div>
<nav class="navbar navbar-light bg-faded">
  <button class="navbar-toggler hidden-sm-up" type="button" aria-
controls="exCollapsingNavbar2" aria-expanded="false" aria-label="Toggle
navigation">
      ≡
  </button>
  <div class="navbar-toggleable-xs">
  <div class="container">
    <ul class="nav navbar-nav">
      <li class="nav-item">
        <a class="nav-link active" [routerLink]="['/home']"
routerLinkActive="active">Home</a>
      </li>
      <li class="nav-item">
        <a class="nav-link" [routerLink]="['/features']"
routerLinkActive="active">Features</a>
      </li>
      <li class="nav-item">
        <a class="nav-link" [routerLink]="['/pricing']"
routerLinkActive="active">Pricing</a>
      </li>
      <li class="nav-item">
        <a class="nav-link" [routerLink]="['/about']"
routerLinkActive="active">About</a>
```

```
        </li>
      </ul>
    </div>
    </div>
</nav>
<main class="container">
  <router-outlet></router-outlet>
</main>
<footer class="container">
    <div class="row">
        <div class="col-xs-12 text-xs-center">
              &copy; 2016 {{title}}
        </div>
    </div>
</footer>
```

You can read more about Bootstrap's navbar markup in Chapter 1, *Getting Started with Bootstrap.*

Inspect the result in your browser again. You'll find that it now looks like that shown in the following screenshot:

As you can see in the preceding screenshot, it does not look well yet. Bootstrap's CSS code is not loaded into the application, so the HTML is not styled. In the next step, we'll add Bootstrap's CSS code to the application.

Integrating Bootstrap's CSS code into the application

Now we'll have to add Bootstrap's CSS code to our application. Of course ,we can simply add a link to the CSS code on CDN in `index.html`, but doing that does not enable us to profit from the underlying Sass code.

Each component in our app can have its own styles sheets. The main styles of our app are loaded via the `styles.css` file in the root. We'll set up a build system that compiles Bootstrap's SCSS code and our own modification into the styles.css file.

First, we install Bootstrap's source code via npm by running the following command:

```
npm install bootstrap --save-dev
```

Then we set up a similar file structure as we have done already in the preceding chapters of this book:

```
scss/styles.scss
scss/includes/_bootstrap.sccs
scss/includes/_variables.sccs
```

The `scss/_includes/_variables.scss` file enables us to override Bootstrap's default values and the `scss/_includes/_bootstrap.scss` file is a copy of the original `bootstrap.scss` file. In the `scss/_includes/_bootstrap.scss` file each Bootstrap component of the module is loaded separately, enabling us to comment out the parts we do not need. Files are loaded from the source code in the `node_modules` folder, which is possible by setting the `includePath` option to the `node_modules` folder for the Sass compiler. We will set up the Sass compiler in the next section.

Setting up the Sass compiler

Run the following command in your console to set up the node-sass Sass compiler:

```
npm install node-sass --save-dev
```

The `node-sass` module compiles your Sass code with **libSass**. Note that **Compass** is not compatible with libSass. More information about the node-sass module can be found at the following URL: `https://github.com/sass/node-sass`.

In `Chapter 2`, *Creating Your Own Build Process with Gulp*, you can read how to use node-sass via gulp-sass in a Gulp build process.

Edit the `package.json` file of your project after installing node-sass and create a new entry in the scripts property as follows:

```
"compile-scss": "node-sass --output-style expanded --precision 6 --source-
comments false --source-map true --include-path node_modules -o . scss"
```

Now you can run the following command to compile `scss/styles.scss` into styles.css:

```
npm compile-scss
```

Add the `compile-scss` command to the start command in the file as follows:

```
"start": "npm run compile-scss & tsc && concurrently "tsc -w" "lite-server"
",
```

Now the `scss/styles.scss` files compiles into the styles.css file when we run the `npm start` command. The start command did already run the `tsc -w` command, which watches for file changes in the TypeScript files. The web server automatically reloads when any HTML, CSS, or JavaScript file changes. The CSS should also recompile when we change one or more of the Sass files. We can use the **Nodemon** module to watch the `.scss` files.

Nodemon watches for file changes and can restart a program when this happens. You can install Nodemon by running the following command in your console:

```
npm install nodemon --save-dev
```

Change the scripts property in your package.json file after installing Nodemon as follows:

```
"start": "concurrently "npm run watch-scss" & tsc && concurrently "tsc -w"
"lite-server" ", "watch-scss": "nodemon -e scss -x "npm run compile-scss"",
```

Notice that `node-sass` also has a built-in `watch` option, but we cannot run the post-processors when using this option. We'll set up the post-process in the next section.
Test your new commands; first run the `npm start` command, then change and save your `scss/styles.scss` file. After saving the `scss/styles.scss` file, the Sass compiler should start and your browser windows should automatically reload.

Adding the post-processors

As you know the `postcss autoprefixer` post-processor is required to compile Bootstrap's Sass code into CSS. By default, Bootstrap also runs the `postcss-flexbugs-fixes post processor`.

> The `postcss-flexbugs-fixes post processor` tries to fix browser bugs for the Flexbox Layout. More information can be found at: `https://github.com/luisrudge/postcss-flexbugs-fixes`.

First we have to install postcss and the post-processors by running the following command in your console:

```
npm install postcss-cli autoprefixer postcss-flexbugs-fixes --save-dev
```

After installing this module, we can simply reuse Bootstrap's post process settings. Add the following entry to the scripts property of your package.json file:

```
"postcss": "postcss --config node_modules/bootstrap/grunt/postcss.js --replace styles.css"
```

Then we add a new command, which runs the post-processor after the Sass compiler as follows:

```
"build:css" : "npm run compile-scss && npm run postcss"
```

Do not forget to change the watch-scss command too, because `nodemon` should execute the `build:css` command now:

```
"watch-scss": "nodemon -e scss -x "npm run build:css""
```

Finally, the scripts property in the `package.json` file should look like the following:

```
"scripts": {
  "start": "concurrently "npm run watch-scss" & tsc && concurrently "tsc -w" "lite-server" ",
  "docker-build": "docker build -t ng2-quickstart .",
  "docker": "npm run docker-build && docker run -it --rm -p 3000:3000 -p 3001:3001 ng2-quickstart",
  "pree2e": "npm run webdriver:update",
  "e2e": "tsc && concurrently "http-server -s" "protractor protractor.config.js" --kill-others --success first",
  "lint": "tslint ./app/**/*.ts -t verbose",
  "lite": "lite-server",
  "postinstall": "typings install",
```

```
    "test": "tsc && concurrently "tsc -w" "karma start karma.conf.js"",
    "test-once": "tsc && karma start karma.conf.js --single-run",
    "tsc": "tsc",
    "tsc:w": "tsc -w",
    "typings": "typings",
    "webdriver:update": "webdriver-manager update",
    "build:css": "npm run compile-scss && npm run postcss",
    "postcss": "postcss --config node_modules/bootstrap/grunt/postcss.js --
replace styles.css",
    "watch-scss": "nodemon -e scss -x "npm run build:css"",
    "compile-scss": "node-sass --output-style expanded --precision 6 --
source-comments false --source-map true --include-path node_modules -o .
scss"
    },
```

And at the end, the result of your work should look like that shown in the following screenshot:

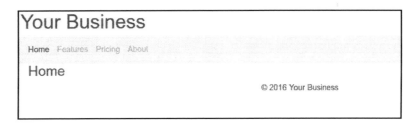

Using the ng-bootstrap directives

Resize your browser window and make sure that the width of the viewport becomes smaller than 768 pixels. You will find that your navbar stacks like that shown in the following screenshot:

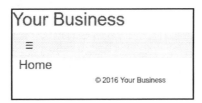

The *hamburger* menu button, which should open the menu, does not work. The menu button requires the Bootstrap JavaScript Collapse plugin. As discussed before, we can't use Bootstrap JavaScript plugins and should replace them with Angular directives.

Remember that Angular directives are markers on DOM elements that tell the compiler what to attach or how to transform it.

We can use the ng-bootstrap directives to replace the Bootstrap jQuery plugins. More information about the ng-bootstrap directives can be found at the following URL: `https://ng-bootstrap.github.io/`.

Use the following steps to integrate the ng-bootstrap directives into your project.

First install the ng-bootstrap directives by running the following command in your console:

```
npm install @ng-bootstrap/ng-bootstrap --save-dev
```

Then open the `angular-cli-build.js` file in the root folder of your project and add the following lines into it:

```
// map tells the System loader where to look for things
var map = {
  'app':                       'app', // 'dist',
  '@angular':                  'node_modules/@angular',
  'angular2-in-memory-web-api': 'node_modules/angular2-in-memory-web-
api',
  'rxjs':                      'node_modules/rxjs',
  '@ng-bootstrap/ng-bootstrap': 'node_modules/@ng-bootstrap/ng-
bootstrap'
};
// packages tells the System loader how to load when no filename
and/or no extension
var packages = {
  'app':                       { main: 'main.js', defaultExtension:
'js' },
  'rxjs':                      { defaultExtension: 'js' },
  'angular2-in-memory-web-api': { main: 'index.js', defaultExtension:
'js' },
  '@ng-bootstrap/ng-bootstrap': { defaultExtension: 'js', main:
'index.js' }
};
```

In subsequent steps, we'll change the app component and its HTML template. First edit the `app.components.ts` file, so that its TypeScript code looks like that shown here:

```
import { Component } from '@angular/core';
import { ROUTER_DIRECTIVES } from '@angular/router';
import {NGB_COLLAPSE_DIRECTIVES} from '@ng-bootstrap/ng-bootstrap';
@Component({
    selector: 'my-app',
    templateUrl: 'app/app.component.html',
```

```
          directives: [ ROUTER_DIRECTIVES, NGB_COLLAPSE_DIRECTIVES]
        })
export class AppComponent {
  title = 'Your Business';
  private isCollapsed = true;
}
```

As you can see, in the above we've made the Collapse directive available for the component. Now change the HTML code in the app.components.html the file according to this change:

```
        <button class="navbar-toggler hidden-sm-up" type="button"
(click)="isCollapsed = !isCollapsed" aria-expanded="false" aria-
label="Toggle navigation">
             ≡
        </button>
        <div class="navbar-toggleable-xs" [ngbCollapse]="isCollapsed">
```

Run the `npm start` command and inspect the result in your browser. You'll find that the *hamburger* menu in the small viewports works as expected now.

Now the skeleton for your Angular 2 website is ready. You have learned how to integrate Bootstrap in an Angular 2 project.

Using other directives

The list of directives at the ng-bootstrap website does not contain a directive for each Bootstrap component yet. On the other hand, some of the directives are not available as Bootstrap components, but are only available as ng-bootstrap directives.

The rating component is an example of a component which is only available in ng-bootstrap. To use the rating component in your project use the following steps.

Open the `home.componet.ts` in your editor. Add the directive and required HTML code for the rating, component. Take a look at for some example code. At the end, the TypeScript code should look like the following:

```
import { Component } from '@angular/core';
import {NGB_RATING_DIRECTIVES} from '@ng-bootstrap/ng-bootstrap';
@Component({
  selector: 'home',
  template: `<h3>Home</h3>
    <ngb-rating [(rate)]="currentRate"></ngb-rating>
  <hr>
  <pre>Rate: <b>{{currentRate}}</b></pre>`,
  directives: [NGB_RATING_DIRECTIVES]
  })
```

```
export class HomeComponent {
  currentRate = 10;
}
```

After your changes, the Home view should look like that shown in the following screenshot:

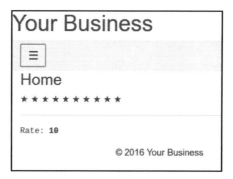

Using the ng2-bootstrap directives as an alternative

The ng-bootstrap directives are the successor to the Angular UI Bootstrap library and are maintained by Google's Angular 2 team. There's also the ng2-bootstrap module maintained by Valor Software. The native Angular 2 directives for Bootstrap work with both Bootstrap 3 and Bootstrap 4.

To use the ng2-bootstrap directives instead of the ng-bootstrap directives, you can repeat the step we've used to integrate ng-bootstrap. First install ng2-bootstrap by running the following command in your console:

```
npm install ng2-bootstrap --save
```

After installing the ng2-bootstrap directives, you also have to modify the angular-cli-build.js, app.components.ts, and app.components.html files. Also read the instructions at the following URL: https://github.com/valor-software/ng2-bootstrap #quick-start. These instructions describe how to use the ng2-bootstrap module with the Angular2 5 min quickstart guide.

The `ng2-bootstrap` module contains among others a `datepicker` and `timepicker`. The `datepicker` looks like that shown in the following screenshot:

Downloading the complete code

As with all the projects in this book, the source code for this project can be downloaded from the Packt Publishing website at `http://www.packtpub.com/support`. You'll find the files for this project in the `chapter9/finish` folder.

Navigate to the `chapter9/finish` folder and run the following command to start:

```
npm install && npm start
```

I have also published the source at GitHub. You will find it at the following URL:

`https://github.com/bassjobsen/angular2-bootstrap4-website-buil der.`

You can install it by simply running the following command in your console:

```
git clone
https://github.com/bassjobsen/angular2-bootstrap4-website
-builder.git yourproject
```

What about Angular CLI?

Angular CLI is a **Command Line Interface (CLI)** for Angular 2 applications based on the `ember-cli` project. The tool helps you set up and develop an Angular 2 project with more ease.

You can use the ng-bootstrap and ng2-Bootstrap directives as described in the previous sections with Angular CLI too. The Angular CLI tool use the webpack module bundler. Webpack uses plugin loaders to preprocess Sass files. If you do not load Bootstrap's CSS code from CDN, you will have to configure webpack to pre- and post-process Bootstrap's Sass code.

Using React.js with Bootstrap

React is another popular JavaScript library for building user interface (UI) components for web applications. In contrast to Angular, React uses composable components in instead of template logic. When using composable components your logic is not in a separate template file. The technique of not introducing any logic into the template is achieved through a technique called **JSX (JavaScript syntax extension)**. JSX is an HTML-like syntax that compiles down to JavaScript.

Probably the easiest way to get started with React is to include the necessary libraries from a CDN. React supports most popular browsers, including Internet Explorer 9 and above. React's documentation points you to a JSFiddle Hello World example to start hacking React. You can find this JSFiddle at the following URL: `https://jsfiddle.net/reactjs/69z2wep o/`. This example only prints `"help world"`.

As this book is about Bootstrap, I cannot discus JSX in detail here. You can learn more about React and JSX by watching Samer Buna's Learning ReactJS video, which can be found at `https://www.packtpub.com/web-development/learning-reactjs-video`. Now it's time to add Bootstrap to our React application.

Using React Bootstrap 4 components

Reactstrap is a library containing React Bootstrap 4 components that favor composition and control. The documentation for Reactstrap can be found at the following URL: `https://reactstrap.github.io`.

A demo can be found at the following URL: `http://output.jsbin.com/dimive/latest`. To install Reactstrap on your local system, perform the following steps:

- Run the following command in your console:

  git clone https://github.com/reactstrap/reactstrap.git reactstrap

- Then navigate to the new reactstrap folder and run the following commands:

  npm install && npm start

The `npm start` command starts a webpack develop server at `http://localhost:8080/webpack-dev-server/`. Webpack is a module bundler for JavaScript. When you point your browser to `http://localhost:8080/webpack-dev-server/` it should look like the following screenshot:

Notice that Reactstrap depends on Bootstrap's CSS code but not jQuery or Bootstrap JavaScript.

Now we can use Reactstrap in the JSFiddle Hello World example too. Let's go to the following URL again: and create a fork in it.

Then add the following external resources:

- `https://npmcdn.com/bootstrap@4.0.0-alpha.3/dist/css/bootstrap.min.css` (Bootstap's CSS)
- `https://npmcdn.com/reactstrap@2/dist/reactstrap.min.js` (the Reactstrap library)

At the end, the resources should look like those shown in the following screenshot:

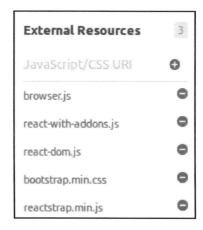

After that you may edit the JavaScript code. To show a Bootstrap button in the danger state use the following JavaScript code:

```javascript
const {
  Button
} = Reactstrap;
var Hello = React.createClass({
  render: function() {
    return <Button color="danger">danger</Button>;
  }
});
ReactDOM.render(
  <Hello name="World" />,
  document.getElementById('container')
);
```

At the end, press the **run** button and find that your button indeed looks like that shown in the following screenshot:

You can find the modified JSFiddle at the following URL: `https://jsfiddle.net/bassjob sen/2fz6aLrv/`.

Other tools for deploying Bootstrap 4

A Brunch skeleton using Bootstrap 4 is available at the following URL: `https://github.co m/bassjobsen/brunch-bootstrap4`. Brunch is a frontend web app build tool. It builds lints, compiles, concatenates, and shrinks your HTML5 apps.

Read more about Brunch at the official website, which can be found at the following URL: `h ttp://brunch.io/`. You can try Brunch by running the following commands in your console:

```
npm install -g brunch
brunch new -s https://github.com/bassjobsen/brunch-bootstrap4
```

Notice that the first command requires administrator rights to run. After installing the tool, you can run the following command to build your project:

```
brunch build
```

The preceding command creates a new `public/index.html` file. Open it in your browser. You'll find that it should look like the following screenshot:

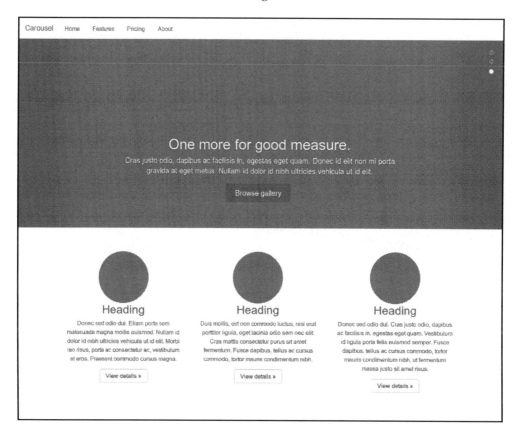

Yeoman

Yeoman is another build tool. It's is a command line utility allowing the creation of projects utilizing scaffolding templates, called generators. A Yeoman generator that scaffolds out a frontend Bootstrap 4 web app can be found at the following URL: `https://github.com/bassjobsen/generator-bootstrap4`.

You can run the Yeoman Bootstrap 4 generator by running the following commands in your console:

```
npm install -g yo
npm install -g generator-bootstrap4
yo bootstrap4grunt serve
```

Again notice that the first two commands require administrator rights.

The grunt serve command runs a local web server at `http://localhost:9000`. Point your browser to that address and you will find that it looks as follows:

Summary

You are at the end of the book now. I hope you have enjoyed it and have learned a lot. You can create your own Bootstrap 4 projects now and your knowledge extends to a set of tools for deploying them.

In this chapter, you have learned how to set up an Angular 2 app with Bootstrap 4. At the end, you were introduced to some other tools to deploy your projects. Happy Bootstrapping'!

Beyond this, there are a plethora of resources available for pushing further with Bootstrap. The Bootstrap community is an active and exciting one. This is truly an exciting point in the history of frontend web development. Bootstrap has made its mark on history, and for a good reason. Check my GitHub pages at `http://github.com/bassjobsen` for new projects and updated sources or ask me a question on Stack Overflow (`http://stackoverflow.com/users/1596547/bass-jobsen`).

Index

&

& parent reference 78

A

Accessible Rich Internet Applications (ARIA) 19,
    272
Adobe
  reference 207
Affix plugin 9
Amazon
  reference 265, 290
AMD 13
AMPPS
  about 116
  reference 116
Angular 2
  reference 357, 358
Angular app
  Bootstrap's CSS code, integrating into 364
  Bootstrap's HTML markup code, adding 362
  routing, adding 359
  setting up 358
Angular Command Line Interface (CLI) 372
Angular
  overview 357
AngularJS 358
attention-grabbing pricing tables
  adjusting, for small viewports 345
  body, styling 341
  creating 336
  files, setting up 336
  foot, styling 341
  head, beautifying 339, 340
  markup, setting up 336, 338
  packages, differentiating 342, 343, 344
  variables, setting up 336, 338

visual hierarchy, providing 346
autoprefixer 8

B

before pseudo-element
  reference 293
beginning files
  sizing up 210, 211
blog page
  main part 100
blog posts
  styling 102
blog
  page header, adding 132
  posts, styling 135
  side bar 136
Bootply
  reference 35
Bootstrap 4
  deploying, tools 375
  reference 375
Bootstrap button classes
  reference 292
Bootstrap CLI
  prerequisites 17
  used, for running starter template 72
  using 17
Bootstrap drop-down documentation
  reference 218
Bootstrap navbar
  navigation, turning on 125
Bootstrap project
  preparing 17
Bootstrap slider
  reference 156
Bootstrap's CSS code integration
  ng-bootstrap directives, using 367, 368

post-processors, adding 366
Sass compiler, setting up 364
Bootstrap's CSS code
integrating, into Angular app 364
Bootstrap's HTML markup code
adding, to Angular app 362
Bootstrap's Media object
reference 151
Bootstrap's Sass files
customizing 182
variables, customizing 184
Bootstrap, running from CDN
about 10
Subresource Integrity (SRI) 11
Bootstrap
about 7
build process 39
carousel documentation, reference 172
compile version, reference link 10
compiled code, downloading 10
cons 8
documentation, reference 287, 301
Flexbox enabled version 10
grid 127
grid only versions 10
improvements 8
installing, via Bower 43
predefined classes 123
pros 8
React.js, using 372
reference 9, 11, 141
running, from CDN 10
Sass 9
source files, downloading 11
Bootstrappin E-Commerce
designing 265, 266, 267
Bower
Bootstrap, installing via 43
reference 117
breadcrum styles
reference 269
breadcrumbs
styling 269, 270, 271, 272
browser support
about 32

flexible boxes 33
reference 33
vendor prefixes 32
Browsersync 55
Brunch
reference 375
BST 4 theme
installing 117, 118
build process
creating 38
layout template 59
page header 60
requisites 39
used, for finishing project 59
business home page design
basics, setting up 211
bottom border, setting up for page header 214
drop-down menus, adding to navbar 212
images, adding with header.js 215
images, adding with holder.js 214
business home page
creating 208, 209
buttons
links, turning 181
style, applying 147

C

Can I Use database
reference 47
caption position
refining 333
tiny screens, adjusting 335
Card module
about 278, 280
using, with CSS3 Flexbox layout module 281, 284
carousel markup
reference 154
carousel
adding, to page 153
indicators, repositioning 193
JavaScript events 177
marking up 169
markup. reference 169
modifying, by new animation additions 173

styling 192, 194
  top and bottom padding, adding 192
  working 173
child theming 160
Chrome's V8 JavaScript engine 39
code
  writing, reference 84
codepen
  reference 35
collapsed navbar
  drop-down menus, customizing 230
  p-down menus, customizing 231
  styling 229
color scheme
  implementing 227
columns
  content, tweaking 196
  tweaking 196
Command Line Interface (CLI) 372
comment_form() PHP function
  reference 148
CommonJS 13
Compass
  about 88, 364
  reference 89
complex banner area
  creating 215
  logo, placing above navbar 216, 218
  navbar drop-down items, checking 218, 219, 220
  navbar drop-down items, reviewing 218, 219, 220
complex footer
  laying out 252
complex responsive layout
  buttons, adjusting 242, 243, 244
  designing 233
  fine touches, adding for multiple viewports 252
  font sizes, adjusting 242, 243, 244
  headings, adjusting 242, 243, 244
  large and extra-large layout, adjusting 236, 237
  medium layout, adjusting for tablet-width viewports 237, 238, 239, 241
  primary column, enhancing 246, 247, 248
  tertiary column, adjusting 249, 251

Content Delivery Network (CDN) 10
Content Management System (CMS) 115
CSS animations
  reference 173
CSS multi-column layout 329
CSS normalize 8
CSS position
  fixed:reference 112
CSS properties 32
CSS sourcemaps 42
css-mqpacker
  reference 239
CSS3 animations
  reference 173
CSS3 flexbox layout module
  reference 285
CSS3 Flexible Box Layout Module 32
custom SCSS code
  color scheme, selecting 89
  HTML templates, preparing 90
  navbar, styling 94
  page header, styling 92
  writing 89
customer reviews
  caption position, refining 333
  captions, positioning 332, 333
  captions, styling 332, 333
  tackling 329, 331
customization strategies, Sass
  Bootstrap's mixins, using 87
  Bootstrap's predefined CSS classes, extending 86
  other codes, reusing 88
  Sass functions 88
  variables, using 84

D

data-attributes, HTML5
  reference 351
data-URIs
  reference 69
default tasks
  creating 57
deployment tools, Bootstrap
  about 375

Yeoman 376
DOM element 358
Don't Repeat Yourselff (DRY) 9
Dropdown plugin
  reference 213

E

environments
  setting up for development 42
  setting up, for production 42
ES6 8
exercise files
  surveying 164

F

features list
  beautifying 325, 326
features
  styling 68
file permissions
  reference 135
files
  importing 83
  modular organization 83
final touches
  adding, to design 348, 349, 350
Flexbox Layout 33
Flexbox support
  enabling 232
floats
  reference 87
Font Awesome
  about 190
  adding, to project 315
  documentation, reference 197
  icon page, reference 192
  reference 190, 200, 223, 294
  used, for building social links 156
  using, in theme 156
footer
  styling 200

G

GitHub
  CLI, using 113

code, running 113
  download link 160
  project link 12
  reference 73
  work, publishing 72
Glyphicon Halflings set 9
Glyphicons 190
Grunt 7, 39
gulp-environments plugin
  reference 42
gulp-imagemin plugin
  reference 57
Gulp
  about 39, 116
  clean task 41
  Gulpfile.js, creating 41
  installing 40
  reference 55
  using 39

H

h-review
  reference 329
holder.js
  reference 215
horizontal navbar
  styling 231
HP
  reference 207
HTML starter template
  about 15
  Bootstrap's CSS code 16
  JavaScript files 16
  responsive meta tag 15
  X-UA-Compatible meta tag 16
HTML
  compiled HTML code, validating 54
  Gulp task installation, for compiling Panini HTML
    templates 54
  modularization 53

I

icons
  adding 190
inline forms

reference 305
Internet Explorer 32

J

JavaScript Collapse plugin 95
JavaScript plugins
  JavaScript code, making ready 52
  preparing 51
JavaScript syntax extension (JSX) 372
JavaScript task runners
  avoiding 72
JBST 4 WordPress theme 116
jQuery 19
jQuery lite (jqLite) 358
jQuery's animations
  reference 354
JSFiddle
  reference 372, 374
jumbotron
  customizing 318, 319, 320, 321, 322
  message design, refining 322, 323, 324, 325
  reference 318

L

last-child pseud-class
  reference 283
Leaner CSS (Less) 8
libSass 9, 364
links
  turning, into buttons 181
logo image
  adding 187

M

major structural elements, setting up
  navbar markup, providing 19
major structural elements
  Normalize.css 28
  setting up 18
markup
  adjusting, for tablet-width viewports 256, 257
  details, refining 258, 259, 261, 262
  setting up 252, 253, 255
  targeted responsive clearfix 257
  targeted responsive clearfix, adding 258

masonry template
  using 158
material design, Bootstrap
  reference 72
MaxCDN
  reference 10
media queries
  testing, reference 322
mixins
  about 81
  reference 97
  version, reference 95
mobile-first responsive grid
  reference 178
mock-up, for tables
  features 164
Model-View-Controller (MVC) 357

N

navbar configuration
  about 128
  HTML code 130
  photo, adding to middle of navbar 130
navbar markup
  breakpoints 23
  collapsible content, adding 22
  CSS classes 21
  placements 22
  providing 20
  reference 21
  responsive features 24
  responsive navbar, completing 25
  responsive utility classes 25
navbar
  adjusting 315, 317, 318
  configuring 128
  ScrollSpy, adding 351
  styling 94
  without Bootstrap predefined CSS classes 99
navigation
  setting up 361
nested rules
  about 78
ng-bootstrap directives
  other directives, using 369

reference 368
using 367, 368
using, as alternative 370, 371
ng2-bootstrap directives
  reference 370
node-sass module
  reference 364
Node.js
  about 7, 39
  reference 39, 116
Nodemon module 365
Normalize.css
  reference 28
npm 39
npm script objects
  reference 72

O

off-canvas side bar 141
one-page marketing website
  overview 309, 312
online portfolio
  building 161
  recommended steps 204
operations 82
options sidebar
  basic styles, setting up 286
  Clearance Sale link, styling 287, 288
  Font Awesome checkboxes, adding to option
    links 292
  Font Awesome, adding to option links 293, 294
  options list layout for tablets and phones,
    adjusting 298, 299, 300
  options list, styling 290
  options panel for phone users, collapsing 301,
    302, 303, 304
  Sass mixins, used for arrange option links in
    columns 296, 297
  styling 285, 286

P

page content
  viewing 314
page footer
  about 107
  adding 133
  left footer column 109
  right footer column 110
  styling 70
page header
  about 60
  adding, to blog 133
  CSS code, fine tuning 63
  custom CSS code, building 62
  hero unit, styling 64
  HTML code, fine tuning 63
  navbar, styling 64
page title
  styling 269, 270, 271
page
  carousel, adding 153
  user comments, styling 149
pagination styles
  reference 271
pagination
  styling 269, 270, 271, 272
Panini HTML templates
  compiling, with installation of Gulp task 54
Panini
  reference 18, 53, 59, 165, 213, 296, 314
PHP Tech Page
  reference 154
PhpMyAdmin 116
Pixabay
  reference 154
plugin directory
  reference 156
PostCSS autoprefixer 33
postcss-flexbugs-fixes
  reference 366
products grid
  adjusting 273, 274, 275, 276, 278
  Card module 278, 279
products page markup
  surveying 268, 269
project
  requisites 77
  setting up 77
pseudo element
  reference 340

R

React Bootstrap 4 components
  using 373, 374
React.js
  using, with Bootstrap 372
Reactstrap library
  reference 374
Reactstrap
  about 373
  installation link 373
  reference 373
Reboot module
  about 8
  box-sizing 29
  predefined CSS classes 29
  Sass variables and mixins 30
responsive adjustments
  creating 225
responsive breakpoints
  reference 320
responsive columns
  creating 178
routing
  adding, to Angular 2 app 359
Ruby 88

S

Sass code
  reusing 120
Sass structure
  creating 43
  CSS code, making ready 48
  CSS sourcemaps, for debugging 46
  postCSS autoprefixer, running 47
  Sass code, compiling into CSS code 45
  SCSS code, limiting 49
Sass
  about 9, 75
  built-in functions, reference 82
  customization, strategies 84
  importance 78, 182
  mixins 81
  nested rules 78
  operations 82

reference 182
tweaks 148
variable interpolation, reference 293
variables 80
ScrollSpy
  adding, to navbar 351, 353
  page scrolls, adding 354
  page scrolls, animating 353
  reference 351
SCSS code, social buttons
  reusing 111
SCSS syntax 9
SCSS-linter
  using 84
search form
  adding, to designing 304
  Typeahead plugin, using 305, 306, 307
selector inheritance 78
shim
  reference 47
side bar
  reference 137
  styling 106
single page applications (SPAs) 357
sizing classes
  reference 287
social links
  building, with Font Awesome 156
source code
  reference 113, 372
source files, Bootstrap
  about 12
  downloading 11
  downloading, alternatives 14
sr-only utility class
  reference 226
Stack Overflow
  reference link 35
starter files
  surveying 312, 313, 314
starter templates
  running, with Bootstrap CLI 72
static web server
  creating 55
  file changes, monitoring 56

images, copying 56
images, minifying 57
sticky polyfill
    reference 9
Subresource Integrity
    reference 11

T

tables
    reference 338
Tether 8, 19
text capitalization classes
    reference 317
tooling setup
    about 14
    HTML starter template 15
transition property
    reference 33
transition-timing-function
    reference 173
translate3ds
    reference 173
troubleshooting 34
tweaks, Sass
    pagination 148
    search button 149
typeahead plugin
    reference 305, 307
TypeScript 358
typography and heading classes
    reference 271

U

Universal Module Definition (UMD) 8, 13
user comments
    styling, on pages 149
utility navigation
    adding 222, 223, 224

V

variables
    about 80
    customizing 184
    navbar, customizing 185
vendor-specific rules 32

W

WampServer
    about 116
    reference 116
web blog
    design, deploying with Bootstrap 75
website
    banner/masthead 207
    footer 207
    main content area 207
WordPress themes
    testing, reference 158
WordPress
    installing 116
    predefined classes 123
    reference 116
    template hierarchy, reference 123
    template system, reference 147
World Wide Web Consortium (W3C)
    reference 272

Y

YAML
    reference 212
Yeoman generator
    reference 34
Yeoman workflow 34
Yeoman
    about 376, 377
    reference 376

Z

Zappos
    reference 207, 265, 290